skinnytaste™
FAST AND SLOW

CLARKSON POTTER/PUBLISHERS
NEW YORK

Knockout Quick-Fix and
Slow Cooker Recipes

skinnytaste™
FAST AND SLOW

Gina Homolka

with Heather K. Jones, R.D.

CONTENTS

Introduction **6**

Cooking Fast and Slow **9**

A Month of Good-for-You Meals **14**

HEALTHY MORNINGS
18

CHILIS, SOUPS, AND STEWS
38

ONE-BOWL MEALS
74

ZOODLES, SQUASHTA, PASTA, AND SAUCE
96

TACO NIGHT
124

POULTRY MAINS
146

MEAT LOVER MAINS
178

FISH AND SEAFOOD MAINS
206

MEATLESS MAINS
224

ON THE SIDE
250

THE SWEETER SIDE
277

Acknowledgments **300**

Index **301**

INTRODUCTION

I COOK BECAUSE I LOVE TO EAT. I'm not talking about just good-for-you foods like salads and quinoa—although, yes, those are great. The foods I crave range from classic comfort dishes to global cuisine, and everything in between. At the same time, I try to eat a light and balanced diet, and these two things don't necessarily go together. That's what led me to start experimenting in my own kitchen eight years ago. I wanted to find ways to eat the foods I craved, but without throwing off all of my hard work to lose weight and keep it off. Plus, as a mom, I had to find a way to please not only my palate, but my picky family's preferences as well, because cooking separate meals is just not an option for me. The results of those experiments ultimately became my blog Skinnytaste.com, and later inspired my first cookbook, *The Skinnytaste Cookbook.*

My mission with my first cookbook was to help people create low-calorie food without sacrificing flavor. I also wanted to help take away some of the fear and intimidation that people—especially beginners—feel about cooking. I was thrilled that the book was received so well—thanks to loyal Skinnytaste fans and so many others, it was a bestseller. What a dream come true! But, as I talked with people about the book, I kept fielding similar questions: "Are the recipes easy?" and "Are the recipes fast? I don't have time to cook." At the same time, I was receiving emails and Facebook requests for more superquick weeknight ideas, as well as recipes for the slow cooker. With all of this feedback, I knew exactly what my next book should be about.

Skinnytaste Fast and Slow is filled with two types of recipes: quick and easy dishes that are ready in 30 minutes or less, and those that are made in a slow cooker. With this book, no matter how busy you are, you *can* enjoy a delicious home-cooked meal. Tasty, light, and time-saving! I want everything in these pages to help simplify your life, because I totally get it—I understand the stress of having to come up with healthy meals the whole family will enjoy on a limited time schedule. Talk about pressure!

TAKE A TASTE

In this book, you'll find 140 recipes that are light on calories and packed with nutrients and satisfying flavors, while being simple enough to make anytime. Many of these dishes are versions of the comfort foods I loved during my childhood, and others are my current favorites. All of them have been simplified and skinny-fied, so they slim your waistline *and* fit into your busy schedule. I've spent a year testing and tweaking everything here, and I learned a lot along the way (you'd be amazed what you can make in a slow cooker . . . hello, brownies [see page 296]!). I hope that as you flip through this book, you'll discover that you can enjoy great taste and good health, even when time is tight.

In each chapter, I've dished out fast recipes, so you can get your meal on the table in less time than it takes to watch your favorite TV show, as well as slow-toss all the ingredients into your slow cooker in the morning and come home to a fabulous masterpiece. If Slow Cooker Hamburger Stroganoff (page 119), Pizza-Stuffed Chicken Roll-Ups (page 157), and Slow Cooker

Peach-Strawberry Crumble (page 288) don't whet your appetite, then I don't know what will! And, of course, I've covered you from breakfast to dessert, and every meal in between. You'll even find some special chapters, um, sandwiched in between, including one on bowls—because I love the convenience and ease of tossing a bunch of yummy ingredients into a single bowl—and one devoted entirely to tacos. I've peppered in time-saving tips, served up some prep and cooking strategies, and even whipped up a meal plan to give you a day-by-day map for eating well. I've given you all the info you need to achieve your health and diet goals: Each recipe has a full set of nutrition facts as well as icons that indicate which dishes are vegetarian, dairy-free, gluten-free, and freezer-friendly. And the photography . . . well, don't be surprised if your stomach starts growling as you begin to turn the pages!

RECIPE KEY

Look for these helpful icons throughout the book:

Q Quick (ready in 30 minutes or less)

PC Pressure Cooker

SC Slow Cooker

V Vegetarian

GF Gluten-Free

DF Dairy-Free

FF Freezer-Friendly

TACKLING THE TIME OBSTACLE

The truth is that most of us would love to cook or make all of our meals at home. Research shows that home cooking is healthier than dining out. That's no surprise to me, considering that restaurant and take-out meals are enormous and typically loaded with calories, fat, and sodium. But despite these facts, many of us are still unable to make it happen. What's the main issue? For most of us, it's time.

With this cookbook, I hope to help you eliminate that excuse once and for all. If you have 15 minutes, then you have more than enough time to whip up my kid-friendly Easiest One-Pot Pasta and Broccoli (page 238), for example. So many of these recipes take very little time to make; just look for the ones under the "fast" sections of each chapter. On the other end of the spectrum, the thrill of slow cooker meals is that you do some prep work—sometimes as little as tossing everything in the cooker, though some recipes need a little sautéing to build flavor—and then you set the timer and head out the door! While you go to work, run errands, work out, or hang out with your kids, your dinner cooks itself. Sounds pretty great to me!

Taking charge of your cooking and eating habits can make a big impact on your health and weight. I hope that *Skinnytaste Fast and Slow* is a helpful tool to getting on the road to your very best self—and having fun while you're at it.

There's one final point I'd like to make about this book—and this one is crucial. The good-for-you food here actually tastes really good! Who wants to eat "diet" food and ditch all the good stuff? Not me! Remember, if you don't enjoy the process, it isn't likely to become a lifelong habit. I kept this thought in the back of my mind as I was in my kitchen testing recipes. Every dish had to meet three criteria: Deliver great taste, without many calories, and in a small amount of prep time. For you, it's a weight loss win-win . . . win!

Ready to dig in? Let's go!

GINA HOMOLKA

COOKING FAST AND SLOW

NO TIME TO COOK? NO PROBLEM!

Getting dinner on the table when time is tight might seem like nothing short of a miracle. Most of us would never even try to put these two things—insane schedule and homemade meals—in the same sentence, let alone imagine them coming together in our own kitchens. Well, hold on to your spatula because I'm about to let you in on a little secret: It's more than possible—no spells or wishes required. Even better, these meals can also be good for you and your waistline. Talk about a terrific trifecta: trim and tasty meals that can fit into your busy schedule! You can totally do it with the right recipes, a slow cooker, and a few time-saving tips.

As a mother of two (with one still in grade school), I totally understand what it's like to be time-pressed. Every day, I'm faced with the juggle struggle—you know, trying to keep all the balls in the air: family life, full-time career, exercise, date nights, time with friends, and so on. It can be challenging. Toss meal planning into the mix and, often, all the balls come crashing to the ground. But not anymore! This book is jam-packed with recipes you can make in 30 minutes or less, or fuss-free meals you can simply throw into a slow cooker. I'm talking *easy*!

Don't worry for a second about sacrificing quality for convenience. Sure, it can seem like everything comes at a cost, but there are no trade-offs with these delicious dishes. I've kept it healthy with whole foods, lots of veggies, and other ingredients that are widely available. In fact, my entire food philosophy is based on choosing in-season whole (and *wholesome*) picks. I love food in its natural state, rather than things that are packaged and processed. If something contains ingredients I can't pronounce, I leave it on the shelf. That's because I know that real food is not only better for my family and me, but it tastes a heck of a lot better, too. I stock up on the good stuff at my local farmers' market, the organic produce section of my nearby supermarket, and my CSA (community supported agriculture). There are fish dishes, as well as meals that contain lean meat and dairy (if you enjoy these foods), and even dessert, because let's face it, eliminating the occasional treat will only lead to overeating later.

Before you get cooking, I want to arm you with some time-saving strategies. These tips and tricks help me be efficient in the kitchen, while boosting my enjoyment of cooking, and I hope they'll do the same for you. Start using them today and you can chop precious minutes off prep!

MAKE A PLAN

Meal planning requires a little effort, but it pays you back big time in the forms of saved time and cash. It also helps keep you on track to avoid last-minute schedule changes that often lead to drive-through or delivery. It's easy and anyone (yes, even you!) can do it. Here's how to become a planning pro:

Step 1: Grab a meal planner—my journal, *The Skinnytaste Meal Planner*, was made for this, though any notebook will work perfectly. Take an inventory of what you have in the fridge and pantry.

Step 2: Flip through this cookbook and select a few recipes that suit your taste. I usually start by choosing three major proteins—such as chicken, seafood, and beef—as well as at least one meatless meal. Also, I try to incorporate a dish or two that allows me to cook once and eat twice (or three times), like Slow Cooker Chicken Cacciatore (page 112) and Slow Cooker Beef and Two-Bean Chili (page 66). And I use my slow cooker for many dishes (a total time-saver).

Step 3: Make a shopping list, then head to the grocery store.

Step 4: Prep for the week. There are many ways to get ready for the coming week: You can prep foods (such as beans, hard-boiled eggs, chopped veggies, and grains), you can batch-cook (double recipes and freeze half for later), and you can cook ahead for the week. This comes in handy when you know your schedule is going to be crazy. If you're super motivated (and have room in the freezer), you can cook ahead for the month! Look for the recipes that are labeled FF (Freezer-Friendly).

It's really that simple!

COOK IN-SEASON

I can't stress this enough: Cooking with locally grown produce that is in season will always give you the best results. Fruit is sweeter and vegetables taste better because they have been harvested shortly before you purchase them. It takes less effort to make your food taste great when you're starting with fresh produce. Less work + more flavor = a winning equation! Although this might not always be possible year-round, depending on where you live, it's a great guideline to shop and eat by. Your best bets for the freshest picks: shopping at farmers' markets, planting your own garden (go ahead and embrace that green thumb), or joining a CSA.

PACK YOUR PANTRY

Having a well-stocked pantry will mean you're in a good position to handle curveballs, aka those evenings that don't go according to plan. You'll always have ingredients on hand to whip up a home-cooked meal if you prepare! Here are a few staples I always have in my kitchen cabinets:

Grains: Oats, quinoa, brown rice, assorted pastas

Canned and Jarred Goods: Broths (chicken, vegetable, beef), tomato products (sauce, diced, crushed, paste), capers, olives, canned tuna, sun-dried tomatoes, dried fruit

Nuts and Seeds: Walnuts, pecans, cashews, peanuts, chia seeds, pumpkin seeds, almond butter, peanut butter

Sweeteners and Baking Products: Honey, pure maple syrup, stevia, raw sugar, cocoa powder, baking powder, baking soda, all-purpose flour (wheat or gluten-free), white whole wheat flour

Beans and Legumes: Dried beans, dried lentils, canned beans

Oils, Vinegars, and Seasonings: Olive oil, sesame oil, canola oil, coconut oil, grapeseed oil, balsamic glaze, red wine vinegar, balsamic vinegar, rice vinegar, dried spices and herbs

Produce: Onions, shallots, garlic

A NOTE ABOUT SALT

You may be surprised to learn that different brands and different types of salt can vary widely. For consistency in my recipes—both for flavor and for the nutrition information—I use Diamond Crystal Kosher. If you use another kind, just remember to taste as you go.

FILL YOUR FRIDGE AND FREEZER

What's true for the pantry is also true for the fridge and freezer—load them up! I've found that replenishing a few items as I use them, so that I always have them on hand, really helps me be ready to whip up healthy and speedy meals. Take a look at my essentials:

Fridge: Milk, eggs, cheese, fruits, fresh herbs, and seasonal vegetables. Flavor-boosting staples that have a longer shelf life are various hot sauces, condiments, soy sauce, and tomato paste.

Freezer: When winter rolls around and fresh produce is limited—or expensive—in much of the country, many of us turn to canned or frozen options. While canned vegetables tend to lose nutrients during the preservation process (exceptions include tomatoes and pumpkin), frozen vegetables that are flash-frozen at their peak may be even more nutrient-packed than some fresh produce. Here are a few examples of what I keep in my freezer: chopped spinach, butternut squash, corn, peas, fresh ginger, and fresh herbs wrapped in plastic. Other fantastic things to keep tucked away are frozen shrimp, chicken, cooked rice, and cooked quinoa.

The freezer can also be your friend when you want to stock up on sale items. You can freeze extra milk, butter, bread, and meat (out of the packaging and stored in plastic freezer bags) whenever the price is right. Save cash and be prepared—it's a win-win.

FAST COOKING BASICS

I always feel so accomplished in the kitchen when I manage to "throw together" a delicious, wholesome meal that makes everyone happy. It can feel like I pulled a meal out of thin air! The recipes in this book that are listed as "fast" really can make you feel this way, too—but I have a few tips that are key to mastering this kind of efficiency.

Make a Mental Game Plan

Read through your recipe before you get started to figure out the timing of all steps. Doing so can ensure that your meal comes together when it's supposed to. There's nothing worse than watching one food get cold as you wait for another to finish cooking. Not to mention, you can take advantage of every minute—prepping one ingredient as another cooks.

Get Set Before You Go

A little organization goes a long way. Having all your ingredients out on the counter, prepped and ready to go before you begin, is huge. In fact, chefs have a special term for this, *mise en place*, which is French for "setting in place." It will save you time and stress in the long run.

Arm Yourself with the Right Tools

If you've been slicing and dicing with a dull knife, you might be amazed at the difference when you pick up a sharp new knife. It truly makes a big difference in the amount of effort that goes into prepping foods! Other time-saving gadgets that you may consider investing in: an immersion blender, a slow cooker (of course), a sturdy spiralizer, a mini chopper, and a pressure cooker (I love my Instant Pot!).

Enlist Help

Have little ones (or even big kids) who you can recruit to help? Put them to work! Cleaning veggies, making a salad, setting the table—find the right age-appropriate job for the right kid, and save a little time. Bonus: You'll also get your kids involved in the kitchen, an important first step that can help set them up for a lifetime of healthy eating.

Clean Up Your Act

If I could send a thank-you note to the person who invented aluminum foil, I would. Use this handy kitchen staple to line baking sheets, and you'll cut cleanup to almost nothing! They also sell a nonstick version, which allows you to use less oil. Parchment paper is another helpful kitchen staple for easy cleanup.

Slow Cooker to Stovetop, and Back Again

You might be wondering if you can make slow cooker dishes without a slow cooker. The answer is yes! All my slow cooker recipes can be made on the stovetop, in a Dutch oven, or even with a pressure cooker. When converting, you'll need to add more liquid, as needed, and adjust the cooking time as follows:

SLOW COOKER HIGH	SLOW COOKER LOW	STOVETOP/ LOW SIMMER OVEN/350°F
2 to 3 hours	4 to 6 hours	15 to 30 minutes
3 to 4 hours	6 to 8 hours	35 to 45 minutes
4 to 6 hours	8 to 12 hours	50 minutes or more

SLOW COOKER SECRETS

The slow cooker is a huge part of my dinnertime successes. Recipes for this kitchen tool are also my number one request from Skinnytaste fans, and that's why I've included 59 of them in this book. Though the gadget is super convenient, often the slow, low heat can dull or change the flavors of a dish. Here are my tips for achieving the best-tasting results:

Get to Know Your Slow Cooker
The cooking temperatures of different models can vary, which can affect the cook time and success of a recipe. For consistency, I tested the recipes in this book with a 6-quart Hamilton Beach Set & Forget programmable slow cooker.

Size Matters
All the recipes in this book were tested in an oval 6-quart slow cooker. In many cases, a smaller slow cooker will be fine, though some recipes may require a large pot to be sure everything fits—especially when baking in a loaf pan.

Watch Your Heat
Setting recommendations will vary depending on what you're making. Use the high setting only when I specify; use the low setting as much as possible—when in doubt, cook low and slow.

Don't Skip the Sautéing Step . . .
Sautéing aromatics, such as onions and garlic, before adding them to the slow cooker will always result in the best flavor. Although it's not 100 percent necessary, it is a *must* for me.

. . . or the Searing Step
While browning meats before adding them to a slow cooker is not always required, searing gives dishes a greater depth of flavor and adds color, which makes it look more appetizing.

Hands Off!
Opening the slow cooker breaks the seal and lets heat and steam escape, which can slow down the cooking. Open it only 30 to 45 minutes before the low end of the cooking range to check for doneness, or as instructed by a recipe.

Finish with Flavor
In most cases, you'll notice that I finish a recipe with a fresh element, such as herbs, lemon or lime juice, or a garnish. This step is crucial for giving the final dish that extra hit of flavor.

Prep and Dump
To save time in the morning (I know how frenzied those can be), have everything prepped the night before and keep it all in the refrigerator so it's ready to simply dump in, turn on, and walk away.

Cook While You Sleep
If you know your mornings will be nuts, cook overnight! Toss all the ingredients into the cooker before you hit the sack, and when you wake, let the meal cool, and then stash it in the fridge.

PERFECT FOR PARTIES

Put your slow cooker to work when you're entertaining! It can help free up space when your stove and oven are in use. Plus, how great for you to be able to enjoy the food and company instead of slaving over the stove all evening The slow cooker will keep your meal warm until you're ready to feast.

A MONTH OF GOOD-FOR-YOU MEALS

These four weeks of meals are around 1,500 calories per day.
Feel free to adjust these menus for whatever your goals may be.

WEEK 1		SUNDAY	MONDAY (Meatless Monday!)	TUESDAY (Taco Tuesday!)
	BREAKFAST	Whole Wheat Crêpes with Strawberry Sauce (page 20)	Avocado Toast—Put an Egg on It! (page 23) and an apple	Banana-Almond Smoothie Bowl (page 30) and a hard-boiled egg
	LUNCH	Grilled Cheese with Havarti, Brussels Sprouts, and Apple (page 229) with Cream of Zucchini Soup (page 43)	Spiralized Lemon-Basil Zucchini Mason Jar Salads (page 98)	Slow Cooker Pollo in Potacchio (page 115), leftovers from Sunday, over 1 cup pasta
	SNACK	1 apple with ½ tablespoon peanut butter	2 tablespoons mixed nuts and a banana	1 cup berries
	DINNER	Slow Cooker Pollo in Potacchio (page 115) over 1 cup pasta	Slow Cooker Chana Masala (page 248) and ¾ cup basmati rice	Grilled Cumin-Rubbed Skirt Steak Tacos with Pickled Red Onions (page 128) and Pineapple Jicama Slaw (page 269)
	TREAT	Grilled Piña Colada Delight with whipped coconut cream (page 284)		

WEEK 2		SUNDAY	MONDAY (Meatless Monday!)	TUESDAY (Taco Tuesday!)
	BREAKFAST	Slow Cooker Chocolate Swirl Banana Bread (page 36), and 1 cup berries	Slow Cooker Chocolate Swirl Banana Bread (page 36) leftovers from Sunday, and 1 cup berries	Avocado Toast—South of the Border Huevos Revueltos (page 25)
	LUNCH	Grilled Cheese with Havarti, Brussels Sprouts, and Apple (page 229) and an orange	Cream of Zucchini Soup (page 43) and Italian House Salad (page 252)	Slow Cooker Loaded "Baked" Sweet Potatoes (page 246) leftovers from Monday, topped with 1 tablespoon 0% Greek yogurt
	SNACK	2 tablespoons mixed nuts and a banana	½ cup sugar snap peas and ½ cup baby carrots dipped in ¼ cup hummus	1 ounce baked tortilla chips (about 18 chips) and ½ cup salsa
	DINNER	Slow Cooker Carne Desmechada (page 195) with Baked Sweet Plantains with Cheese (page 259) and ¾ cup brown rice	Slow Cooker Loaded "Baked" Sweet Potatoes (page 246) topped with 1 tablespoon 0% Greek yogurt and Italian House Salad (page 252)	Grilled Greek Chicken Tostadas (page 127)
	TREAT			Macerated Berries with Whipped Cream (page 280)

WEDNESDAY	THURSDAY	FRIDAY	SATURDAY
Avocade Toast—Karina's Special (page 24) and a pear	**Breakfast Banana Split** (page 34)	2 hard-boiled eggs with a banana and a whole-grain English muffin	**Savory Quinoa Breakfast Bowls** (page 33)
Spiralized Lemon-Basil Zucchini Mason Jar Salads (page 98)	**Slow Cooker Chicken Burrito Bowls** (page 93) leftovers from Wednesday	**Roasted Brussels Bowls with Spicy Sausage** (page 82) and an orange	**Dad's Peppers and Egg Sandwiches** (page 242)
1 ounce baked tortilla chips (about 18 chips) with ½ cup salsa	½ cup sugar snap peas and ½ cup baby carrots dipped in ¼ cup hummus	2 tablespoons mixed nuts and 1 ounce cheese	2 cups air-popped popcorn topped with 2 tablespoons grated Parmesan
Slow Cooker Chicken Burrito Bowls (page 93)	**Sweet 'n' Spicy Salmon with Stir-Fried Veggies** (page 211) with ¾ cup brown rice	**Slow Cooker BBQ Pulled Chicken** (page 168), 1 corn on the cob, and ½ cup baked beans	Dinner out!
Easy No-Cook Mango Fool (page 283)	6 ounces 0% Greek yogurt mixed with 1 tablespoon shaved dark chocolate and ½ tablespoon raspberry preserves		

WEDNESDAY	THURSDAY	FRIDAY	SATURDAY
2 hard-boiled eggs with whole-grain toast and a banana	**Avocado Toast—Cucumber, Tomato, and Lox** (page 25)	6 ounces 0% Greek yogurt topped with 1 cup berries and ¼ cup low-fat granola	**Mexican Huevos Shakshukos** (page 29)
Grilled Greek Chicken Tostadas (page 127), leftovers from Tuesday	**Slow Cooker Chicken Taco Chili** (page 62) leftovers from Wednesday, over ¾ cup brown rice, topped with 2 tablespoons reduced-fat cheese and 2 tablespoons reduced-fat sour cream	**Greek Panzanella Salad** (page 233) with **Dad's Cauliflower Soup** (page 40) leftovers from Thursday	**Roasted Pepper and Orzo Soup** (page 45)
1 apple and 1 ounce cheese	½ cup sugar snap peas and ½ cup baby carrots dipped in ¼ cup hummus	2 tablespoons mixed nuts and a hard-boiled egg	1 apple with ½ tablespoon peanut butter
Slow Cooker Chicken Taco Chili (page 62) over ¾ cup brown rice, topped with 2 tablespoons reduced-fat cheese and 2 tablespoons reduced-fat sour cream	**Greek Panzanella Salad** (page 233) with **Dad's Cauliflower Soup** (page 40)	**Veggie-Stuffed Flounder Sheet Pan Dinner** (page 215)	Dinner out!
	Banana Pudding Cups (page 279)	**Banana Pudding Cups** (page 279)	

	SUNDAY	MONDAY (Meatless Monday!)	TUESDAY (Taco Tuesday!)
BREAKFAST	**Slow Cooker Oatmeal with Coconut, Blueberries, and Bananas** (page 35)	**Slow Cooker Oatmeal with Coconut, Blueberries, and Bananas** (page 35), leftovers from Sunday	**Avocado Toast—Cucumber, Tomato, and Lox** (page 25) and an apple
LUNCH	**Korean-Inspired Chicken Lettuce Wraps** (page 151) and sliced cucumbers	**Spiralized Lemon-Basil Zucchini Mason Jar Salads** (page 98)	**Spiralized Lemon-Basil Zucchini Mason Jar Salads** (page 98)
SNACK	2 cups grapes	2 cups grapes	6 ounces 0% Greek yogurt topped with 1 cup berries, ¼ cup low-fat granola
DINNER	**Pork Tenderloin with Potatoes and Caraway Seeds** (page 191) and **Braised Red Cabbage with Vinegar** (page 265)	**Coconut Veggie Curry** (page 241) with ¾ cup basmati rice	**Ahi Tuna Poke Jicama Tacos** (page 132) with 1 ounce baked tortilla chips (about 18 chips) and **Pineapple Jicama Slaw** (page 269)
TREAT	**Vanilla Bean Cheesecake Shooters** (page 287)	**Vanilla Bean Cheesecake Shooters** (page 287)	

WEEK 3

	SUNDAY	MONDAY (Meatless Monday!)	TUESDAY (Taco Tuesday!)
BREAKFAST	**Brussels Sprout Hash with Bacon and Eggs** (page 26) with 1 cup sliced strawberries	**Banana-Almond Smoothie Bowl** (page 30)	**Avocado Toast—Chunky Loaded Guac Toast** (page 24) and an apple
LUNCH	**Pizza-Stuffed Chicken Roll-Ups** (page 157) with baby carrots	**Greek Panzanella Salad** (page 233)	**Kale Caesar and Grilled Chicken Bowls** (page 77)
SNACK	2 cups air-popped popcorn topped with 2 tablespoons grated Parmesan	6 ounces 0% Greek yogurt topped with 1 cup berries	6 ounces 0% Greek yogurt topped with 1 cup berries
DINNER	**Slow Cooker Hamburger Stroganoff** (page 119) with 1 cup noodles and **Italian House Salad** (page 252)	**Cauliflower-Potato Tacos with Lime-Cilantro Chutney** (page 135)	**Slow Cooker Hawaiian Pork Tacos with Charred Pineapple Salsa** (page 142) with 1 ounce baked tortilla chips (about 18 chips) and ¼ avocado mashed with a pinch of salt and pepper
TREAT	1 ounce good-quality dark chocolate		

WEEK 4

WEDNESDAY	THURSDAY	FRIDAY	SATURDAY
Avocado Toast—Cucumber, Tomato, and Lox (page 25) and a grapefruit	1 slice whole wheat toast with 1 tablespoon peanut butter and a banana	6 ounces 0% Greek yogurt topped with 1 cup berries and ¼ cup low-fat granola	1 slice whole wheat toast with 1 tablespoon peanut butter and a banana
Zesty Lime Shrimp and Avocado Salad (page 208) with 1 ounce baked tortilla chips (about 18 chips)	**Slow Cooker Chicken and Dumpling Soup** (page 54) leftovers from Wednesday	**Salad Pizza** (page 230)	**Egg Roll Bowls** (page 85)
½ cup sugar snap peas and ½ cup baby carrots dipped in ¼ cup hummus	1 pear and 1 ounce cheese	½ cup sugar snap peas and ½ cup baby carrots dipped in ¼ cup hummus	1 cup sliced strawberries
Slow Cooker Chicken and Dumpling Soup (page 54), and **Italian House Salad** (page 252)	**Fork-and-Knife Cheeseburgers** (page 181)	**Slow Cooker Adobo Chicken with Sriracha, Ginger, and Scallions** (page 163), ¾ cup brown rice, and sliced cucumbers	Dinner out!
1 ounce good-quality dark chocolate	1 ounce good-quality dark chocolate		

WEDNESDAY	THURSDAY	FRIDAY	SATURDAY
6 ounces 0% Greek yogurt topped with 1 cup berries, ¼ cup low-fat granola, and 1 tablespoon sliced almonds	**Banana-Almond Smoothie Bowl** (page 30)	**Avocado Toast—Karina's Special** (page 24) and a banana	**Whole Wheat Crêpes with Strawberry Sauce** (page 20)
Slow Cooker Hawaiian Pork Tacos with Charred Pineapple Salsa (page 142) leftovers from Tuesday, and an apple	**Italian House Salad** (page 252) and 4 ounces cooked salmon	**Zoodles with Shrimp and Feta** (page 105)	**Cold Peanut-Sesame Chicken and Spiralized Cucumber Noodle Salad** (page 101)
½ cup sugar snap peas and ½ cup baby carrots dipped in ¼ cup hummus	½ cup sugar snap peas and ½ cup baby carrots dipped in ¼ cup hummus	1 cup sliced strawberries and 2 tablespoons mixed nuts	1 pear and 1 ounce cheese
Steak and Onions (page 182) over ¾ cup brown rice with **Zucchini Wedges with Lemon and Fresh Oregano** (page 256)	**Slow Cooker Turkey Meatloaf** (page 177) with **Whipped Parmesan Cauliflower Puree** (page 264)	**Baked Fish and Chips** (page 212) with **Italian House Salad** (page 252)	Dinner out!
		Slow Cooker Peach-Strawberry Crumble (page 288) with ½ cup nonfat vanilla frozen yogurt	

HEALTHY MORNINGS

FAST

Q	V		Whole Wheat Crêpes with Strawberry Sauce	**20**

Avocado Toast Obsession—5 Ways! **23**

Q	V	DF	Put an Egg on It!	**23**
Q	V	DF	Karina's Special	**24**
Q	V	DF	Chunky Loaded Guac Toast	**24**
Q		DF	Cucumber, Tomato, and Lox	**25**
Q	V	DF	South of the Border Huevos Revueltos	**25**

Q	GF	DF	Brussels Sprout Hash with Bacon and Eggs	**26**
Q	V GF	DF	Mexican Huevos Shakshukos	**29**
Q	V GF	DF	Banana-Almond Smoothie Bowl	**30**
Q	V GF	DF	Savory Quinoa Breakfast Bowls	**33**
Q	V		Breakfast Banana Split	**34**

SLOW

SC	V GF	DF	Slow Cooker "Baked" Oatmeal with Coconut, Blueberries, and Bananas	**35**
SC	V	GF	Slow Cooker Chocolate Swirl Banana Bread	**36**

WHOLE WHEAT CRÊPES WITH STRAWBERRY SAUCE   SERVES 6

Q V

Crêpes are my favorite solution for pancake cravings. Light and thin, they can be filled with just about anything your heart desires. They also reheat really well, so they're perfect to make ahead for busy weekdays. This simple protein-packed cottage cheese filling is delicious and has just a hint of lemon flavor. Topped with an easy homemade strawberry sauce, it's great for breakfast, and even dessert.

FILLING

1½ cups 1% unsalted small curd cottage cheese

1 tablespoon sugar

¼ teaspoon grated lemon zest

½ teaspoon vanilla extract

STRAWBERRY SAUCE

4 cups (18 ounces) strawberries, cut into ¼-inch-thick slices

2 tablespoons plus 1 teaspoon sugar

½ teaspoon white balsamic vinegar

CRÊPES

1¾ cups fat-free milk

2 large egg whites

1 large egg

1 teaspoon vegetable or coconut oil

1 teaspoon vanilla extract

1 cup white whole wheat flour (I like King Arthur)

1 teaspoon ground cinnamon

Cooking spray or oil mister

Confectioners' sugar, for serving (optional)

For the filling: In a blender, combine the cottage cheese, sugar, lemon zest, and vanilla and blend until smooth. Transfer to a medium bowl.

For the strawberry sauce: In a saucepan, combine the strawberries, sugar, balsamic vinegar, and 2 tablespoons water. Bring to a simmer over medium heat and cook for 2 to 3 minutes until the sugar dissolves. Reduce the heat to medium-low, cover, and simmer until the strawberries are soft and the sauce thickens, about 15 minutes.

For the crêpes: In a blender, combine the milk, egg whites, egg, oil, and vanilla. Add the flour and cinnamon and blend until smooth, using a spatula to scrape down the sides of the blender.

Heat a 10-inch nonstick skillet over medium-low heat. When hot, lightly coat with cooking spray. Pour ¼ cup of batter into the skillet, swirling the pan slightly to form a thin, even coating on the bottom of the skillet. Cook until the bottom of the crêpe is golden, about 2 minutes. Gently flip with a spatula and cook until the second side is golden, about 1 minute. Transfer to a plate. Repeat with the remaining batter.

SKINNY SCOOP Crêpes can be refrigerated for up to 3 days, and then reheated in the microwave for a quick weekday breakfast. This recipe makes 3 cups of batter, which can be refrigerated for up to 2 days.

PER SERVING	2 crêpes
CALORIES	223
FAT	3 g
SATURATED FAT	1 g
CHOLESTEROL	35 mg
CARBOHYDRATE	37 g
FIBER	5 g
PROTEIN	15 g
SUGARS	18 g
SODIUM	69 mg

To serve, place 2 tablespoons of the filling in the center of each crêpe, then roll them up. Place 2 rolled crêpes, seam side down, on each of 6 plates. Top each with 1/3 cup of the strawberry sauce and dust lightly with confectioners' sugar, if desired. Serve immediately.

AVOCADO TOAST OBSESSION—5 WAYS!

I've never been much of a breakfast person. Most weekday mornings start with a cup of coffee (or two) and something quick to sustain me, like hard-boiled eggs, fruit, a smoothie, or oatmeal. But then I discovered avocado toast and became *obsessed*! I always have avocados in my house, so this dish is perfect when I have leftovers in my fridge that need to be used up. And the best part: Each of these takes less than 5 minutes to whip up! My older daughter, Karina, and my husband, Tommy, now share my A.T. obsession. Here are some of our favorites!

SKINNY SCOOP For the best-tasting toast, I like to buy multigrain bread from my local bakery.

PUT AN EGG ON IT! SERVES 1

Q V DF

1 ounce (¼ small) Hass avocado

¼ teaspoon kosher salt

Freshly ground black pepper

1 slice (1½ ounces) multigrain bread, toasted

Cooking spray or oil mister

1 large egg

A few dashes of hot sauce (optional)

In a small bowl, mash the avocado with ⅛ teaspoon of the salt and pepper to taste. Spread the avocado on the toast.

Heat a small nonstick skillet over low heat. Coat with cooking spray and gently crack the egg into the skillet. Cover and cook until the white is set and the yolk runny, 2 to 3 minutes, or to your liking. Slide the egg on top of the avocado toast and top with the remaining ⅛ teaspoon salt, pepper to taste, and hot sauce (if using).

CALORIES	239
FAT	11 g
SATURATED FAT	2.5 g
CHOLESTEROL	186 mg
CARBOHYDRATE	23 g
FIBER	5.5 g
PROTEIN	13 g
SUGARS	3 g
SODIUM	547 mg

KARINA'S SPECIAL   SERVES 1

1 ounce (¼ small) Hass avocado

¼ teaspoon kosher salt

Freshly ground black pepper

1 slice (1½ ounces) multigrain bread, toasted

2 thin slices tomato

1 large egg, hard-boiled, peeled, and sliced

½ tablespoon chopped scallions, green parts only

CALORIES	248
FAT	11 g
SATURATED FAT	2.5 g
CHOLESTEROL	186 mg
CARBOHYDRATE	25 g
FIBER	6 g
PROTEIN	13 g
SUGARS	4 g
SODIUM	550 mg

In a small bowl, mash the avocado with ⅛ teaspoon of the salt and pepper to taste. Spread the avocado on the toast and top with the tomato slices, egg slices, and scallions. Sprinkle with the remaining ⅛ teaspoon salt and pepper to taste.

CHUNKY LOADED GUAC TOAST   SERVES 1

2 ounces (½ small) Hass avocado

2 tablespoons chopped tomato

1 tablespoon chopped red onion

1 teaspoon fresh lime juice

1 teaspoon chopped fresh cilantro

¼ teaspoon kosher salt

Freshly ground black pepper

1 slice (1½ ounces) multigrain bread, toasted

3 or 4 thin slices jalapeño pepper

CALORIES	236
FAT	10.5 g
SATURATED FAT	1.5 g
CHOLESTEROL	0 mg
CARBOHYDRATE	30 g
FIBER	8 g
PROTEIN	8 g
SUGARS	6 g
SODIUM	483 mg

In a small bowl, mash the avocado. Add the tomato, onion, lime juice, cilantro, salt, and pepper to taste and stir well. Spread the mixture on the toast and top with the jalapeño.

CUCUMBER, TOMATO, AND LOX   SERVES 1

1 ounce (¼ small) Hass avocado

½ tablespoon chopped scallions or chives

⅛ teaspoon plus a pinch of kosher salt

Freshly ground black pepper

1 slice (1½ ounces) multigrain bread, toasted

2 thin slices tomato

3 slices cucumber

½ ounce thinly sliced Nova lox or smoked salmon

CALORIES	195
FAT	7 g
SATURATED FAT	1 g
CHOLESTEROL	3 mg
CARBOHYDRATE	25 g
FIBER	6 g
PROTEIN	10 g
SUGARS	5 g
SODIUM	520 mg

In a small bowl, mash the avocado with the scallions, a pinch of salt, and pepper to taste. Spread the avocado on the toast and top with the tomato slices, cucumber slices, and lox. Sprinkle with the remaining ⅛ teaspoon salt and pepper to taste.

SOUTH OF THE BORDER HUEVOS REVUELTOS   SERVES 1

1 ounce (¼ small) Hass avocado

¼ teaspoon kosher salt

Freshly ground black pepper

1 slice (1½ ounces) multigrain bread, toasted

1 large egg

1 tablespoon chopped scallions

Cooking spray or oil mister

1 tablespoon jarred mild salsa

CALORIES	245
FAT	11 g
SATURATED FAT	2.5 g
CHOLESTEROL	186 mg
CARBOHYDRATE	24 g
FIBER	5.5 g
PROTEIN	13 g
SUGARS	4 g
SODIUM	636 mg

In a small bowl, mash the avocado with ⅛ teaspoon of the salt and pepper to taste. Spread the avocado on the toast.

In a separate bowl, beat together the egg, scallions, remaining ⅛ teaspoon salt, and pepper to taste.

Heat a small nonstick skillet over low heat. Coat with cooking spray and add the egg mixture. Cook, stirring with a wooden spoon, until cooked through, 2 to 3 minutes. Slide the scrambled egg on top of the avocado toast and top with the salsa and pepper to taste.

BRUSSELS SPROUT HASH WITH BACON AND EGGS SERVES 2

Q GF DF

These pan-roasted sprouts are perfectly charred and crispy on the outside and slightly tender on the inside. Cooked with just enough bacon to add flavor, they're then topped with a fried egg, which I prefer a little runny. Tommy and I are obsessed with Brussels sprouts—for breakfast, lunch, or dinner. Though I can serve this any time of day, I especially love making it for Sunday brunch, because as much as I enjoy going out for brunch with my family, it's really hard to find healthy options at my local spots. So instead, I whip up the dishes I *wish* they would serve!

2 slices center-cut bacon, cut into ½-inch pieces

1 tablespoon olive oil

10 ounces Brussels sprouts, quartered

1 large shallot, quartered lengthwise and halved crosswise

½ teaspoon plus a pinch of kosher salt

Freshly ground black pepper

Cooking spray or oil mister

2 large eggs

Preheat the oven to 425°F.

Heat a 12-inch cast iron or ovenproof nonstick skillet over medium heat. Add the bacon and cook, stirring, until crisp, 3 to 4 minutes. Using a slotted spoon, transfer to a plate lined with a paper towel.

Add the oil to the skillet with the bacon fat, then add the Brussels sprouts, shallot, ¼ teaspoon of the salt, and pepper to taste. Increase the heat to medium-high and cook, undisturbed, until beginning to caramelize, about 3 minutes. Flip the vegetables, add another ¼ teaspoon salt and pepper to taste, and cook until golden all over, 2 to 3 more minutes. Return the bacon to the skillet and transfer to the oven.

Roast until the sprouts have softened but still have bite, 6 to 8 minutes.

Meanwhile, heat a nonstick skillet over medium heat. Coat lightly with cooking spray and crack the eggs into the skillet. Cover and cook until the eggs are set, about 2 minutes, or to your desired doneness.

Divide the sprouts between 2 plates and top each with an egg, a pinch of salt, and pepper to taste.

PER SERVING	1½ cups hash + 1 large egg
CALORIES	267
FAT	15.5 g
SATURATED FAT	4 g
CHOLESTEROL	191 mg
CARBOHYDRATE	16 g
FIBER	6 g
PROTEIN	18 g
SUGARS	5 g
SODIUM	669 mg

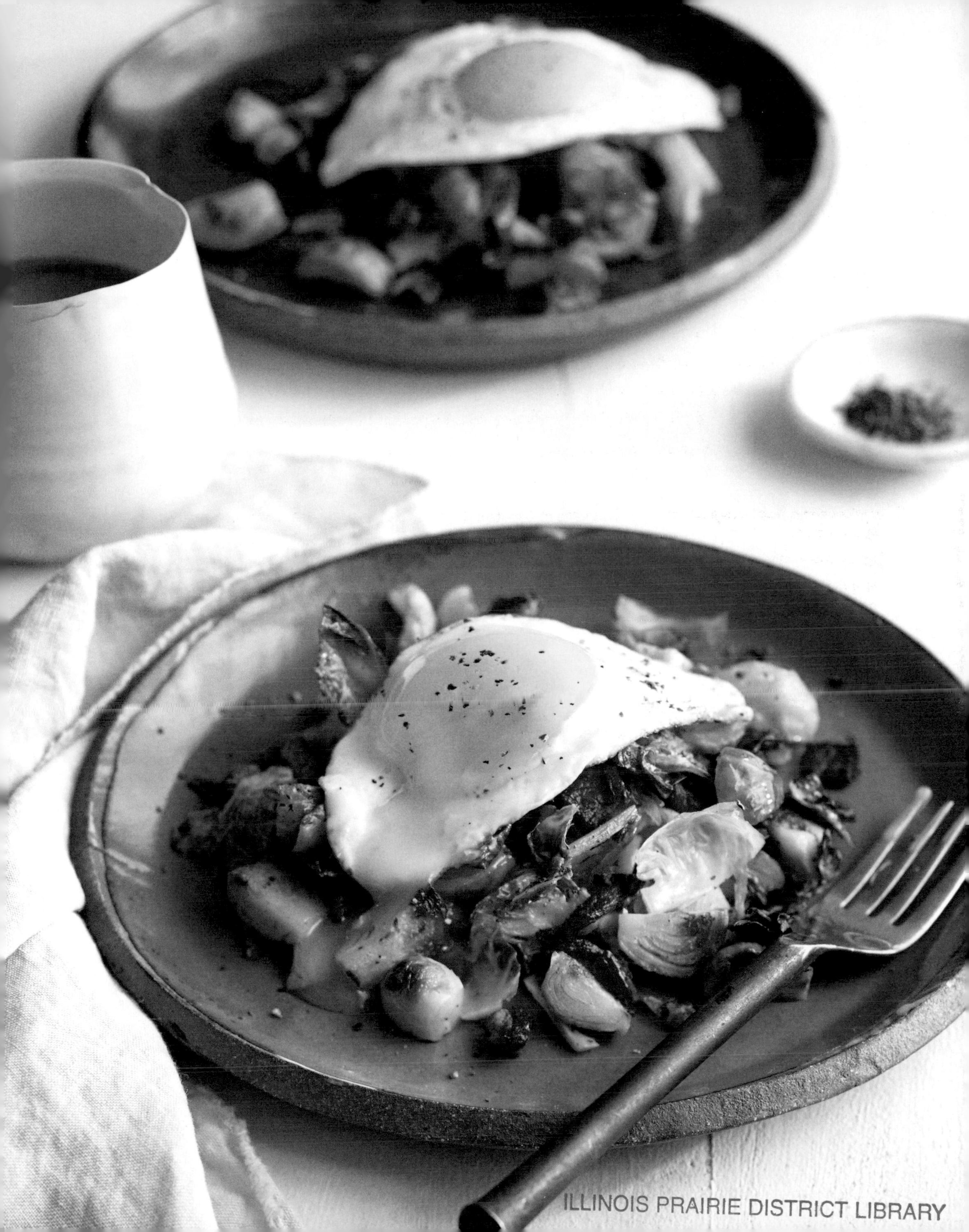

MEXICAN HUEVOS SHAKSHUKOS

SERVES 4

Q V GF DF

Shakshuka is a simple one-skillet stew of slow-cooked tomatoes and spices with eggs poached directly in the sauce. This North African dish can be adapted hundreds of different ways. I love this Mexican twist, where I add diced green chiles and cumin to the sauce, and serve it on a charred tortilla topped with lettuce, avocado, and cilantro. This is an easy, inexpensive dish you can serve for breakfast, brunch, lunch, or dinner.

1 teaspoon olive oil

½ medium onion, finely chopped

1 (14.5-ounce) can no-salt-added petite diced tomatoes

1 (4.25-ounce) can diced green chiles

¼ teaspoon ground cumin

¾ teaspoon kosher salt

Freshly ground black pepper

4 corn tortillas

Olive oil spray (such as Bertolli) or a mister

4 large eggs

1 cup shredded romaine lettuce

1 small Hass avocado (4 ounces), cubed

2 tablespoons chopped fresh cilantro

Tabasco sauce (optional)

In a 10-inch nonstick skillet, heat the oil over medium heat. Add the onion and cook, stirring, until softened, about 3 minutes. Add the tomatoes, chiles, cumin, ½ teaspoon of the salt, and pepper to taste. Bring to a boil, reduce the heat to medium-low, cover, and simmer for 5 minutes.

Meanwhile, heat a nonstick griddle or skillet over high heat. Lightly spray both sides of the tortillas with oil, put them in the skillet, and heat until crisp and pockets of air start to form, about 30 seconds per side. Transfer to 4 plates.

Carefully break the eggs into the tomato sauce. Cover and cook until the egg whites are opaque and the yolks are cooked to your liking, 4 to 5 minutes for runny yolks.

To serve, carefully spoon some sauce with an egg over each tortilla. Top each with a pinch of salt, the lettuce, avocado, cilantro, and Tabasco (if using).

FOOD FACTS: EGGS
The egg is a powerhouse of lean protein, healthy fats, and disease-fighting nutrients. One egg has around 6 grams of high-quality protein, along with vitamins, minerals, and heart-healthy omega-3 fatty acids. Eggs are also a rich source of antioxidants that help protect the eyes.

PER SERVING	1 egg + 1 tortilla + ½ cup sauce
CALORIES	**218**
FAT	**11 g**
SATURATED FAT	**2.5 g**
CHOLESTEROL	**186 mg**
CARBOHYDRATE	**21 g**
FIBER	**4.5 g**
PROTEIN	**9 g**
SUGARS	**4 g**
SODIUM	**392 mg**

BANANA-ALMOND
SMOOTHIE BOWL SERVES 2

(Q) (V) (GF) (DF)

Instead of drinking your smoothie with a straw, try making it thicker and serving it in a bowl to eat with a spoon! I love to add all sorts of toppings: seeds, nuts, oats, granola, coconut flakes—the list goes on! And you can switch up the fruit, too. Sometimes I throw in a handful of spinach to make a green smoothie bowl! Though the color may be off-putting, the taste isn't any different.

2 medium bananas, sliced and frozen

½ cup unsweetened almond milk

1 tablespoon vanilla almond butter (I like Justin's)

2 teaspoons chia seeds

½ cup sliced strawberries

½ cup blueberries

1 tablespoon chopped almonds

In a high-speed blender, combine the bananas, almond milk, almond butter, and 1 teaspoon of the chia seeds and blend until smooth (if you don't have a high-speed blender, thaw the bananas a bit first). Pour the smoothie into 2 bowls and top with the strawberries, blueberries, chopped almonds, and remaining 1 teaspoon chia seeds.

PER SERVING	1 bowl
CALORIES	231
FAT	7.5 g
SATURATED FAT	1 g
CHOLESTEROL	0 mg
CARBOHYDRATE	41 g
FIBER	7.5 g
PROTEIN	5 g
SUGARS	22 g
SODIUM	65 mg

SAVORY QUINOA BREAKFAST BOWLS

SERVES 4

Q V GF DF

Here's a little breakfast bowl that will definitely help you get through your day. Protein-packed quinoa and nutrient-rich spinach are topped with a soft-boiled egg with a slightly runny yolk. You can also add any leftover vegetables you have on hand (asparagus or roasted squash are both delicious choices).

4 large eggs

2/3 cup vegetable broth*

1/3 cup quinoa, rinsed well

4 cups baby spinach

4 ounces (1 small) Hass avocado, sliced

16 grape tomatoes, halved

4 teaspoons olive oil

1 tablespoon chopped fresh chives

1/4 teaspoon kosher salt

Freshly ground black pepper

Read the label to be sure this product is gluten-free.

Bring a small pot of water to a boil. Add the eggs, cover, and remove the pan from the heat. Let stand for 10 minutes for slightly soft yolks. Drain and rinse the eggs under cold water. Peel the eggs and cut them in half lengthwise.

Meanwhile, in a second small pot, bring the broth to a boil over high heat. Reduce the heat to low, add the quinoa, cover, and cook on low until the liquid is absorbed, about 15 minutes. Fluff with a fork.

Place 1 cup of the spinach in the bottom of each of 4 serving bowls. Top each with 1/4 cup hot quinoa, 1 sliced egg, a quarter of the avocado, and a quarter of the tomatoes. Drizzle each with 1 teaspoon olive oil, sprinkle with chives, and season each with a pinch of salt and pepper to taste.

FOOD FACTS: QUINOA

This nutty-tasting and gluten-free ancient grain provides a healthy (and tasty!) dose of protein, fiber, and nutrients. Quinoa is also one of the only plant foods that is a complete protein, meaning it contains all nine essential amino acids.

PER SERVING	1 bowl
CALORIES	**236**
FAT	**14.5 g**
SATURATED FAT	**3 g**
CHOLESTEROL	**186 mg**
CARBOHYDRATE	**17 g**
FIBER	**4.5 g**
PROTEIN	**10 g**
SUGARS	**4 g**
SODIUM	**312 mg**

BREAKFAST BANANA SPLIT   SERVES 2

Q V

Banana splits for breakfast? Coming right up! This superquick and (yes!) healthy breakfast is loaded with fruit, sweet vanilla yogurt, crunchy granola, and coconut chips. You can use any combination of berries you like. If I'm making this for my daughter Madison, I add a little whipped cream on top, a drizzle of chocolate syrup, and a few colored sprinkles—it makes her feel like she's having dessert for breakfast.

2 small peeled bananas
(2½ ounces each)

½ cup sliced strawberries

½ cup blackberries

½ cup chopped pineapple

1 cup 0% vanilla Greek yogurt
(I like Stonyfield)

2 tablespoons low-fat granola
(I use Back to Nature Classic)

¼ ounce roasted coconut chips
(I like Trader Joe's) or sweetened
coconut flakes

Halve the bananas lengthwise and place 2 halves in each of 2 shallow bowls. Using half the fruit, divide the strawberries, blackberries, and pineapple evenly, placing it in the bottom of each bowl, between the banana slices. Top each with ½ cup of the yogurt, and then with the remaining fruit. Divide the granola and coconut chips between the bowls and serve.

PER SERVING	1 banana split
CALORIES	256
FAT	2 g
SATURATED FAT	1.5 g
CHOLESTEROL	0 mg
CARBOHYDRATE	50 g
FIBER	6 g
PROTEIN	12 g
SUGARS	34 g
SODIUM	56 mg

SLOW COOKER "BAKED" OATMEAL WITH COCONUT, BLUEBERRIES, AND BANANAS SERVES 6

SC V GF DF

If you've ever tried baked oatmeal, you'll love this slow cooker version. I layer it with lots of fruit, add a little honey for sweetness, and then top it with nuts and shredded coconut for a healthy breakfast that's not only high in fiber, but also delicious. I've tested this with different types of oats and have found that quick oats work best and take less time. Any type of milk will work, so you can use whatever you normally drink. I use coconut milk to keep it dairy-free, but you can easily swap in almond milk or dairy milk. Good morning, indeed!

Cooking spray or oil mister

2 medium bananas (the riper the better), cut into ½-inch-thick slices

1½ cups blueberries

1 cup quick-cooking oats*
(I like Bob's Red Mill Quick Gluten Free Oats)

¼ cup chopped walnuts

½ teaspoon ground cinnamon

Pinch of kosher salt

1 cup canned light coconut milk

3 tablespoons honey

1 teaspoon vanilla extract

¼ cup sweetened shredded coconut

Read the label to be sure this product is gluten-free.

Coat the bottom of a 6-quart slow cooker with cooking spray. Arrange the banana slices in a single layer on the bottom and top with half of the blueberries.

In a medium bowl, combine the oats, 2 tablespoons of the walnuts, the cinnamon, and salt.

In a separate bowl, whisk together the coconut milk, honey, and vanilla. Pour the liquid mixture over the oats, stir well, and pour into the slow cooker. Sprinkle the remaining ¾ cup blueberries, the remaining 2 tablespoons walnuts, and the coconut over the top.

Cover and cook on low for 2 to 2½ hours, until the oatmeal is cooked through. Serve warm.

PER SERVING	⅔ cup
CALORIES	219
FAT	8 g
SATURATED FAT	3.5 g
CHOLESTEROL	0 mg
CARBOHYDRATE	35 g
FIBER	4 g
PROTEIN	3 g
SUGARS	19 g
SODIUM	27 mg

SLOW COOKER CHOCOLATE SWIRL BANANA BREAD SERVES 12

SC V GF

My younger daughter, Madison, loves banana bread, so I always keep extra bananas on hand and let them get super ripe (almost black!) just to make it for her. Overripe bananas are very sweet, which means you can cut back on the sugar without missing any sweetness. The first time I tried making a quick bread in my slow cooker, I was blown away! I couldn't believe how perfectly it turned out. It's really great during the warmer months when I don't want to heat up my kitchen by turning the oven on.

Baking spray

1 cup all-purpose flour*
(I like Bob's Red Mill)

¾ teaspoon baking soda

¼ teaspoon kosher salt

2 tablespoons unsalted butter,
at room temperature

½ cup packed light brown sugar

3 overripe medium bananas,
mashed

2 tablespoons unsweetened
applesauce

2 large egg whites

1 teaspoon vanilla extract

¼ cup semisweet chocolate
chips*

*Read the labels to be sure these products are gluten-free.

Lightly coat an 8 x 4-inch loaf pan with baking spray. Place a small rack or 3 or 4 foil balls (see opposite) into a slow cooker.

In a medium bowl, whisk together the flour, baking soda, and salt.

In a large bowl, with an electric mixer, beat the butter and brown sugar. Add the bananas, applesauce, egg whites, and vanilla and beat on medium speed until combined. Scrape down the sides of the bowl with a rubber spatula. Add the flour mixture and mix on low speed until just combined. Pour the batter into the prepared pan.

Place the chocolate chips in a microwave-safe bowl and microwave in 15-second increments, stirring after each, until the chips are melted. Add dollops of the melted chocolate to the top of the batter. Using a butter knife, swirl the chocolate into the batter. Place the pan in the slow cooker on the rack and cover.

Cover and cook on high for 2½ to 3 hours, until a toothpick inserted in the center comes out clean. Remove the pan from the slow cooker and let cool at least 20 minutes in the pan before turning the bread out of the pan. Cut into 12 slices to serve.

SKINNY SCOOP If you want to bake it in the oven instead, bake in a 350°F oven for about 50 minutes.

PER SERVING	1 slice
CALORIES	134
FAT	3.5 g
SATURATED FAT	2 g
CHOLESTEROL	5 mg
CARBOHYDRATE	26 g
FIBER	2.5 g
PROTEIN	2 g
SUGARS	15 g
SODIUM	115 mg

SKINNY SCOOP This recipe works best in a 6-quart oval or rectangular slow cooker that can hold a loaf pan and a small rack. If you don't have a rack that will fit into your slow cooker, cut 3 or 4 sheets of foil about 12 inches long and roll them into individual balls, flattening the top of each ball slightly so that the loaf pan can sit on top of the foil balls.

FAST

Q V GF FF Dad's Cauliflower Soup **40**

Q V GF FF Cream of Zucchini Soup **43**

Q PC GF DF FF Pressure Cooker Chicken Soup for My Soul **44**

Q V FF Roasted Pepper and Orzo Soup **45**

Q V GF FF Pasta e Fagioli **47**

Q GF DF Drunken Seafood Stew **48**

SLOW

SC GF DF FF Slow Cooker Stuffed Pepper Soup **50**

SC GF FF Slow Cooker Italian Sausage and White Bean Soup with Escarole **51**

SC GF FF Slow Cooker Lasagna Soup **53**

SC FF Slow Cooker Chicken and Dumpling Soup **54**

SC V GF DF FF Slow Cooker Butternut-Apple Soup with Crispy Leeks **57**

SC V GF FF Slow Cooker Creamy Tomato Soup **58**

SC V GF FF Slow Cooker Vegetable Yellow Split Pea Soup **61**

SC GF DF FF Slow Cooker Chicken Taco Chili **62**

SC GF DF FF Slow Cooker Turkey, White Bean, and Pumpkin Chili **65**

SC GF FF Slow Cooker Beef and Two-Bean Chili **66**

SC GF DF FF Slow Cooker Beef Stew with Sweet Potatoes **69**

SC DF FF Slow Cooker Venison Stew **70**

SC GF DF FF Roasted Chicken Stock in the Slow Cooker **72**

SC GF DF FF Beef Stock in the Slow Cooker **73**

CHILIS, SOUPS, AND STEWS

DAD'S CAULIFLOWER SOUP   SERVES 4

Q V GF FF

As I was growing up, my family had homemade soup for dinner practically every night, either as a first course or a main dish. I wasn't always happy about this, but on the nights we had this soup, I never complained. Dad lost his vision a few years ago, so sadly he no longer cooks, but thankfully, he is still with us and I've been making it a point to learn some of the dishes he once cooked. This one is very easy, with few ingredients, and it's ready in under 30 minutes.

1 tablespoon unsalted butter

1 tablespoon all-purpose flour*

4 cups reduced-sodium chicken or vegetable broth*

1 medium head cauliflower, chopped (about 20 ounces)

½ cup chopped onions

½ teaspoon kosher salt

Microgreens, for garnish (optional)

Read the labels to be sure these products are gluten-free.

In a medium nonstick pot, melt the butter over low heat. Add the flour and cook, stirring with a wooden spoon, until golden in color, about 2 minutes. Add the broth, cauliflower, and onions. Increase the heat to medium, bring to a boil, then cover and reduce the heat to medium-low. Cook until the vegetables are tender, about 20 minutes. Remove the pan from the heat. Puree the soup in the pot with an immersion blender until smooth (or in a stand blender, in two batches). Season with the salt. Serve hot. Ladle 1½ cups into each of 4 bowls and garnish with microgreens, if desired.

PERFECT PAIRINGS This soup is wonderful served as a first course. To make it a meal, serve with crusty bread and a salad or paired with a sandwich on the side.

PER SERVING	1½ cups
CALORIES	91
FAT	3 g
SATURATED FAT	2 g
CHOLESTEROL	8 mg
CARBOHYDRATE	11 g
FIBER	4 g
PROTEIN	5 g
SUGARS	4 g
SODIUM	754 mg

CREAM OF ZUCCHINI SOUP   SERVES 4

Q V GF FF

Creamy and light, this fan favorite was one of the first recipes I shared when I started blogging. Because it's ridiculously easy and quick to make, I knew it belonged in this book. I use chicken broth, but vegetable broth works well, too, if you want to keep it vegetarian. The Parmesan cheese and drizzle of oil on top are musts, so don't skip them!

4 cups reduced-sodium vegetable or chicken broth*

3 medium zucchini (8 ounces each), cut into chunks

½ small onion, quartered

2 garlic cloves

2 tablespoons reduced-fat sour cream

4 tablespoons shredded Parmesan cheese,* for serving

2 teaspoons extra-virgin olive oil

Freshly ground black pepper

Read the labels to be sure these products are gluten-free.

In a large pot, combine the broth, zucchini, onion, and garlic. Bring to a boil over medium heat. Reduce the heat to low, cover, and simmer until the vegetables are tender, about 20 minutes. Remove the pan from the heat. Puree the soup in the pot with an immersion blender (or in a regular blender, in batches). Add the sour cream and puree again until smooth.

To serve, ladle 1½ cups into each of 4 bowls. Top each with 1 tablespoon Parmesan, ½ teaspoon olive oil, and pepper to taste.

PER SERVING	1½ cups
CALORIES	101
FAT	5 g
SATURATED FAT	2 g
CHOLESTEROL	6 mg
CARBOHYDRATE	7 g
FIBER	2 g
PROTEIN	6 g
SUGARS	5 g
SODIUM	675 mg

PRESSURE COOKER CHICKEN SOUP FOR MY SOUL   SERVES 6

Q PC GF DF FF

When my family's in the mood for chicken soup, this is the bowl they crave. You'll need a spoon, a fork, *and* your hands to eat it—I make it with a side of rice so it's a full meal. On lazy Sundays, I whip up a big pot and let it simmer for hours. Need it finished faster? With a pressure cooker (I'm loving my Instant Pot), it's ready in just 30 minutes. I swear this soup tastes even better the next day . . . if we're lucky enough to have any leftovers.

6 bone-in, skinless chicken thighs (28 ounces total)

1 teaspoon kosher salt

½ teaspoon ground cumin

1 teaspoon olive oil

1 cup chopped scallions

4 garlic cloves, minced

1 medium tomato, chopped

6 baby red potatoes (about 1 ounce each), halved

½ red bell pepper, cut into 1-inch pieces

⅓ cup chopped fresh cilantro (stems and leaves)

1 tablespoon chicken bouillon*

2 bay leaves

3 medium ears corn, husked and halved

5 ounces Hass avocado, cut into 6 slices

*Read the label to be sure this product is gluten-free.

Season the chicken with ½ teaspoon of the salt and the cumin.

Press the sauté button if using the Instant Pot, or heat a standard pressure cooker over medium heat. Add the oil, scallions, and garlic and cook, stirring, until softened, about 2 minutes. Add the tomato and cook, stirring, until soft, about 1 minute. Add the chicken, potatoes, bell pepper, ¼ cup of the cilantro, 5½ cups water, the bouillon, bay leaves, and remaining ½ teaspoon salt. Cover and lock the lid.

Cook on high pressure for 25 minutes. Quick-release the lid. Add the corn and cook on high pressure until the potatoes are tender, 3 more minutes. Discard the bay leaves.

To serve, place 1 thigh, 1 piece of corn, and 2 potato halves in each of 6 bowls. Ladle 1 cup of broth into the bowls, top with a slice of avocado, and sprinkle with the remaining cilantro.

SKINNY SCOOP Although this soup can be made in a slow cooker, it loses some of its flavor. So for the best results, make this recipe in a pressure cooker (as here) or on the stovetop. If you're making this on the stove, add a little more water and increase the cook time to about 1 hour.

PER SERVING	1 bowl
CALORIES	280
FAT	10.5 g
SATURATED FAT	2 g
CHOLESTEROL	115 mg
CARBOHYDRATE	20 g
FIBER	4.5 g
PROTEIN	30 g
SUGARS	3 g
SODIUM	555 mg

ROASTED PEPPER AND ORZO SOUP SERVES 4

Q V FF

Orzo and roasted peppers are a perfect pair in this simple, hearty soup. It's filling, yet light enough to eat with a salad or half a sandwich—two of my favorite lunch combinations. Using jarred roasted peppers is the trick to getting this soup on the table in under 30 minutes. If you prefer to roast the peppers yourself, use two large red bell peppers and add an additional cup of broth.

1 teaspoon olive oil

2 large shallots, chopped

2 garlic cloves, chopped

2 (12-ounce) jars water-packed roasted red peppers

1²/₃ cups reduced-sodium vegetable or chicken broth

2 tablespoons freshly grated Pecorino Romano cheese

2 ounces (about ¹/₃ cup) orzo

1 cup baby spinach

1 tablespoon chopped fresh basil

Heat a medium pot over medium heat. Add the oil, shallots, and garlic and cook, stirring, until lightly golden, 3 to 4 minutes. Transfer to a blender and add the roasted red peppers and the liquid from the jars. Blend until smooth. Pour the mixture into the pot, add the broth and Romano, and bring to a boil. Add the orzo and cook according to package directions. Stir in the spinach and basil and cook 1 more minute. Serve hot.

PER SERVING	1 cup
CALORIES	127
FAT	2 g
SATURATED FAT	0.5 g
CHOLESTEROL	2 mg
CARBOHYDRATE	15 g
FIBER	1.5 g
PROTEIN	4 g
SUGARS	2 g
SODIUM	772 mg

PASTA e FAGIOLI   SERVES 6

Q V GF FF

I've been making this soup for years, and it's a true triple threat: delicious, easy to make, *and* easy on your wallet. Oh, and it also freezes like a champ. As a kid I hated beans, and it's funny how my children also dislike them. So I do what my mom always did, which is to puree them—a sneaky way to add nutrition that also helps thicken the soup and give it great body, as if it had simmered all day. Soup's on!

1 (15-ounce) can cannellini beans,* rinsed and drained

1 tablespoon olive oil

½ onion, chopped

3 garlic cloves, chopped

3½ cups reduced-sodium vegetable or chicken broth*

1 (15-ounce) can tomato sauce

1 celery stalk, chopped

1 carrot, finely chopped

2 tablespoons chopped fresh basil, plus more for serving

1 tablespoon dried parsley flakes

1 teaspoon dried oregano

1 bay leaf

½ teaspoon kosher salt

Freshly ground black pepper

Parmesan cheese rind (optional)

6 ounces small pasta (such as ditalini)*

Freshly grated Parmesan cheese, for serving (optional)

Read the labels to be sure these products are gluten-free.

Place the beans in a blender. Fill the can with water and pour it into the blender. Blend until almost smooth.

Heat a large pot or Dutch oven over medium heat. Add the oil, onion, and garlic and cook, stirring, until soft, about 3 minutes. Add the pureed beans, broth, tomato sauce, 1 cup water, the celery, carrot, basil, parsley, oregano, bay leaf, salt, pepper to taste, and Parmesan rind (if using). Increase the heat to high and bring to a boil. Reduce the heat to medium-low, cover, and cook, stirring occasionally, for 15 minutes. Add the pasta and cook, uncovered, until the pasta is al dente according to the package directions. Discard the bay leaf.

Ladle the soup into 6 serving bowls and top with fresh basil and grated Parmesan (if using).

PER SERVING	1½ cups
CALORIES	263
FAT	4.5 g
SATURATED FAT	1 g
CHOLESTEROL	1 mg
CARBOHYDRATE	44 g
FIBER	7 g
PROTEIN	10 g
SUGARS	8 g
SODIUM	816 mg

DRUNKEN SEAFOOD STEW

SERVES 4

Q GF DF

What do you get when you mix booze, seafood, and garlic? The makings of a good meal. This is honestly the easiest dish to make. You can use any combo of seafood you like—scallops, mussels, and lobster tails could easily be swapped for anything in this recipe. But be sure to keep the anchovies! Though tempting to leave out, they're the secret ingredient in this stew and completely disintegrate into it.

1 tablespoon olive oil

6 garlic cloves, chopped

5 whole anchovy fillets in oil, drained

¼ teaspoon crushed red pepper flakes

1½ cups canned whole peeled tomatoes (I like San Marzano), crushed by hand

1 cup clam juice

½ cup dry white wine

2 tablespoons fresh lemon juice

12 littleneck clams

½ pound saltwater fish fillets (such as cod or halibut), skinned and cut into 4 pieces

20 jumbo peeled, deveined shrimp (10 ounces total)

2 tablespoons chopped fresh parsley

2 tablespoons chopped fresh basil

4 ounces crusty whole wheat bread, for serving (optional)

In a 4- to 6-quart Dutch oven or saucepan, heat the oil over low heat. Add the garlic, anchovies, and pepper flakes and cook, stirring, until the garlic and anchovies fall apart, about 5 minutes. Add the tomatoes, clam juice, wine, and lemon juice. Increase the heat to medium, bring to a boil, and simmer for about 10 minutes. Add the clams, cover, and cook for 4 minutes. Add the fish and shrimp, cover, and simmer until the shrimp are opaque and the clams open (discard any that don't open), about 5 minutes (be careful not to overcook). Stir in the parsley and basil.

To serve, place 1 piece of fish, 5 shrimp, 3 clams, and ¾ cup broth in each of 4 serving bowls and serve with the crusty bread on the side, if desired.

TIME-SAVING TIP
I buy shrimp peeled and deveined. They cost slightly more, but it's worth the time saved in the kitchen.

PER SERVING	1 bowl + 1 ounce bread
CALORIES	301
FAT	6 g
SATURATED FAT	1 g
CHOLESTEROL	123 mg
CARBOHYDRATE	22 g
FIBER	2.5 g
PROTEIN	32 g
SUGARS	4 g
SODIUM	774 mg

SLOW COOKER STUFFED PEPPER SOUP · SERVES 6

SC · GF · DF · FF

I grew up eating stuffed peppers. Mom would stuff them with ground beef, rice, and tomato sauce and bake them in the oven. I love taking some of my favorite comfort foods and turning them into a hearty bowl of soup—and that's just what I've done here. It's not just a great way to cut calories, it cuts down on prep time, too. This recipe is extremely popular on Skinnytaste.com (where I share my stovetop version). My kids love it—Madison especially—and because it makes a lot, I usually pack the extras in her thermos for lunch. Gotta love leftovers!

1 pound 95% lean ground beef

3/4 teaspoon kosher salt

1 cup chopped onion

2/3 cup chopped green bell pepper

2/3 cup chopped red bell pepper

3 garlic cloves, chopped

2 cups reduced-sodium chicken broth*

2 (14.5-ounce) cans petite diced tomatoes

1 3/4 cups canned tomato sauce

1/2 teaspoon dried marjoram

Freshly ground black pepper

3 cups cooked brown rice (see below)

Read the label to be sure this product is gluten-free.

Heat a large nonstick skillet over high heat. Add the ground beef and salt, and cook, using a wooden spoon to break the meat into pieces as it browns, 4 to 5 minutes. Drain the fat from the pan. Return the pan to medium-low heat and add the onion, bell pepper, and garlic and cook, stirring, until soft, 6 to 8 minutes. Transfer to a slow cooker and add the broth, tomatoes, tomato sauce, marjoram, and black pepper to taste.

Cover and cook on high for 4 hours or on low for 8 hours.

Ladle the soup into 6 serving bowls. Top each with 1/2 cup of the cooked brown rice and serve hot.

PERFECT BROWN RICE IN THE SLOW COOKER

Cooking brown rice in the slow cooker is easy and foolproof. Place 1 1/2 cups water, 1 cup rinsed brown rice, 1 teaspoon olive oil, and 1 teaspoon kosher salt (if you want it) in a slow cooker. Cover and cook on high for 2 hours.

PER SERVING	about 1 1/2 cups soup + 1/2 cup rice
CALORIES	347
FAT	7.5 g
SATURATED FAT	2.5 g
CHOLESTEROL	48 mg
CARBOHYDRATE	45 g
FIBER	6 g
PROTEIN	23 g
SUGARS	12 g
SODIUM	927 mg

SLOW COOKER ITALIAN SAUSAGE AND WHITE BEAN SOUP WITH ESCAROLE SERVES 6

SC GF FF

This soup is hearty *without* being heavy. Made with classic Italian ingredients, it's the kind of meal you want to come home to on a cold evening because it will warm you up in a flash. If you can't find escarole, use any dark leafy green such as kale or Swiss chard. Serve with crusty bread on the side and some extra Pecorino Romano to pass around the table.

11 ounces sweet Italian chicken sausage,* casings removed

½ cup chopped onion

½ cup chopped celery

½ cup chopped carrots

2 garlic cloves, crushed

Pinch of crushed red pepper flakes

3 cups reduced-sodium chicken broth*

1 (28-ounce) can crushed tomatoes (I like Tuttorosso)

1 (15-ounce) can no-salt added white beans,* such as cannellini, rinsed and drained

2 bay leaves

Freshly ground black pepper

4 cups shredded escarole

3 tablespoons freshly grated Pecorino Romano cheese

Read the labels to be sure these products are gluten-free.

Heat a nonstick skillet over medium heat. Add the sausage and cook, using a wooden spoon to break the meat into small pieces as it browns, about 5 minutes. Add the onion, celery, carrots, garlic, and pepper flakes. Cook, stirring, until the vegetables soften, 2 to 3 minutes. Transfer to a slow cooker and add the broth, tomatoes, white beans, bay leaves, and black pepper to taste.

Cover and cook on high for 4 hours or on low for 8 hours. Discard the bay leaves, add the escarole and Romano, and cook until the escarole is wilted, about 30 minutes.

PER SERVING	1⅓ cups
CALORIES	207
FAT	5 g
SATURATED FAT	1.5 g
CHOLESTEROL	42 mg
CARBOHYDRATE	23 g
FIBER	7 g
PROTEIN	17 g
SUGARS	8 g
SODIUM	914 mg

SKINNY SCOOP To make quick marinara: In a medium pan over medium-low heat, sauté 3 smashed garlic cloves in 1 teaspoon oil until golden. Add 1 (28-ounce) can crushed tomatoes, season with salt and pepper, and simmer for about 5 minutes. Remove the pan from the heat and add 1 tablespoon chopped fresh basil.

SLOW COOKER LASAGNA SOUP SERVES 6

SC **GF** **FF**

I love taking classic dishes, such as lasagna, and turning them into soup. It's a wonderful way to enjoy some of my favorite meals for a fraction of the calories—but don't let the sound of that fool you. This soup has everything you love about lasagna in one big bowl. Plus, it's finished with a big dollop of a ricotta-Parmesan-mozzarella blend that's so creamy and cheesy you won't believe it's good for you.

TOPPING

½ cup part-skim ricotta cheese

3 tablespoons freshly grated Parmesan cheese

2 tablespoons chopped fresh parsley

SOUP

Cooking spray or oil mister

14 ounces sweet Italian chicken sausage,* casings removed

½ onion, chopped

2 garlic cloves, chopped

3 cups reduced-sodium chicken broth*

2 cups marinara sauce, homemade (see Skinny Scoop) or store-bought

¼ cup chopped fresh parsley

2 bay leaves

Freshly ground black pepper

2 cups baby spinach, chopped

6 ounces lasagna noodles,* broken into small pieces

6 tablespoons shredded part-skim mozzarella cheese*

¼ cup chopped fresh basil

Freshly ground black pepper

*Read the labels to be sure these products are gluten-free.

For the topping: In a medium bowl, combine the ricotta, Parmesan, and parsley. Refrigerate until the soup is ready.

For the soup: Heat a large nonstick skillet over medium-high heat and coat with cooking spray. Add the sausage and cook, using a wooden spoon to break the meat into small pieces as it browns, 3 to 4 minutes. Add the onion and garlic and cook, stirring, until soft, 3 to 4 minutes. Transfer to a slow cooker and add the broth, 2¼ cups water, the marinara sauce, parsley, bay leaves, and pepper to taste.

Cover and cook on high for 4 hours or on low for 8 hours.

About 30 minutes before the soup is ready, remove the bay leaves and add the spinach and broken pasta. Cover and cook on high until the pasta is cooked, about 30 minutes.

Divide the soup among 6 bowls and top each with 2 tablespoons of the ricotta mixture, and sprinkle with the mozzarella, basil, and pepper to taste.

TIME-SAVING TIP

Using a mini chopper or food processor saves time in the kitchen. I keep mine on my counter to slice and dice all my vegetables.

PER SERVING	about 1½ cups
CALORIES	310
FAT	10 g
SATURATED FAT	3.5 g
CHOLESTEROL	72 mg
CARBOHYDRATE	30 g
FIBER	3 g
PROTEIN	23 g
SUGARS	2 g
SODIUM	959 mg

CHILIS, SOUPS, AND STEWS

SLOW COOKER CHICKEN AND DUMPLING SOUP   SERVES 6

SC **FF**

Although I grew up on dumplings, having them in a soup is something I discovered later in life. Make sure that the soup is boiling before dropping in the dough. Once I shred the chicken and put it all back in the pot, I cover it and keep the slow cooker on high while I prepare the dumpling dough. The dumplings really expand when they cook, so use less than a teaspoon of batter for each. Madison tells me I make the *best* soup every time she eats this. I hope you'll agree.

SOUP

1 tablespoon unsalted butter

1 cup chopped celery

1 cup chopped carrots

½ cup chopped onion

1 garlic clove, minced

2 tablespoons all-purpose flour

7 cups reduced-sodium chicken broth

1 pound boneless, skinless chicken breasts

2 bay leaves

Freshly ground black pepper

DUMPLINGS

1 cup all-purpose flour

1 teaspoon baking powder

1 tablespoon chopped fresh chives

½ teaspoon kosher salt

⅛ teaspoon freshly ground black pepper

1 large egg yolk, beaten

½ cup chilled reduced-sodium chicken broth

¼ cup chopped fresh parsley, for garnish

For the soup: In a large nonstick skillet, melt the butter over medium heat. Add the celery, carrots, onion, and garlic and cook, stirring, until soft and fragrant, about 12 minutes. Sprinkle the flour over the vegetables and cook, stirring, 1 to 2 more minutes. Transfer to a slow cooker. Add the broth, chicken breasts, bay leaves, and pepper to taste.

Cover and cook on high for 4 hours (for best results) or low for 8 hours. Remove the chicken, shred with 2 forks, and return to the slow cooker. Discard the bay leaves. Cover and set to high.

For the dumplings: In a large bowl, combine the flour, baking powder, chives, salt, and pepper. In a small bowl, whisk together the egg yolk and broth, then add the liquid to the flour mixture. Mix until just blended (the dough will be thick).

Drop scant teaspoons of dough into the soup (they will expand). Cover and cook without removing the lid for 30 to 40 minutes. The dumplings should expand and float to the surface when done.

Ladle the soup into 6 serving bowls. Serve garnished with the parsley.

PER SERVING	1²/₃ cups
CALORIES	236
FAT	5 g
SATURATED FAT	2 g
CHOLESTEROL	84 mg
CARBOHYDRATE	23 g
FIBER	2 g
PROTEIN	22 g
SUGARS	2 g
SODIUM	1,026 mg

SKINNY SCOOP I tested the soup recipes in this book using Swanson 33% Less Sodium Chicken Broth (570 mg of sodium per cup), but if you're watching the salt in your diet, you can use Imagine Organic Low-Sodium Free-Range Chicken Broth (115 mg), Trader Joe's Organic Low-Sodium Chicken Broth (90 mg), or Pacific Organic Low-Sodium Free-Range Chicken Broth (70 mg).

SLOW COOKER BUTTERNUT-APPLE SOUP WITH CRISPY LEEKS SERVES 6

SC V GF DF FF

Simple and easy, this hearty fall soup combines sweet butternut squash with mild leeks and tart green apple to make a creamy, delightful, warm meal. The golden, just-crisp leeks do double duty in this dish: They add texture and flavor. Because peeling and cutting butternut squash can be time consuming, I often buy it precut to save time.

SOUP

2 pounds butternut squash, peeled, seeded, and cubed

1 leek (white parts only), rinsed well and roughly chopped

1 medium Granny Smith apple, peeled and roughly chopped

1 medium carrot, roughly chopped

2½ cups reduced-sodium chicken or vegetable broth*

½ cup canned coconut milk

GARNISH

1 tablespoon olive oil

¾ cup thinly sliced leeks (white parts only), rinsed well

⅛ teaspoon kosher salt

Coconut milk, for drizzling (optional)

Read the label to be sure this product is gluten-free.

For the soup: Place the squash, leek, apple, carrot, and broth in a slow cooker. Cover and cook on high for 4 hours or on low for 8 hours, until the squash is soft and cooked through.

Stir the coconut milk into the soup mixture. Puree the soup in the cooker with an immersion blender until smooth (or in a stand blender, in batches).

For the garnish: Heat a medium nonstick skillet over medium-low heat. Add the oil and leeks and cook, stirring occasionally, until golden and crisp, about 10 minutes. Season with the salt.

To serve, pour the soup into 6 serving bowls and garnish with the crispy leeks. If desired, drizzle with a little coconut milk.

PER SERVING	1 generous cup + 1 tablespoon crisp leeks
CALORIES	145
FAT	6 g
SATURATED FAT	3.5 g
CHOLESTEROL	0 mg
CARBOHYDRATE	22 g
FIBER	3.5 g
PROTEIN	3 g
SUGARS	8 g
SODIUM	284 mg

SKINNY SCOOP This soup can be made ahead of time and frozen for future meals. To freeze, let it cool completely before storing portions in airtight containers. Thaw overnight in the refrigerator before reheating.

SLOW COOKER CREAMY TOMATO SOUP SERVES 6

SC V GF FF

I'm a bit of a soup snob, thanks to the fact that my parents always made it from scratch when I was growing up. One of my favorite ones that my mom made was tomato soup, a recipe that had been passed down from my grandmother. Her version is a bit more labor intensive, so I've simplified it for the slow cooker.

1 tablespoon olive oil

1 cup finely chopped celery

1 cup finely chopped carrots

1 cup finely chopped onions

1 (28-ounce) can whole peeled tomatoes (I like San Marzano)

3½ cups reduced-sodium vegetable or chicken broth*

1 sprig of fresh thyme

¼ cup chopped fresh basil, plus more for garnish

1 bay leaf

Parmesan or Pecorino Romano cheese rind (optional)

2 tablespoons unsalted butter

2 tablespoons all-purpose flour*

1¾ cups 2% milk, warmed

⅓ cup freshly grated Pecorino Romano cheese

¾ teaspoon kosher salt

Freshly ground black pepper

*Read the labels to be sure these products are gluten-free.

Heat a large nonstick skillet over medium heat. Add the oil, celery, carrots, and onions and cook, stirring, until soft, 7 to 8 minutes. Transfer to a slow cooker.

Pour the juice from the tomato can into the slow cooker. Roughly crush the tomatoes with your hands as you add them to the cooker. Add the broth, thyme, basil, bay leaf, and cheese rind (if using).

Cover and cook on low for 6 hours. Remove the bay leaf and cheese rind. Puree the soup in the cooker with an immersion blender until smooth (or in a stand blender, in batches).

In a large skillet, melt the butter over low heat. Whisk in the flour and cook, whisking constantly, until the flour becomes golden, 4 to 5 minutes. Slowly whisk in about 1 cup of the hot soup. Add the warmed milk and stir until smooth. Pour the mixture into the slow cooker and stir. Add the Romano, salt, and pepper to taste. Cover and cook on low for 30 more minutes.

To serve, divide the soup among 6 bowls and garnish with basil.

PERFECT PAIRINGS I like to serve this with garlic bread and a simple garden salad, such as Italian House Salad with Dijon Vinaigrette (page 252). For lunch, I reduce the serving to 1 cup and serve it with a half sandwich, like Grilled Cheese with Havarti, Brussels Sprouts, and Apple (page 229).

PER SERVING	1⅔ cups
CALORIES	177
FAT	9.5 g
SATURATED FAT	4.5 g
CHOLESTEROL	21 mg
CARBOHYDRATE	16 g
FIBER	3 g
PROTEIN	8 g
SUGARS	9 g
SODIUM	807 mg

SLOW COOKER VEGETABLE YELLOW SPLIT PEA SOUP

SERVES 8

SC V GF FF

Split pea soup—one of my favorite cold-weather soups—is so easy to make in a slow cooker. Yellow split peas are often used in an Indian dish called dal, which inspired the flavors in this soup. I added turmeric to enhance the golden color of the dish, which turns out velvety, satisfying, and warming with just a hint of fragrant spices. You can refrigerate it for about a week, but note that it will thicken up. To loosen, simply reheat with a touch more liquid.

16 ounces yellow split peas, rinsed well

1 cup diced peeled butternut squash, fresh or frozen

1 cup sliced carrots

1 cup chopped celery

6 cups reduced-sodium vegetable or chicken broth*

1 tablespoon unsalted butter

1 cup chopped yellow onion

6 garlic cloves, crushed

1/2 tablespoon grated fresh ginger

1 teaspoon ground cumin

1 1/2 teaspoons ground turmeric

3/4 teaspoon kosher salt

4 cups coarsely chopped baby spinach

Read the label to be sure this product is gluten-free.

Combine the split peas, butternut squash, carrots, celery, and broth in a slow cooker. Cover and cook on high for 4 hours or on low for 9 to 10 hours, until the peas are very soft.

In a medium skillet, melt the butter over medium heat. Add the onion, garlic, ginger, cumin, turmeric, and 1/4 teaspoon of the salt and cook, stirring occasionally, until the vegetables are soft and fragrant, 3 to 4 minutes. Transfer to the slow cooker with the remaining 1/2 teaspoon salt and the spinach. Stir well and cook until the spinach wilts, 15 minutes. Serve hot.

TIME-SAVING TIP For easy prep, there's nothing better than precut diced vegetables, which are available in most supermarkets. Frozen diced butternut squash works extremely well in this dish, too.

PER SERVING	1 1/4 cups
CALORIES	247
FAT	1.5 g
SATURATED FAT	1 g
CHOLESTEROL	4 mg
CARBOHYDRATE	43 g
FIBER	9.5 g
PROTEIN	17 g
SUGARS	7 g
SODIUM	599 mg

SLOW COOKER CHICKEN TACO CHILI SERVES 10

SC GF DF FF

This recipe is one of the most popular slow cooker dishes on Skinnytaste.com, and it's no wonder! It's one of those perfect slow cooker dishes that requires no precooking—just throw everything in (you probably already have most of the ingredients in your pantry) and you'll have a delicious meal in a few hours. The key to the great flavor here is the homemade taco seasoning. Not only is my version much tastier and healthier than the premixed packets, but it's also much cheaper.

TACO SEASONING

1½ tablespoons ground cumin

1½ tablespoons chili powder*

¼ teaspoon garlic powder

¼ teaspoon onion powder

¼ teaspoon dried oregano

½ teaspoon sweet paprika

1 teaspoon kosher salt

½ teaspoon freshly ground black pepper

CHILI

1 (8-ounce) can tomato sauce

1 (15-ounce) can black beans,* rinsed and drained

1 (15.25-ounce) can kidney beans,* rinsed and drained

1 (10-ounce) package frozen corn kernels

2 (10-ounce) cans diced tomatoes with chiles

1 (4-ounce) can chopped green chiles

1 small onion, chopped

3 large boneless, skinless chicken breasts (8 ounces each)

¼ cup chopped fresh cilantro, for serving

*Read the labels to be sure these products are gluten-free.

For the taco seasoning: In a small bowl, combine the cumin, chili powder, garlic powder, onion powder, oregano, paprika, salt, and pepper.

For the chili: In a 5- or 6-quart slow cooker, combine the tomato sauce, beans, corn, tomatoes, green chiles, onion, and taco seasoning. Stir well. Nestle the chicken on top and cover.

Cook on high for 6 hours or on low for 10 hours. About 30 minutes before it's done, remove the chicken and shred. Return the chicken to the slow cooker and stir well.

To serve, scoop the chili into individual serving bowls and top with the cilantro.

PER SERVING	about 1 cup
CALORIES	221
FAT	3 g
SATURATED FAT	0.5 g
CHOLESTEROL	44 mg
CARBOHYDRATE	28 g
FIBER	8.5 g
PROTEIN	21 g
SUGARS	6 g
SODIUM	729 mg

PERFECT PAIRINGS I love this chili over brown rice or served with baked tortilla chips. You can top it with shredded cheese, diced avocado, or a dollop of sour cream.

SLOW COOKER TURKEY, WHITE BEAN, AND PUMPKIN CHILI   SERVES 9

SC **GF** **DF** **FF**

Pumpkin in chili? Yup! The pumpkin not only sneaks in extra vitamins and nutrients, it also gives the chili a beautiful golden hue and a rich creamy texture. And my kids don't even know it's in there! This dish is very mild, which makes it family friendly. If you want to kick up the heat a bit, just add jalapeño or serrano peppers along with the mild green chiles.

Cooking spray or oil mister

2 pounds 93% lean ground turkey

2½ teaspoons kosher salt

1 teaspoon olive oil

1 small onion, chopped

3 garlic cloves, minced

2 cups reduced-sodium chicken broth*

2 (15-ounce) cans Great Northern or navy beans, rinsed and drained

1 (15-ounce) can unsweetened pumpkin puree

2 (4-ounce) cans chopped mild green chiles

1½ tablespoons ground cumin

2 teaspoons chili powder*

1 teaspoon dried oregano

2 bay leaves

Read the labels to be sure these products are gluten-free.

Heat a large nonstick skillet over high heat. Coat with cooking spray and add the ground turkey and 1 teaspoon of the salt and cook, using a wooden spoon to break the meat into pieces as it browns, about 5 minutes. Transfer to a slow cooker.

Add the oil to the skillet, reduce the heat to medium, and add the onion and garlic. Cook, stirring, until the onion is translucent, 3 to 4 minutes. Transfer to the slow cooker.

To the slow cooker, add the broth, beans, pumpkin, green chiles, cumin, chili powder, oregano, bay leaves, and the remaining 1½ teaspoons salt. Stir well. Cover and cook on high for 4 hours or on low for 8 hours.

Remove the bay leaves and adjust the seasoning to taste before serving.

SKINNY SCOOP Here are some of my favorite toppings for chili, and you can use any combination you like: chopped red onions, chopped scallions, fresh cilantro, diced avocado, diced jalapeño, light sour cream, and/or shredded cheddar cheese.

PER SERVING	1 cup
CALORIES	268
FAT	9.5 g
SATURATED FAT	2.5 g
CHOLESTEROL	75 mg
CARBOHYDRATE	22 g
FIBER	6.5 g
PROTEIN	25 g
SUGARS	4 g
SODIUM	832 mg

CHILIS, SOUPS, AND STEWS

SLOW COOKER BEEF AND TWO-BEAN CHILI SERVES 8

(SC) (GF) (FF)

This chili pleases all palates in my house—it's not too spicy or too mild, but it's loaded with flavor. I love the combination of black beans and chickpeas, but you can use any type of legumes you like. What really makes the chili, in my opinion, are the toppings! Some sharp cheddar, a dollop of cumin-cilantro sour cream, and diced red onions are a must. Sometimes I even add some crushed tortilla chips.

2 pounds 93% lean ground beef

2¼ teaspoons kosher salt

Freshly ground black pepper

1 tablespoon tomato paste

1 cup chopped onion

1 cup chopped red bell peppers

3 garlic cloves, minced

1 (15-ounce) can no-salt-added black beans,* rinsed and drained

1 (15.5-ounce) can chickpeas,* rinsed and drained

1 (10-ounce) can diced tomatoes with mild green chiles (I like Rotel Original)

1 (8-ounce) can no-salt-added tomato sauce

2 teaspoons ground cumin

1 teaspoon chili powder*

1 teaspoon sweet paprika

½ teaspoon garlic powder

2 bay leaves

CUMIN-CILANTRO SOUR CREAM

½ cup light sour cream

2 tablespoons chopped fresh cilantro

¼ teaspoon ground cumin

TOPPINGS

½ cup grated reduced-fat sharp cheddar cheese

⅓ cup chopped red onion

Crushed tortilla chips (optional)*

*Read the labels to be sure these products are gluten-free.

Set a large deep skillet over medium-high heat. Add the beef, salt, and pepper to taste. Cook, using a wooden spoon to break the meat into pieces as it browns, 4 to 5 minutes. Drain all the liquid from the pan. Add the tomato paste, onion, bell peppers, and garlic, and cook, stirring, until the vegetables have softened, 3 to 4 minutes. Transfer to a slow cooker. Add 1 cup water, the black beans, chickpeas, tomatoes, tomato sauce, cumin, chili powder, paprika, garlic powder, and bay leaves.

Cover and cook on high for 5 hours or on low for 8 to 10 hours.

For the cumin-cilantro sour cream: In a small bowl, combine the sour cream, cilantro, and cumin. Refrigerate until ready to serve.

Discard the bay leaves. To serve, ladle the chili into 8 serving bowls. Top each with 1 tablespoon of the sour cream mixture, 1 tablespoon of the cheddar, the red onion, and tortilla chips, if desired.

PER SERVING	1 cup chili + toppings
CALORIES	349
FAT	12 g
SATURATED FAT	5 g
CHOLESTEROL	77 mg
CARBOHYDRATE	25 g
FIBER	7 g
PROTEIN	34 g
SUGARS	4 g
SODIUM	725 mg

PERFECT PAIRINGS
Serve this with some crusty whole-grain bread on the side.

SLOW COOKER BEEF STEW WITH SWEET POTATOES SERVES 6

SC GF DF FF

Nothing is more comforting on a cold winter night than coming home to a warm bowl of hearty stew. This is a great dish to make in a slow cooker because the low heat makes the meat melt-in-your-mouth tender. Everyone in my house loves beef stew with potatoes, except for my husband, Tommy (go figure!). Interestingly enough, though, when I make it with sweet potatoes instead of the usual white potatoes, he gobbles it up and usually goes back for seconds!

1 teaspoon olive oil

1 medium onion, chopped

1 celery stalk, chopped

1½ tablespoons tomato paste

2 pounds boneless beef chuck shoulder steak, trimmed and cut into 1½-inch cubes

1½ teaspoons kosher salt

1 tablespoon all-purpose flour, wheat or gluten-free

1¾ cups unsalted beef stock*

½ tablespoon Worcestershire sauce*

9 ounces (about 1 large) sweet potato, peeled and cut into 1-inch cubes

6 ounces small cremini or white mushrooms

12 baby carrots (about 4 ounces)

3 sprigs of fresh thyme

2 bay leaves

Freshly ground black pepper

¾ cup frozen peas

*Read the labels to be sure these products are gluten-free.

Heat a large nonstick skillet over medium-low heat. Add the oil, onion, and celery. Cook until tender, 7 to 8 minutes. Stir in the tomato paste and transfer to a slow cooker.

Return the skillet to the heat, increase the heat to high, add the beef to the pan, and season with the salt. Cook until the meat is browned, 4 to 5 minutes. Sprinkle in the flour and cook, stirring, for 1 minute.

Into the slow cooker, pour the stock, Worcestershire sauce, sweet potato, mushrooms, carrots, thyme, and bay leaves. Season with pepper and stir. Nestle the beef into the mixture.

Cover and cook on high for 4 to 6 hours or on low for 8 to 10 hours, until the beef and potatoes are tender. Add the peas and cook until heated through, about 10 minutes. Discard the thyme sprigs and bay leaves. To serve, divide among 6 serving bowls.

SKINNY SCOOP Beef chuck shoulder steak is a boneless cut of beef that might be alternatively labeled London broil, chuck top blade roast, or shoulder roast.

PER SERVING	about 1 cup
CALORIES	311
FAT	10 g
SATURATED FAT	3.5 g
CHOLESTEROL	86 mg
CARBOHYDRATE	19 g
FIBER	3.5 g
PROTEIN	40 g
SUGARS	6 g
SODIUM	478 mg

CHILIS, SOUPS, AND STEWS

SLOW COOKER VENISON STEW

SERVES 6

SC DF FF

My friend Nalini makes the best venison stew with the meat that our friend gives us when he comes back from deer hunting. It's so tender, and not gamy at all. She was kind enough to share her recipe with me, which I tweaked for the slow cooker. Every time I make it, I tell my family members it's beef, and no one has a clue it's deer meat until after they've wiped their plates clean. They are always surprised. That said, this recipe does work great with beef, too. I love to serve this stew with roasted vegetables and brown rice, mashed potatoes, or noodles.

1 large onion, cut into chunks

6 garlic cloves

1¾ pounds leg of venison, cut into ½-inch cubes

½ teaspoon kosher salt

Freshly ground black pepper

Cooking spray or oil mister

1 teaspoon olive oil

¼ cup canned crushed tomatoes

1 tablespoon dark mushroom soy sauce (I like Pearl River Bridge)

1 sprig of fresh thyme or 1 teaspoon dried thyme

Chopped fresh thyme or parsley, for garnish

In a blender, combine ¼ cup water, the onion, and garlic and blend until pureed, 20 to 30 seconds.

Season the venison with the salt and pepper. Heat a large nonstick skillet over high heat. Coat with cooking spray, add the meat, and cook until browned on all sides, 3 to 4 minutes per side. Transfer the meat to a slow cooker.

Discard any liquid in the skillet and wipe it out. Heat the skillet over medium heat. Add the oil and onion puree and cook until thickened, about 5 minutes. Add the tomatoes and mushroom soy sauce, and cook, stirring, for 1 minute. Pour the sauce over the meat, add 1 cup water, and stir well. Add the thyme sprig.

Cover and cook on high for 4 to 5 hours or on low for 8 to 9 hours. Discard the thyme sprig.

To serve, ladle into 6 serving bowls and garnish with chopped thyme.

SKINNY SCOOP Mushroom soy sauce is darker and much thicker than regular soy sauce. It's worth buying because it gives the stew a great brown color and wonderful, rich flavor. You can find it at any Asian grocery store or online at Amazon.com.

PER SERVING	½ cup
CALORIES	187
FAT	4 g
SATURATED FAT	1.5 g
CHOLESTEROL	112 mg
CARBOHYDRATE	5 g
FIBER	0.5 g
PROTEIN	31 g
SUGARS	2 g
SODIUM	401 mg

FOOD FACTS: VENISON

Venison (or, meat from a deer) is an excellent source of protein that's lower in calories and fat than beef, lamb, or pork. Wild game, such as deer, elk, and antelope, tend to be very lean due to their active lifestyles and natural diets.

ROASTED CHICKEN STOCK IN THE SLOW COOKER

MAKES ABOUT 5 CUPS

SC GF DF FF

One of the easiest ways to make chicken stock is in the slow cooker. On nights when I roast a chicken, I place the carcass in the slow cooker with vegetables and water, and then let it cook overnight. In the morning, I let it cool, and then transfer it to jars, if I don't plan on making soup that day. This stock can be used in any recipe that calls for broth or stock. Just keep in mind that you'll have to add salt to taste, if you're replacing canned broth in a recipe.

Bones from a roasted chicken

1 large onion, quartered

4 celery stalks

2 medium carrots

4 garlic cloves

2 bay leaves

3 or 4 sprigs of fresh parsley

1 sprig of fresh thyme or rosemary

Place the chicken bones, onion, celery, carrots, garlic, bay leaves, parsley, and thyme in a slow cooker. Fill with just enough water to cover everything (about 6 cups).

Cover and cook on high for 6 to 8 hours or on low for 12 hours, or longer if desired. Discard the vegetables, bones, and herbs and strain the liquid through a fine-mesh sieve. Let cool to room temperature, then refrigerate until cold, 2 to 3 hours. Skim the top layer of fat off with a spoon and discard. Divide the stock into lidded storage containers or jars and refrigerate for up to 1 week or freeze for up to 6 months.

PER SERVING	1 cup
CALORIES	20
FAT	0 g
SATURATED FAT	0 g
CHOLESTEROL	0 mg
CARBOHYDRATE	1 g
FIBER	0 g
PROTEIN	4 g
SUGARS	1 g
SODIUM	130 mg

BEEF STOCK IN THE SLOW COOKER   MAKES ABOUT 5½ CUPS

SC **GF** **DF** **FF**

Growing up, nothing went to waste in my mom's kitchen. And because she was a stay-at-home mom on a budget, there was always some type of broth with vegetables and inexpensive beef or chicken bones simmering away on the stove, which would later be turned into a scrumptious soup. Life is so different now. In many households, both parents work full-time, so we don't always have the luxury of being home to make long-cooked meals—but using a slow cooker is a great solution. In fact, you can use it to whip up a delicious broth with very little work required. Keep in mind that you'll have to add salt to taste on recipes where you're replacing canned broth with homemade.

2 pounds marrow bones, fat trimmed

1 large onion, quartered

1 whole leek, quartered

2 celery stalks with tops

2 medium carrots

4 garlic cloves

2 bay leaves

3 or 4 sprigs of fresh flat-leaf parsley

1 sprig of fresh thyme

1 sprig of fresh rosemary

1 tablespoon black peppercorns

Preheat the oven to 450°F.

Place the bones on a rimmed baking sheet and roast, turning halfway, until browned, 20 to 25 minutes.

Transfer the bones to a slow cooker. Add the onion, leek, celery, carrots, garlic, bay leaves, parsley, thyme, rosemary, and peppercorns. Fill with just enough water to cover everything (about 6 cups).

Cover and cook on high for 8 hours or on low for 12 hours, or longer if desired. Discard the vegetables, bones, and herbs and strain the liquid through a fine-mesh sieve. Let cool to room temperature, then refrigerate until cold. Skim the top layer of fat off with a spoon and discard. Divide the stock into lidded storage containers or jars and refrigerate for up to 1 week or freeze for up to 6 months.

SKINNY SCOOP This is best made in a 5- or 6-quart slow cooker. It can be refrigerated for up to 1 week or frozen for about 6 months.

PER SERVING	1 cup
CALORIES	15
FAT	0 g
SATURATED FAT	0 g
CHOLESTEROL	0 mg
CARBOHYDRATE	1 g
FIBER	0 g
PROTEIN	2 g
SUGARS	1 g
SODIUM	150 mg

CHILIS, SOUPS, AND STEWS

ONE-BOWL
MEALS

FAST

(Q) (GF) Kale Caesar and Grilled Chicken Bowls **77**

(Q) (DF) Chicken and Couscous Bowls with Piri Piri **78**

(Q) (GF) (DF) Teriyaki Chicken Bowls **81**

(Q) (GF) (DF) Roasted Brussels Bowls with Spicy Sausage **82**

(Q) (GF) (DF) Egg Roll Bowls **85**

(Q) (GF) (DF) Spicy Seared Tuna Sushi Bowls **86**

(Q) (GF) Shrimp and Artichoke Quinoa Bowls **89**

(Q) (V) (GF) (DF) Sunny-Side-Up Egg and Avocado Rice Bowls **90**

SLOW

(SC) (GF) (FF) Slow Cooker Chicken Burrito Bowls **93**

(SC) (GF) (DF) Slow Cooker Banh Mi Rice Bowls **94**

KALE CAESAR AND GRILLED CHICKEN BOWLS SERVES 4

Q GF

Replacing romaine with kale increases the health factor of your salad *big* time! Kale can be pretty tough, so the trick is to soften it by letting the dressed leaves sit at least a minute before eating. My family loves lots of anchovies in our Caesar dressing, but rather than making it with a raw egg, I prefer to serve it with hard-boiled eggs instead.

DRESSING

½ cup freshly grated Parmesan cheese

4 anchovy fillets

1 garlic clove

3 tablespoons extra-virgin olive oil

Juice of ½ lemon

1 tablespoon red wine vinegar

1 tablespoon Dijon mustard

Freshly ground black pepper

SALAD

1 bunch kale, preferably lacinato, ribs removed and (6 ounces without ribs) sliced ¼ inch wide

2 large eggs

4 thin chicken breast cutlets (14 ounces total)

Juice of ½ lemon

2 teaspoons extra-virgin olive oil

1 garlic clove, crushed

½ teaspoon dried oregano

½ teaspoon kosher salt, plus a pinch for each bowl

Freshly ground black pepper

Cooking spray or oil mister

1 cup halved cherry tomatoes

Shaved Parmesan cheese, for serving (optional)

For the dressing: In a blender, blend together the Parmesan, anchovies, garlic clove, olive oil, lemon juice, vinegar, mustard, and pepper to taste until smooth (add 1 tablespoon water if needed to loosen it up). Pour the dressing over the kale in a large bowl and toss well.

Place the eggs in a saucepan and cover with 1 inch of cold water. Bring to a boil over medium heat. Turn off the heat, cover, and let sit for 20 minutes. Cool the eggs under cold water. Peel and cut into quarters.

Season the chicken with lemon juice, 1 teaspoon of the oil, the garlic, oregano, ½ teaspoon of the salt, and pepper to taste.

Heat a grill pan over high heat and coat with cooking spray. Grill the chicken until cooked through, 2 to 3 minutes per side. Transfer to a cutting board and let rest for 10 minutes. Cut into bite-size pieces.

Divide the kale among 4 bowls. Top each with 2½ ounces grilled chicken, 2 wedges of egg, and ¼ cup tomatoes. Divide the remaining 1 teaspoon oil among the bowls and season each with a pinch of salt and pepper. Top with shaved Parmesan, if desired, and serve.

PER SERVING	1 bowl
CALORIES	347
FAT	21 g
SATURATED FAT	5 g
CHOLESTEROL	167 mg
CARBOHYDRATE	8 g
FIBER	1.5 g
PROTEIN	31 g
SUGARS	1 g
SODIUM	783 mg

ONE-BOWL MEALS

CHICKEN AND COUSCOUS BOWLS WITH PIRI PIRI SERVES 4

Q DF

I'm a little obsessed with the Instagram account of the tiny Manhattan restaurant Jack's Wife Freda, which led me to have lunch there. Their chicken kebab dish was simple, yet wonderful. It is served on top of couscous and a chopped salad, with piri piri sauce on the side, which is delicious slathered all over (if you like it hot). This is my rendition, with a red-hued hot sauce—instead of green, as at the restaurant.

CHICKEN

1 pound boneless, skinless chicken breast, cut into 1-inch cubes

Juice of ½ lemon

½ teaspoon olive oil

1 garlic clove, crushed

½ teaspoon dried oregano

½ teaspoon kosher salt

Freshly ground black pepper

PIRI PIRI SAUCE

2 tablespoons fresh lemon juice

2 tablespoons olive oil

1 tablespoon red wine vinegar

2 medium fresh red jalapeño or other chile peppers, seeded if you like a milder sauce

¼ medium red bell pepper

2 garlic cloves, peeled

1 teaspoon smoked paprika

½ teaspoon kosher salt

COUSCOUS

1½ cups reduced-sodium chicken broth

1 teaspoon olive oil

1 cup uncooked couscous

CHOPPED SALAD

2 cups chopped cucumber

1 cup chopped seeded tomatoes

¼ cup chopped red onion

2 tablespoons fresh lemon juice

1 tablespoon extra-virgin olive oil

½ tablespoon finely chopped fresh parsley

¼ teaspoon kosher salt

Freshly ground black pepper

Cooking spray or oil mister

1 tablespoon chopped fresh parsley, for garnish

For the chicken: In a medium bowl, combine the chicken, lemon juice, olive oil, garlic, oregano, salt, and pepper to taste.

For the piri piri sauce: In a blender, combine the lemon juice, olive oil, vinegar, chiles, bell pepper, garlic, smoked paprika, and salt and puree until smooth.

For the couscous: In a medium saucepan, bring the broth and olive oil to a boil over high heat. Add the couscous, cover, and remove the pan from the heat. Let stand for 5 minutes, then lightly fluff with a fork.

For the chopped salad: In a medium bowl, combine the cucumber, tomatoes, onion, lemon juice, olive oil, parsley, salt, and pepper to taste.

PER SERVING	1 bowl
CALORIES	444
FAT	15.5 g
SATURATED FAT	2.5 g
CHOLESTEROL	73 mg
CARBOHYDRATE	43 g
FIBER	4 g
PROTEIN	32 g
SUGARS	5 g
SODIUM	708 mg

Preheat a grill to high (or preheat a grill pan over high heat). Lightly rub the grates with oil (or coat the grill pan with cooking spray).

Thread the chicken onto 4 metal skewers. Grill the chicken until browned on the edges and no longer pink in the center, about 3 minutes per side.

To serve, place a generous ¾ cup couscous in each of 4 bowls. Top with ¾ cup of the salad and 1 chicken skewer. Garnish with the parsley. Serve with the piri piri sauce on the side for dipping.

TERIYAKI CHICKEN BOWLS   SERVES 4

Q GF DF

Teriyaki chicken is so easy to make yourself that you'll never order it out again. It takes only a few ingredients to create this flavorful dish that has a savory-sweet sauce the whole family will love. Plus, it's cheaper and healthier when you cook it at home! I prefer using chicken thighs, which are much juicier than breasts. Serving this recipe over cauliflower "rice" is a great way to incorporate more vegetables into your meal, and (bonus!) it's low in carbs.

1 small head cauliflower (about 1½ pounds)

1 tablespoon olive oil

¾ teaspoon kosher salt

2 tablespoons reduced-sodium soy sauce*

1½ tablespoons mirin

1 tablespoon honey

1 teaspoon grated fresh ginger

Cooking spray or oil mister

4 boneless, skinless chicken thighs (about 4 ounces each), trimmed of fat

2 scallions, chopped, for garnish

½ teaspoon sesame seeds, for garnish

Read the label to be sure this product is gluten-free.

Cut out and discard the core of the cauliflower, then break the cauliflower into florets. Pulse the florets in a food processor until you have rice-size pieces. (Alternatively, grate the florets on the large holes of a box grater.)

Heat the oil in a large nonstick skillet over medium heat. Add the cauliflower and salt. Cook, stirring, until the "rice" is crisp-tender, 6 to 8 minutes. Remove the pan from the heat.

In a small bowl, combine the soy sauce, mirin, honey, and ginger.

Heat a nonstick 10-inch skillet over medium-high heat and coat with cooking spray. Add the chicken and cook until browned and cooked through, 5 minutes per side. Reduce the heat to low and pour the sauce over the chicken. Cook until the sauce thickens slightly, turning the chicken halfway, 20 to 30 more seconds. Remove the pan from the heat to prevent the sauce from drying out.

To serve, place 1 cup cauliflower "rice" in each of 4 serving bowls. Slice each chicken thigh on an angle and place over the cauliflower rice. Top each with 1 tablespoon of sauce from the pan, and sprinkle with the scallions and sesame seeds.

PER SERVING	1 bowl
CALORIES	243
FAT	8.5 g
SATURATED FAT	1.5 g
CHOLESTEROL	108 mg
CARBOHYDRATE	17 g
FIBER	4.5 g
PROTEIN	26 g
SUGARS	10 g
SODIUM	679 mg

ONE-BOWL MEALS

ROASTED BRUSSELS BOWLS WITH SPICY SAUSAGE   SERVES 4

Q GF DF

I often replace pasta with vegetable noodles, so why not try the same trick with roasted vegetables? While the vegetables are roasting, I make a quick and simple sauce using spicy Italian chicken sausage and crushed tomatoes. A great big bowl of this fills you up and can be made ahead to reheat throughout the week.

Cooking spray or oil mister

1 pound Brussels sprouts, trimmed and halved

16 ounces white mushrooms, stemmed

2 tablespoons extra-virgin olive oil

¾ teaspoon kosher salt

Freshly ground black pepper

14 ounces spicy Italian chicken sausage,* casings removed

2 garlic cloves, crushed

1½ cups canned crushed tomatoes

2 tablespoons chopped fresh basil, for garnish

*Read the label to be sure this product is gluten-free.

Preheat the oven to 425°F. Coat 2 large nonstick baking sheets with oil.

Place the Brussels sprouts on one of the prepared baking sheets and the mushrooms on the other. Drizzle each with 1 tablespoon of the oil. Season the sprouts with ¼ teaspoon of the salt and pepper to taste, then season the mushrooms with the remaining ½ teaspoon salt and pepper to taste.

Roast both, shaking the pans every 5 minutes and switching the racks halfway through, until the Brussels sprouts are browned and tender and the mushrooms are golden, 20 to 25 minutes for the sprouts and 15 minutes for the mushrooms.

Meanwhile, heat a large deep nonstick skillet over high heat. Add the sausage and cook, using a wooden spoon to break the meat into small pieces as it browns, 6 to 8 minutes. Add the garlic and cook, stirring, for 1 minute. Add the crushed tomatoes and pepper to taste. Cover, reduce the heat to low, and simmer for 10 minutes.

To serve, place ⅔ cup Brussels sprouts and ½ cup mushrooms in each of 4 serving bowls. Spoon ⅔ cup of the sauce over each bowl and garnish with the basil.

PER SERVING	1 bowl
CALORIES	319
FAT	16 g
SATURATED FAT	3.5 g
CHOLESTEROL	76 mg
CARBOHYDRATE	24 g
FIBER	6 g
PROTEIN	25 g
SUGARS	10 g
SODIUM	975 mg

EGG ROLL BOWLS   SERVES 2

(Q) (GF) (DF)

These egg roll bowls are a fun spin on the classic Chinese take-out favorite, without the egg roll wrapper. It's a deconstructed roll in bowl form, loaded with everything you might find in an egg roll's filling. Although it may seem like a lot of vegetables once you start chopping, everything wilts and shrinks in size as it cooks. If you don't love pork, you can swap it with ground chicken or even shrimp. Have all your ingredients prepped and ready, and this dish will come together really fast.

7 ounces ground pork

3 tablespoons reduced-sodium soy sauce*

½ small onion, chopped

2 garlic cloves, minced

½ teaspoon grated fresh ginger

2½ cups finely sliced napa or green cabbage

2 cups finely sliced baby bok choy

½ cup shredded carrots

2½ ounces sliced shiitake mushrooms

½ tablespoon Chinese rice wine or dry sherry

½ teaspoon toasted sesame oil

1 medium scallion, sliced, for garnish

*Read the label to be sure this product is gluten-free.

Set a large nonstick skillet or wok over medium-high heat. Add the pork and 1 tablespoon of the soy sauce and cook, using a wooden spoon to break the meat into small pieces as it browns, about 3 minutes. Add the onion, garlic, and ginger and cook, stirring, until the vegetables are soft, 2 to 3 minutes. Add the cabbage, bok choy, carrots, and mushrooms. Pour in the remaining 2 tablespoons soy sauce, the rice wine, and sesame oil. Cook, stirring occasionally, until the cabbage and bok choy are wilted but still crunchy, 3 to 4 minutes. Serve hot, garnished with the scallions.

PER SERVING	1½ cups
CALORIES	347
FAT	23 g
SATURATED FAT	8 g
CHOLESTEROL	72 mg
CARBOHYDRATE	14 g
FIBER	4 g
PROTEIN	22 g
SUGARS	5 g
SODIUM	987 mg

SPICY SEARED TUNA SUSHI BOWLS   SERVES 4

Q GF DF

Tommy and I share a love of tuna, which is what inspired me to start making these yummy bowls. They're so quick and easy, and perfect for when I want to satisfy my sushi craving at home. If you think making seared tuna is too fancy and complicated, think again. You'll be surprised just how easy it is. I encrusted the tuna in furikake, a Japanese condiment that's delicious. Most grocery stores carry it, and it's also available online. Feel free to substitute with ¼ teaspoon salt and sesame seeds if you can't find it.

VINAIGRETTE

2 tablespoons unseasoned rice vinegar

2 tablespoons reduced-sodium soy sauce*

½ tablespoon toasted sesame oil

1 teaspoon wasabi paste (in a tube)

½ teaspoon grated fresh ginger

SPICY MAYO

2 tablespoons light mayonnaise

2 teaspoons Sriracha sauce

TUNA BOWL

6 tablespoons furikake (I like Eden Shake)

4 (5-ounce) yellowfin tuna steaks

Cooking spray or oil mister

1½ cups cooked short-grain brown rice, warm

1 medium cucumber sliced into matchsticks

1 medium Hass avocado (about 5 ounces), sliced

2 tablespoons chopped fresh chives, for garnish

Read the label to be sure this product is gluten-free.

For the vinaigrette: In a small bowl, whisk together the vinegar, soy sauce, sesame oil, wasabi, and ginger.

For the spicy mayo: In a small bowl, whisk together the mayonnaise, Sriracha, and a little water (enough so that it's thin enough to drizzle).

For the tuna bowl: Place the furikake in a small dish. Press both sides of the tuna steaks into the furikake. Heat a large nonstick skillet over medium-high heat and coat with cooking spray. Put 2 tuna steaks into the skillet, coat the tops with cooking spray, and cook for 1 to 1½ minutes per side for rare, or longer, if desired. Transfer to a cutting board and repeat with the remaining 2 steaks. Slice the steaks into thin strips.

To serve, divide the rice, cucumber, and avocado among 4 bowls. Top with the sliced tuna, drizzle with the vinaigrette and spicy mayo, and then sprinkle with the chives.

PER SERVING	1 bowl
CALORIES	401
FAT	11.5 g
SATURATED FAT	2 g
CHOLESTEROL	58 mg
CARBOHYDRATE	33 g
FIBER	12.5 g
PROTEIN	38 g
SUGARS	2 g
SODIUM	701 mg

TIME-SAVING TIP Buy frozen shrimp that has been peeled and deveined. You can thaw them the night before, or just run them under cold water in a colander in the sink for a few minutes.

SHRIMP and ARTICHOKE QUINOA BOWLS SERVES 5

Q GF

This Italian-inspired stir-fry recipe was given to me by my close friend Doreen, an incredible cook who had to adopt a gluten-free lifestyle a few years ago after learning that both she and her daughter have celiac disease. Most mornings, Doreen and I start our day together on the treadmill talking about—what else—*food!* Quinoa is a great option for people with celiac disease because it's gluten-free. However, quinoa usually turns out mushy if you follow the package directions. You can avoid that problem—and get perfectly cooked quinoa—simply by using less water.

¾ teaspoon kosher salt

1 cup tri-color quinoa, rinsed well

1 tablespoon olive oil

½ small onion, chopped

4 garlic cloves, sliced

1 cup halved grape tomatoes

1 (14-ounce) can artichoke hearts, drained and quartered

6 fresh basil leaves, chopped

⅓ cup chopped fresh parsley

14 ounces (about 24) peeled and deveined extra-large shrimp

¼ teaspoon crushed red pepper flakes

½ cup reduced-sodium chicken broth*

2 heaping cups baby spinach

¼ cup freshly grated Parmesan cheese

Read the label to be sure this product is gluten-free.

In a medium saucepan, bring 1¾ cups water and ½ teaspoon of the salt to a boil over high heat. Add the quinoa and return to a boil. Cover, reduce the heat to low, and cook until all the water is absorbed, about 20 minutes. Uncover and fluff with a fork.

Meanwhile, heat a 12-inch deep nonstick skillet over medium heat. Add the olive oil, onion, and garlic and cook, stirring, until soft and fragrant, about 2 minutes. Add the tomatoes, artichokes, basil, parsley, and remaining ¼ teaspoon salt. Cook, stirring, until the tomatoes soften, about 2 minutes. Increase the heat to medium-high and add the shrimp and pepper flakes. Cook until the shrimp are cooked through, about 2 minutes per side. Add the cooked quinoa, broth, spinach, and Parmesan. Cover and cook until the spinach wilts, about 2 minutes.

To serve, divide among 5 serving bowls.

SKINNY SCOOP For this dish, I prefer the taste of canned artichoke hearts over the marinated ones. If you can find only the marinated kind, rinse them before using.

PER SERVING	generous 1½ cups
CALORIES	**288**
FAT	**6.5 g**
SATURATED FAT	**1.5 g**
CHOLESTEROL	**99 mg**
CARBOHYDRATE	**32 g**
FIBER	**3 g**
PROTEIN	**22 g**
SUGARS	**4 g**
SODIUM	**533 mg**

ONE-BOWL MEALS

SUNNY-SIDE-UP EGG AND AVOCADO RICE BOWLS SERVES 4

Q V GF DF

When I was growing up, my Colombian mom often made me this simple dish for breakfast, lunch, or even dinner using the leftover rice from dinner the night before. But don't let its simplicity fool you! I still crave this meal as an adult, and I whip it up whenever I want something super quick and tasty. Be sure to cook the egg so that it's slightly runny, so that you can mix it up with the rice—delish!

3 cups cooked brown rice, warm

2 tablespoons chopped fresh cilantro

2 tablespoons chopped scallions

¾ teaspoon kosher salt

Olive oil spray (such as Bertolli) or a mister

4 large eggs

Freshly ground black pepper

1 large Hass avocado (6 ounces), sliced

1 medium tomato, halved and thinly sliced

Hot sauce, for serving (optional)

In a medium bowl, combine the rice, cilantro, scallions, and ¼ teaspoon of the salt.

Heat a nonstick skillet over medium-low heat. Coat it with cooking spray, crack the eggs into the skillet, and season each with a pinch of salt and pepper. Cover and cook until the whites are set around the edges but the yolk is still runny, about 2 minutes.

Divide the rice mixture among 4 shallow bowls. Top each with an egg and arrange the avocado and tomato slices on the side. Sprinkle the tomato and avocado with a pinch of salt, and serve right away with hot sauce, if desired.

SKINNY SCOOP If you're lucky enough to live near a Trader Joe's, they sell the best-tasting frozen brown rice I've ever tried. I'm obsessed!

PER SERVING	¾ cup rice + 1 egg + 1½ ounces avocado
CALORIES	327
FAT	13.5 g
SATURATED FAT	3 g
CHOLESTEROL	186 mg
CARBOHYDRATE	41 g
FIBER	5 g
PROTEIN	12 g
SUGARS	2 g
SODIUM	289 mg

SLOW COOKER CHICKEN BURRITO BOWLS   SERVES 8

SC **GF** **FF**

This is my favorite kind of slow cooker recipe: one that requires very little prep in the morning, so it's easy to pull together before heading out the door, and at the end of the day it rewards you with a delicious meal that the whole family loves. The burrito mixture couldn't be simpler, and the taste is delicious. Once it's done, you pile everything into bowls and dig in!

CHICKEN

1½ pounds boneless, skinless chicken thighs, trimmed of fat

1 teaspoon kosher salt

1½ cups store-bought chunky medium salsa

1¼ cups canned black beans,* rinsed and drained

1¼ cups frozen corn kernels

½ teaspoon garlic powder

1 teaspoon ground cumin

2 tablespoons chopped fresh cilantro

PICO DE GALLO

1 cup chopped tomato

¼ cup chopped scallions

¼ cup chopped fresh cilantro

½ fresh jalapeño pepper, seeded and finely chopped

2 tablespoons fresh lime juice

¼ teaspoon kosher salt

BOWLS

4 cups cooked brown rice

2 cups shredded reduced-fat Mexican cheese blend*

2 cups finely shredded romaine lettuce

Read the labels to be sure these products are gluten-free.

For the chicken: Season the chicken with the salt, put it in a slow cooker, and top with the salsa, black beans, corn, garlic powder, and cumin.

Cover and cook on high for 4 hours or on low for 8 hours. Transfer the cooked chicken to a large plate. Shred with 2 forks and return to the slow cooker. Add the cilantro.

For the pico de gallo: In a medium bowl, combine the tomato, scallions, cilantro, jalapeño, lime juice, and salt. Refrigerate until ready to eat.

To serve, place ½ cup brown rice in each of 8 serving bowls. Top with ⅔ cup chicken, ¼ cup shredded cheese, and ¼ cup shredded lettuce. Divide the pico de gallo among the bowls and serve.

PER SERVING	1 bowl
CALORIES	379
FAT	11 g
SATURATED FAT	4.5 g
CHOLESTEROL	98 mg
CARBOHYDRATE	40 g
FIBER	5.5 g
PROTEIN	30 g
SUGARS	3 g
SODIUM	782 mg

SLOW COOKER BANH MI RICE BOWLS SERVES 4

SC GF DF

If you've ever had the classic Vietnamese banh mi sandwich, you know how deliciously the roasted pork, pickled carrots, and pungent vinaigrette go together, but I always feel like the bread gets in the way. So, here, I scrapped the bread and put all the goodies in a bowl over brown rice (it's great over any grain) in my slim remake. Banh appétit!

PORK

1 pound pork tenderloin

¼ teaspoon kosher salt

⅛ teaspoon freshly ground black pepper

¼ cup reduced-sodium soy sauce*

1 tablespoon light brown sugar

3 garlic cloves, crushed

1 fresh jalapeño pepper, sliced

PICKLED CARROTS AND RADISHES

6 tablespoons distilled white vinegar

¼ cup granulated sugar

¼ teaspoon kosher salt

1 cup shredded carrots

2 radishes, cut into matchsticks

3 cups cooked brown rice (see page 50)

1 cup shredded red cabbage

1 cup thinly sliced English cucumber (about ½ small)

1 small fresh jalapeño pepper, thinly sliced

¼ cup fresh cilantro leaves

Read the label to be sure this product is gluten-free.

For the pork: Season the pork with the salt and pepper and place in a slow cooker. In a small bowl, combine the soy sauce, brown sugar, garlic, and jalapeño. Pour the mixture over the pork.

Cover and cook on low for 6 to 8 hours, until the pork is very tender, turning once halfway through, if desired. Transfer the pork to a large plate and shred with 2 forks. Reserve the sauce.

For the pickled carrots and radishes: In a medium glass bowl, combine the vinegar, granulated sugar, and salt and stir until the sugar is dissolved. Add the carrots and radishes, toss well, and let sit for about 30 minutes. Drain well and refrigerate until ready to use.

To serve, place ¾ cup rice in each of 4 serving bowls. Top each with one-fourth of the pork and drizzle each with 2 tablespoons of the sauce from the slow cooker. Top each with ¼ cup shredded cabbage, ¼ cup pickled carrots and radishes, and ¼ cup cucumber. Divide the sliced jalapeños and cilantro among the bowls, and serve.

PER SERVING	1 bowl
CALORIES	372
FAT	6.5 g
SATURATED FAT	2 g
CHOLESTEROL	74 mg
CARBOHYDRATE	48 g
FIBER	3.5 g
PROTEIN	30 g
SUGARS	8 g
SODIUM	692 mg

ZOODLES, SQUASHTA, PASTA, AND SAUCE

FAST

Q V GF DF Spiralized Lemon-Basil Zucchini Mason Jar Salads **98**

Q GF DF Cold Peanut-Sesame Chicken and Spiralized
Cucumber Noodle Salad **101**

Q DF Chicken and Zucchini Noodles with Black Bean Sauce **102**

Q GF Zoodles with Shrimp and Feta **105**

Q GF Shrimp and Summer Squash Noodles Baked in Foil **106**

Q GF Butternut Squash Noodles with Pancetta and Poached Egg **109**

Q GF Spiralized Beet Salad with Seared Scallops and Orange **110**

SLOW

SC GF FF Slow Cooker Spicy Harissa Lamb Ragu with Penne **111**

SC GF FF Slow Cooker Chicken Cacciatore **112**

SC GF FF Slow Cooker Pollo in Potacchio **115**

SC FF Slow Cooker Italian Turkey-Zucchini Meatballs **116**

SC GF FF Slow Cooker Hamburger Stroganoff **119**

SC GF FF Slow Cooker Bolognese Sauce **120**

SC GF FF Slow Cooker Beef Ragu with Pappardelle **123**

SPIRALIZED LEMON-BASIL ZUCCHINI MASON JAR SALADS SERVES 2

Q V GF DF

Want to prepare salad ahead for the week? Make it in a mason jar. Whether you're packing for lunch at the office, a bite at the beach, or a delicious picnic, this is the perfect anytime, anywhere meal. Just start with the dressing on the bottom, then add a layer of ingredients that won't get soggy (like chickpeas), then finish it off with all the salad toppings, leaving the most delicate greens—in this case, the spiralized zucchini—on top. To serve, give everything a good shake, and then transfer it to a bowl or plate so it's easy to eat. Don't forget to pack a fork!

VINAIGRETTE

3 tablespoons fresh lemon juice (about 1 lemon)

4 teaspoons extra-virgin olive oil

¼ teaspoon kosher salt

Freshly ground black pepper

2 large fresh basil leaves, finely chopped

SALAD

1 cup canned chickpeas,* rinsed and drained

¼ cup sliced red onion

1 cup halved grape tomatoes

1 cup packed baby arugula

8 ounces spiralized zucchini, cut with the thin setting, and cut into 6-inch lengths

*Read the label to be sure this product is gluten-free.

For the vinaigrette: In a small bowl, whisk together the lemon juice, oil, salt, and pepper to taste. Add the basil and whisk lightly. Divide the dressing between 2 quart-size mason jars.

For the salad: Dividing the ingredients evenly, layer the salad ingredients into the jars in this order: chickpeas, red onion, tomatoes, arugula, and zucchini noodles. Refrigerate until ready to eat. The salads will last up to 5 days in the refrigerator.

To serve, shake well, and then pour into a large bowl or dish. I prefer to let it sit 4 to 5 minutes after I put it in the bowl to let the zucchini soak in the lemony vinaigrette.

SKINNY SCOOP What is a spiralizer? It's a kitchen tool that makes "noodles" out of solid vegetables, such as zucchini, cucumbers, beets, sweet potatoes, and carrots. There are many brands on the market. The inexpensive ones work fine for cucumbers and zucchini, but I prefer a more durable one—like Inspiralizer or Paderno—that can easily cut through something as tough as a butternut squash and comes with different-size blades that will give you thinner and thicker noodles.

PER SERVING	1-quart mason jar
CALORIES	232
FAT	12 g
SATURATED FAT	1.5 g
CHOLESTEROL	0 mg
CARBOHYDRATE	26 g
FIBER	8 g
PROTEIN	8 g
SUGARS	6 g
SODIUM	490 mg

COLD PEANUT-SESAME CHICKEN AND SPIRALIZED CUCUMBER NOODLE SALAD SERVES 4

Q GF DF

I love cold sesame noodles, but rather than using actual noodles, I spiralize cold cucumbers to keep it lighter and healthier, while also adding a refreshing crunch to the salad. Here, I toss them with leftover shredded chicken (also great with shrimp), diced peppers, and my light peanut-sesame dressing that's so darn tasty, no one will ever guess it's low in fat!

PEANUT DRESSING

¼ cup powdered peanut butter (I like PB2)

2 tablespoons reduced-sodium soy sauce*

1½ tablespoons toasted sesame oil

2 tablespoons unseasoned rice vinegar

1 tablespoon honey

1 tablespoon Sriracha sauce

1 medium garlic clove, minced

1 tablespoon grated fresh ginger

SALAD

2 English cucumbers (about 14 ounces each)

8 ounces cooked chicken breast, shredded

½ red bell pepper, cut into ⅛-inch dice

½ yellow bell pepper, cut into ⅛-inch dice

2 scallions, thinly sliced

1 teaspoon toasted sesame seeds

Read the label to be sure this product is gluten-free.

For the peanut dressing: In a blender, combine 2 tablespoons water, the powdered peanut butter, soy sauce, sesame oil, rice vinegar, honey, Sriracha, garlic, and ginger. Set aside.

For the salad: Cut the cucumbers in half so they fit into the spiralizer. Spiralize the cucumbers into thick noodles with the thickest size noodle blade. Cut the strands into smaller pieces (about 5 inches long) so they're easier to eat. If you don't have a spiralizer, use a knife to cut the cucumbers into small cubes or julienne.

Divide the cucumber and chicken among 4 serving bowls. Top with the bell peppers and drizzle each with 3 tablespoons of the dressing. Serve sprinkled with the scallions and sesame seeds.

PER SERVING	1 salad + 3 tablespoons dressing
CALORIES	**231**
FAT	**8.5 g**
SATURATED FAT	**1.5 g**
CHOLESTEROL	**48 mg**
CARBOHYDRATE	**17 g**
FIBER	**3.5 g**
PROTEIN	**23 g**
SUGARS	**10 g**
SODIUM	**438 mg**

CHICKEN AND ZUCCHINI NOODLES WITH BLACK BEAN SAUCE SERVES 2

Q DF

Fermented black bean sauce is a worthy kitchen staple for any Chinese cooking aficionado. I like to keep a small jar in my refrigerator and use it to add a pungent dimension to stir-fries. But use it sparingly, as a little bit will add a whopping amount of umami to your dish.

CHICKEN

½ pound boneless, skinless chicken breasts, thinly sliced

½ teaspoon cornstarch

1 tablespoon rice wine

SAUCE

¼ cup reduced-sodium chicken broth

2 tablespoons jarred black bean sauce (I prefer KA·ME)

2 tablespoons reduced-sodium soy sauce

½ teaspoon toasted sesame oil

½ teaspoon grated fresh ginger

¼ teaspoon crushed red pepper flakes (optional)

STIR-FRY

3 teaspoons canola oil

⅓ cup (1-inch pieces) red onion

½ cup (1-inch pieces) red bell pepper

3½ ounces sliced shiitake mushrooms

6 ounces asparagus, cut into thirds

3 garlic cloves, crushed

1 medium zucchini (8 ounces), spiralized using the thicker setting and cut into 6-inch lengths

For the chicken: In a medium bowl, combine the chicken, cornstarch, and rice wine.

For the sauce: In a small bowl, combine ¼ cup water, the chicken broth, the black bean sauce, soy sauce, sesame oil, ginger, and pepper flakes (if using).

For the stir-fry: In a large nonstick wok or skillet, heat 1 teaspoon of the oil over high heat. Add the chicken and cook, stirring, until browned and cooked through, 2 minutes. Transfer to a plate.

Add the remaining 2 teaspoons oil to the pan. Add the onion, bell pepper, mushrooms, and asparagus and cook, stirring, for 2 minutes. Add the garlic and cook, stirring, until the vegetables are crisp-tender, 1 more minute. Add the sauce and spiralized zucchini and cook, stirring, until the zucchini is crisp-tender, about 1½ minutes. Return the chicken to the skillet. Divide the mixture between 2 bowls and serve.

SKINNY SCOOP Black bean sauce is available in Asian markets or online at Amazon.com.

PER SERVING	1¾ cups
CALORIES	319
FAT	12 g
SATURATED FAT	1.5 g
CHOLESTEROL	73 mg
CARBOHYDRATE	21 g
FIBER	5.5 g
PROTEIN	31 g
SUGARS	9 g
SODIUM	1,184 mg

ZOODLES WITH SHRIMP AND FETA   SERVES 2

Q GF

This quick dish is all about simplicity. It's made with just a few ingredients and takes less than 15 minutes from start to finish, which makes it perfect for weeknight cooking. I prefer to make my zucchini noodle dishes serve two so I don't overcrowd the pan. If you want to make this for four people, you can just double the recipe and cook it in two batches.

2 teaspoons extra-virgin olive oil

12 peeled and deveined jumbo shrimp (½ pound)

1 teaspoon chopped fresh oregano

¼ teaspoon kosher salt

Freshly ground black pepper

2 garlic cloves, minced

2 medium zucchini (14 ounces total), spiralized using the thick setting and cut into 6-inch lengths

1½ tablespoons fresh lemon juice

1½ ounces crumbled feta cheese

¼ teaspoon grated lemon zest

In a large nonstick skillet, heat 1 teaspoon of the oil over medium-high heat. Season the shrimp with ½ teaspoon of the oregano, ⅛ teaspoon of the salt, and pepper to taste. Add the shrimp to the skillet and cook until they are just opaque, about 2 minutes per side. Transfer to a plate.

Heat the remaining 1 teaspoon oil in the same skillet and add the garlic. Cook, stirring, until golden, 30 to 60 seconds (be careful not to burn it). Add the zucchini noodles, the remaining ½ teaspoon oregano, the remaining ⅛ teaspoon salt, and pepper to taste. Cook, stirring, until the zucchini is crisp-tender, 1½ minutes. Add the lemon juice, stir, and remove the pan from the heat.

Divide the noodles between 2 plates. Dividing evenly, top with the shrimp, feta, and lemon zest. Serve hot.

PER SERVING	1½ cups zoodles + 6 shrimp
CALORIES	238
FAT	10 g
SATURATED FAT	4 g
CHOLESTEROL	154 mg
CARBOHYDRATE	10 g
FIBER	2.5 g
PROTEIN	26 g
SUGARS	6 g
SODIUM	675 mg

SHRIMP AND SUMMER SQUASH NOODLES BAKED IN FOIL   SERVES 2

Q GF

This recipe is inspired by one of my favorite dishes from Areo's in Bay Ridge, Brooklyn: spaghetti al cartoccio, which is spaghetti with shrimp, prosciutto, and cream baked in foil. My lighter version uses zucchini and squash noodles in place of pasta. It's a fun dish to make, since the packets look like giant Hershey's Kisses. The shrimp and zucchini cook in the foil, which means you don't lose a drop of all the juicy flavors. It's a great date-night dish!

16 peeled and deveined extra-large shrimp (9 ounces), tails removed

¼ teaspoon plus ⅛ teaspoon kosher salt

Freshly ground black pepper

½ tablespoon unsalted butter

1 shallot, minced

1 garlic clove, minced

1 ounce pancetta, chopped

1¼ cups marinara sauce, homemade (page 52) or store-bought

3 tablespoons light cream

½ ounce cognac or brandy

1 tablespoon freshly grated Parmesan cheese

1 medium zucchini (7 ounces), spiralized using the thick setting and cut into 6-inch lengths

1 medium yellow squash (7 ounces), spiralized using the thick setting and cut into 6-inch lengths

Season the shrimp with ⅛ teaspoon of the salt and pepper to taste.

Preheat the oven to 350°F.

Cut two 18 x 18-inch pieces of heavy-duty foil and place each over a shallow soup bowl (the bowls help shape the packets).

In a large nonstick skillet, melt the butter over medium heat. Add the shallot, garlic, and pancetta and cook, stirring, until golden, about 2 minutes. Add the marinara, cream, cognac, Parmesan, remaining ¼ teaspoon salt, and pepper to taste. Bring to a boil and cook for 2 minutes. Remove the pan from the heat, add the shrimp and zoodles, and toss in the sauce. Divide the shrimp and zoodles between the foil squares. Seal each foil in the shape of a Hershey's Kiss. Place the packets on a baking sheet.

Bake until the shrimp are opaque and cooked through and the vegetables are tender, 12 to 15 minutes. Serve hot.

SKINNY SCOOP The packets can be prepped ahead of time, several hours before baking, and kept refrigerated.

PER SERVING	1 packet
CALORIES	395
FAT	16 g
SATURATED FAT	8 g
CHOLESTEROL	217 mg
CARBOHYDRATE	22 g
FIBER	5.5 g
PROTEIN	35 g
SUGARS	9 g
SODIUM	1,175 mg

BUTTERNUT SQUASH NOODLES with PANCETTA and POACHED EGG SERVES 2

Q GF

Light and yet still quite filling, "pasta" of butternut squash noodles is a very satisfying substitute for traditional noodles. I also love that they increase my daily veggie quota. In this recipe, I took all the elements of a classic carbonara and created a deconstructed version of it. Rather than making a sauce from eggs, I topped each plate with a poached egg so when you pop the yolk with your fork, it creates a luscious, creamy, and (best part) fuss-free sauce. Be sure to roast the noodles properly (meaning, don't crowd them on your baking sheet) to bring out all of their natural sweetness.

Olive oil spray (such as Bertolli) or a mister

1 large butternut squash, top solid portion (20 ounces), peeled, spiralized with the thickest setting, and cut into 6-inch lengths

2 teaspoons olive oil

½ teaspoon kosher salt

Freshly ground black pepper

2 large eggs

2 ounces pancetta, chopped

¼ cup freshly grated Pecorino Romano cheese

1 tablespoon chopped fresh parsley

Preheat the oven to 400°F. Lightly mist 2 large baking sheets with oil.

Divide the butternut squash between the prepared baking sheets. Toss each with 1 teaspoon oil, ¼ teaspoon salt, and pepper to taste. Roast until soft, 7 to 10 minutes.

Meanwhile, to poach the eggs, fill a large deep skillet with 1½ to 2 inches of water. Bring to a boil over high heat, then reduce the heat until it holds a simmer. Crack the eggs into individual bowls. One at a time, gently slide the eggs into the simmering water. Using a spoon, gently nudge the egg whites toward the yolks. Cook 2 to 3 minutes for a semi-soft yolk or 3 to 4 minutes for a firmer yolk. Using a slotted spoon or spatula, transfer the eggs one at a time to paper towels to drain.

In a large skillet, cook the pancetta over medium heat, stirring, until slightly browned, about 3 minutes. Remove the pan from the heat, add the roasted butternut squash noodles, and stir in the Romano and parsley.

To serve, divide the noodles between 2 plates and top each with a poached egg. Season with more pepper, if desired, and serve.

SKINNY SCOOP Since the hollow bottom part of the butternut squash won't go through the spiralizer, spiralize only the long cylindrical part of the squash.

PER SERVING	about 1½ cups noodles + 1 egg
CALORIES	342
FAT	20 g
SATURATED FAT	7 g
CHOLESTEROL	217 mg
CARBOHYDRATE	25 g
FIBER	4.5 g
PROTEIN	18 g
SUGARS	7 g
SODIUM	790 mg

SPIRALIZED BEET SALAD WITH SEARED SCALLOPS AND ORANGE

SERVES 2

Q GF

Sometimes you just want a salad. But, with seared scallops and roasted beets, this dish isn't *just* a salad. This wonderful blend of flavors is closer to something you'd get at an upscale restaurant—only for a fraction of the price because you're making it yourself. What I love about spiralizing beets is that they cook in a quarter of the time it would take to roast a whole beet and the edges get slightly crisp, which adds nice texture to the dish.

Olive oil spray (such as Bertolli) or a mister

1 medium golden beet (4 ounces), trimmed and peeled

1 medium red beet (4 ounces), trimmed and peeled

1 tablespoon plus 2 teaspoons extra-virgin olive oil

¾ teaspoon kosher salt

Freshly ground black pepper

1 large orange

1 tablespoon golden or white balsamic vinegar

3 cups baby arugula or mixed greens

6 long thin strips red onion

6 large sea scallops (8 ounces total), side muscles removed, rinsed and patted dry

1 teaspoon unsalted butter

Preheat the oven to 375°F. Mist a large baking sheet with olive oil.

Using the thinner noodle blade of your spiralizer, cut the beets into long spaghetti-like strips. Using kitchen scissors, cut the strands into 6-inch pieces. Transfer to the prepared baking sheet and toss with 1 teaspoon of the oil, ⅛ teaspoon of the salt, and pepper to taste. Roast in the center of the oven until tender and the edges begin to get slightly crisp, about 15 minutes.

Peel the orange and cut 6 segments out from between their membranes. Set aside. Squeeze the rest of the orange into a medium bowl. Add the vinegar, 1 tablespoon of the olive oil, ⅛ teaspoon of the salt, and pepper to taste and whisk well. Toss with the greens and red onion, and divide between 2 plates. Top with the beet noodles and orange segments.

Season the scallops with the remaining ½ teaspoon salt and pepper. In a 12-inch skillet, heat the butter and the remaining 1 teaspoon oil over high heat. Once the butter begins to smoke, put the scallops in the pan, making sure they are not touching. Cook until seared on both sides, 1½ minutes per side. Place on top of the salads and serve immediately.

SKINNY SCOOP I recommend using gloves when handling beets so that the red juices won't stain your hands.

PER SERVING	1½ cups salad + 3 scallops
CALORIES	309
FAT	14 g
SATURATED FAT	3 g
CHOLESTEROL	32 mg
CARBOHYDRATE	29 g
FIBER	6.5 g
PROTEIN	18 g
SUGARS	19 g
SODIUM	963 mg

SLOW COOKER SPICY HARISSA LAMB RAGU WITH PENNE SERVES 8

SC GF FF

This hearty, spicy pasta sauce gets its kick from harissa, a North African condiment that's available in the United States jarred and as a paste (Mina harissa, a common brand, is sold online and in many gourmet supermarkets). Topped with chopped scallions and fresh mint, plus lots of grated Pecorino Romano, it's so pretty, we put it on the cover!

SAUCE

1 (14.5-ounce) can diced tomatoes

1 (12-ounce) jar water-packed roasted red peppers, drained

1 tablespoon olive oil

15 ounces ground lamb

1½ teaspoons kosher salt

¼ teaspoon freshly ground black pepper

1 large onion, chopped

1 celery stalk, chopped

1 medium carrot, chopped

6 garlic cloves, chopped

2 tablespoons harissa

1 teaspoon ground coriander

1 teaspoon ground cumin

1 teaspoon sweet paprika

½ teaspoon crushed red pepper flakes

PASTA

Kosher salt

16 ounces penne pasta, whole wheat or gluten-free

2 large scallions, sliced, for garnish

2 tablespoons chopped fresh mint, for garnish

Freshly grated Pecorino Romano cheese, for serving (optional)

For the sauce: In a blender, puree the tomatoes and roasted peppers.

Heat a large nonstick skillet over medium-high heat. Add the oil and lamb, season with the salt and black pepper, and cook, using a wooden spoon to break the meat into small pieces as it browns, 3 to 4 minutes. Add the onion, celery, carrot, and garlic and cook, stirring, until the vegetables are soft, 8 to 10 minutes. Add the harissa, coriander, cumin, and paprika, and cook, stirring, 1 more minute. Transfer to a slow cooker along with the tomato-pepper puree and the pepper flakes.

Cover and cook on high for 4 hours or on low for 8 hours.

For the pasta: Bring a large pot of salted water to a boil. Add the pasta and cook until al dente according to package directions. Drain and return to the pot. Add the sauce from the slow cooker. Increase the heat to medium and stir until hot, about 1 minute.

Divide among 8 pasta bowls and garnish with the scallions and mint. Serve with Romano on the side, if desired.

PER SERVING	1⅓ cups
CALORIES	390
FAT	16 g
SATURATED FAT	5.5 g
CHOLESTEROL	39 mg
CARBOHYDRATE	47 g
FIBER	8 g
PROTEIN	18 g
SUGARS	5 g
SODIUM	484 mg

SLOW COOKER CHICKEN CACCIATORE SERVES 8

SC GF FF

I was always happy when Mom made chicken cacciatore for dinner. We would eat it over pasta with lots of freshly grated cheese on top. Now, whenever I make this dish, I always think of my mom. Since the sauce is hearty and chunky, it's perfect to make in the slow cooker. While any part of the chicken works great, I prefer to use skinless chicken thighs that are still on the bone. The chicken comes out so juicy and tender, and the bones add flavor to the sauce. I find that when you make this without the bone, the meat tends to be dry. Once the sauce is cooked, I remove the chicken from the bone and shred it, so you get chicken in every bite.

8 bone-in, skinless chicken thighs (about 5 ounces each), fat trimmed

¾ teaspoon kosher salt

Freshly ground black pepper

Cooking spray or oil mister

5 garlic cloves, finely chopped

½ large onion, chopped

1 (28-ounce) can crushed tomatoes (I like Tuttorosso)

½ medium red bell pepper, chopped

½ medium green bell pepper, chopped

4 ounces sliced shiitake mushrooms

1 sprig of fresh thyme

1 sprig of fresh oregano

1 bay leaf

1 tablespoon chopped fresh parsley

Freshly grated Pecorino Romano or Parmesan cheese, for serving (optional)

Season the chicken with the salt and pepper to taste. Heat a large nonstick skillet over medium-high heat. Coat with cooking spray, add the chicken, and cook until browned, 2 to 3 minutes per side. Transfer to a slow cooker.

Reduce the heat under the skillet to medium and coat with more cooking spray. Add the garlic and onion and cook, stirring, until soft, 3 to 4 minutes. Transfer to the slow cooker and add the tomatoes, bell peppers, mushrooms, thyme, oregano, and bay leaf. Stir to combine.

Cover and cook on high for 4 hours or on low for 8 hours.

Discard the bay leaf and transfer the chicken to a large plate. Pull the chicken meat from the bones (discard the bones), shred the meat, and return it to the sauce. Stir in the parsley. If desired, serve topped with Romano or Parmesan.

PER SERVING	1 cup
CALORIES	220
FAT	6 g
SATURATED FAT	1.5 g
CHOLESTEROL	123 mg
CARBOHYDRATE	10 g
FIBER	2 g
PROTEIN	31 g
SUGARS	6 g
SODIUM	319 mg

PERFECT PAIRINGS This is great over whole wheat or gluten-free spaghetti (DeLallo is my favorite brand), as well as rice or polenta. For a low-carb option, serve it over spaghetti squash (see page 266).

PERFECT PAIRINGS This is great over noodles, polenta, or even a simple root vegetable puree, like my Whipped Parmesan Cauliflower Puree (page 264).

SLOW COOKER POLLO IN POTACCHIO SERVES 4

(SC) (GF) (FF)

Pollo in potacchio is a traditional braised Italian chicken dish that features tomatoes, rosemary, garlic, and white wine. I first tried it while having lunch in Washington, DC, at the Garden Café Italia, which is in the National Gallery of Art. I have to admit, there's nothing like enjoying a delicious Italian meal in the same building that's home to the only Leonardo da Vinci painting in all of the United States. I loved the dish so much that I re-created it using my slow cooker, lightening it up by using skinless drumsticks. The chicken cooks all day, until the meat literally falls off the bone. It is well worth the wait!

2 teaspoons olive oil

8 bone-in drumsticks (4 ounces each), skin removed

1 teaspoon kosher salt

Freshly ground black pepper

1 large yellow onion, finely chopped

1 celery stalk, chopped

1 carrot, chopped

4 garlic cloves, chopped

Pinch of crushed red pepper flakes (optional)

¼ cup dry white wine

1 (28-ounce) can crushed tomatoes (I like Tuttorosso)

½ cup reduced-sodium chicken broth*

3 small sprigs of fresh rosemary

¼ teaspoon dried marjoram

*Read the label to be sure this product is gluten-free.

In a large nonstick skillet, heat 1 teaspoon of the oil over medium-high heat. Season the chicken with ½ teaspoon of the salt and pepper to taste. Add the chicken to the skillet and cook until browned on all sides, 5 to 7 minutes total. Transfer to a slow cooker.

Add the remaining 1 teaspoon oil to the skillet and reduce the heat to medium-low. Add the onion, celery, carrot, garlic, and pepper flakes (if using). Cook, stirring, until soft, 8 to 10 minutes. Add the wine and cook, scraping any browned bits from the bottom of the pan with a wooden spoon, 3 to 4 minutes to reduce slightly. Transfer to the slow cooker and add the tomatoes, broth, rosemary, marjoram, the remaining ½ teaspoon salt, and pepper to taste.

Cover and cook on low for 8 hours.

SKINNY SCOOP You can use skinless chicken breasts in place of the drumsticks.

PER SERVING	2 drumsticks + 1 cup sauce
CALORIES	400
FAT	11 g
SATURATED FAT	2.5 g
CHOLESTEROL	204 mg
CARBOHYDRATE	23 g
FIBER	4 g
PROTEIN	47 g
SUGARS	15 g
SODIUM	915 mg

SLOW COOKER ITALIAN TURKEY-ZUCCHINI MEATBALLS

SERVES 6

(SC) (FF)

Want the secret to making the juiciest turkey meatballs ever? Add shredded zucchini. And here's the secret to making a really great sauce with very few ingredients: Add some freshly grated Pecorino Romano. Since we're all busy and want dinner on the table with as little prep time as possible, rather than frying or baking the meatballs first, I plop them right into the sauce and let them slowly cook directly in the pot. A 6-quart slow cooker is recommended for this recipe.

MEATBALLS

1 medium zucchini (7 ounces), shredded

1¼ pounds 93% lean ground turkey

¼ cup seasoned dried whole wheat bread crumbs

¼ cup grated Pecorino Romano cheese

¼ cup chopped fresh parsley

1 large garlic clove, crushed

1 large egg, beaten

1 teaspoon kosher salt

Freshly ground black pepper

SAUCE

1 teaspoon olive oil

4 garlic cloves, smashed slightly

1 (28-ounce) can crushed tomatoes (I like Tuttorosso)

2 tablespoons grated Pecorino Romano cheese

1 bay leaf

Freshly ground black pepper

1 tablespoon chopped fresh basil, for garnish

For the meatballs: Using paper towels, squeeze all the excess water from the zucchini. Put the zucchini in a large bowl and add the turkey, bread crumbs, Romano, parsley, garlic, egg, salt, and pepper to taste. Mix well. Gently form 24 meatballs (about 1¼ ounces each). Set aside.

For the sauce: In a small skillet, heat the olive oil over medium heat. Add the garlic and cook, stirring, until golden brown, about 1½ minutes. Transfer to a 6-quart slow cooker and add the tomatoes, Romano, bay leaf, and pepper to taste. Slowly drop the meatballs into the sauce so they are all in a single layer in the bottom of the slow cooker.

Cover and cook on low for 4 to 5 hours, until the meatballs are tender and cooked through. To serve, discard the bay leaf and garnish with the basil.

PERFECT PAIRINGS Serve this over whole wheat pasta, zoodles (see page 120), or squashta (page 266).

PER SERVING	4 meatballs + ²/₃ cup sauce
CALORIES	249
FAT	11 g
SATURATED FAT	3.5 g
CHOLESTEROL	105 mg
CARBOHYDRATE	14 g
FIBER	2.5 g
PROTEIN	24 g
SUGARS	8 g
SODIUM	705 mg

SKINNY SCOOP I love using Tuttorosso crushed tomatoes—you just can't make a bad sauce with them. If you use another brand, you may have to adjust the salt to your taste.

SLOW COOKER HAMBURGER STROGANOFF   SERVES 8

(SC) (GF) (FF)

My entire family loves when I make this budget-friendly dish, which I've successfully adapted for the slow cooker. This recipe makes enough for two meals in my home—perfect for leftovers the next day, or to freeze for another night.

2 pounds 93% lean ground beef

¼ teaspoon kosher salt

Freshly ground black pepper

1 cup chopped onion

2 tablespoons tomato paste

16 ounces sliced cremini mushrooms

2 sprigs of fresh thyme

1 teaspoon Worcestershire sauce*

1 cup light sour cream

¼ cup all-purpose flour*

4 teaspoons chicken bouillon*

1 teaspoon sweet paprika

¼ cup chopped fresh parsley, for garnish

*Read the labels to be sure these products are gluten-free.

Set a large nonstick skillet over high heat. Add the beef and season with the salt and pepper. Cook, using a wooden spoon to break the meat into small pieces as it browns, 4 to 5 minutes. Reduce the heat to medium, add the onion and tomato paste, and cook, stirring, until the onions are soft, 4 to 5 minutes. Transfer to a slow cooker and add the mushrooms, thyme, and Worcestershire sauce.

In a blender, combine 1½ cups water, the sour cream, flour, bouillon, and paprika and blend until smooth. Pour the mixture over the beef.

Cover and cook on low for 6 hours. Discard the thyme. Garnish with the parsley and serve.

HOW TO MAKE ROASTED BUTTERNUT SQUASH NOODLES

Preheat the oven to 400°F. Spray 2 large rimmed baking sheets with oil. Peel the top cylindrical part of the squash (the hollow bottom won't go through the spiralizer) and spiralize it using the thickest noodle setting. Cut the strands into 5- to 6-inch pieces so they're easy to eat. Transfer the noodles to the prepared baking sheets and toss with 1 teaspoon oil, salt, and pepper. Roast until soft, 7 to 10 minutes. One large butternut squash is enough for two 1½-cup servings as a main, or four servings as a side dish.

PERFECT PAIRINGS Serve this over cooked egg noodles (as pictured), or for a lighter, healthier alternative, roasted butternut squash noodles (see below).

PER SERVING	¾ cup
CALORIES	253
FAT	11.5 g
SATURATED FAT	5 g
CHOLESTEROL	82 mg
CARBOHYDRATE	12 g
FIBER	1 g
PROTEIN	28 g
SUGARS	3 g
SODIUM	499 mg

SLOW COOKER BOLOGNESE SAUCE

SERVES 20

SC GF FF

This is my go-to crowd-pleasing recipe whenever I have finicky guests, because everyone *loves* it. I also like to make a big batch of this yummy sauce so I can freeze it for those busy nights when I don't feel like cooking. This Bolognese is so popular on my blog that it's even made an appearance on NBC's *Today* show, thanks to the show's guest Emily, who lost 185 pounds with the help of Skinnytaste recipes!

¼ pound pancetta, chopped

1 tablespoon unsalted butter

1 large white onion, finely chopped

2 celery stalks, finely chopped (about ¾ cup)

2 carrots, finely chopped (about ¾ cup)

2 pounds 95% extra-lean ground beef

1½ teaspoons kosher salt

Freshly ground black pepper

¼ cup dry white wine, such as Pinot Grigio

2 (28-ounce) cans crushed tomatoes (I like Tuttorosso)

3 bay leaves

½ cup half-and-half

¼ cup chopped fresh parsley

Heat a large deep nonstick skillet over medium-low heat. Add the pancetta and cook, stirring, until the fat renders, 4 to 5 minutes. Add the butter, onion, celery, and carrots and cook until soft, 6 to 8 minutes.

Increase the heat to medium-high, add the ground beef, and season it with ¾ teaspoon of the salt and pepper to taste. Cook, using a wooden spoon to break the meat into small pieces as it browns, 4 to 5 minutes. Add the wine and cook 3 to 4 minutes to reduce slightly. Transfer the mixture to a slow cooker. Add the tomatoes, bay leaves, remaining ¾ teaspoon salt, and pepper to taste.

Cover and cook on high for 3 to 4 hours or on low for 6 to 8 hours.

Discard the bay leaves, stir in the half-and-half and parsley, and serve.

HOW TO MAKE ZUCCHINI NOODLES

To make zoodles, spiralize 2 medium zucchini with the thickest noodle setting and cut them into 6-inch lengths. Sauté the noodles over medium-high heat with 1 teaspoon olive oil, 1 crushed garlic clove, ¼ teaspoon salt, and pepper to taste until crisp-tender, 1 to 2 minutes.

PER SERVING	generous ½ cup
CALORIES	126
FAT	5 g
SATURATED FAT	2.5 g
CHOLESTEROL	36 mg
CARBOHYDRATE	7 g
FIBER	1.5 g
PROTEIN	12 g
SUGARS	5 g
SODIUM	340 mg

PERFECT PAIRINGS Serve this over whole wheat pasta, or for a low-carb alternative, I love it over spaghetti squash (page 266) or zucchini noodles (see sidebar).

SLOW COOKER BEEF RAGU WITH PAPPARDELLE   SERVES 8

SC **GF** **FF**

This hearty meat sauce cooks long and slow for an incredible depth of flavor. It was inspired by one of my guilty pleasures that I order only on special occasions at Luigi's, one of my favorite neighborhood Italian restaurants: short rib ragu with pappardelle and a dollop of ricotta. It's so good, but definitely an indulgence, since short ribs have a lot of fat. So I experimented with my slow cooker and discovered that flank steak makes a wonderful substitute for short ribs, as it shreds easily and tastes wonderful. My family loves this served over pappardelle, but penne would also work great.

1 teaspoon olive oil

6 garlic cloves, smashed slightly

1½ pounds flank steak, cut against the grain into 4 pieces

Kosher salt and freshly ground black pepper

1 (28-ounce) can crushed tomatoes (I like Tuttorosso)

¼ cup reduced-sodium beef broth*

1 medium carrot, finely chopped

2 bay leaves

2 sprigs of fresh thyme

16 ounces pappardelle pasta or gluten-free brown rice pasta

½ cup freshly grated Pecorino Romano cheese, for serving

½ cup part-skim ricotta cheese, for serving

Chopped fresh parsley, for garnish

Read the label to be sure this product is gluten-free.

In a small skillet, heat the oil over medium-high heat. Add the garlic and cook, stirring, until golden and lightly browned, about 2 minutes.

Season the beef with 1 teaspoon salt and pepper to taste. Transfer to a 5- to 6-quart slow cooker. Pour the tomatoes and broth over the beef and add the garlic, carrots, bay leaves, and thyme.

Cover and cook on high for 6 hours or on low for 8 to 10 hours. Discard the herbs and shred the beef in the pot using 2 forks.

Bring a large pot of salted water to a boil. Add the pasta and cook until al dente according to package directions. Drain, return to the pot, and add the sauce from the slow cooker. Increase the heat to high and cook, stirring, until the pasta and sauce are combined, about 1 minute.

Divide among 8 pasta bowls and top each with 1 tablespoon Romano and 1 tablespoon ricotta. Sprinkle with parsley and serve hot.

PER SERVING	1½ cups
CALORIES	412
FAT	10 g
SATURATED FAT	4 g
CHOLESTEROL	173 mg
CARBOHYDRATE	48 g
FIBER	3.5 g
PROTEIN	32 g
SUGARS	6 g
SODIUM	555 mg

FAST

Q GF Grilled Greek Chicken Tostadas **127**

Q GF DF Grilled Cumin-Rubbed Skirt Steak Tacos with Pickled Red Onions **128**

Q GF DF Spicy Lump Crab and Charred Corn Flaco "Tacos" **131**

Q GF DF Ahi Tuna Poke Jicama Tacos **132**

Q V GF Cauliflower-Potato Tacos with Lime-Cilantro Chutney **135**

SLOW

SC GF Slow Cooker Salsa Verde Chicken Taquitos **136**

SC GF FF Madison's Favorite Beef Tacos **139**

SC GF DF Slow Cooker Korean-Style Beef Tacos **140**

SC GF DF Slow Cooker Hawaiian Pork Tacos with Charred Pineapple Salsa **142**

SC V GF FF Slow Cooker Vegetarian Black Bean Tacos **145**

TACO

NIGHT

GRILLED GREEK CHICKEN TOSTADAS SERVES 4

Q GF

I've given a classic Mexican dish a fun Greek twist. A tostada is similar to a taco, only the tortilla is flat and it's piled high with lots of fixin's. I love the vibrant, fresh flavors in these Greek-inspired toppings. Leftovers are great to pack for lunch the next day; simply pack the chicken separately from the salad, cheese, and tostada shell. Then you can reheat the chicken, assemble the tostada, and eat!

4 boneless, skinless chicken thighs (3 ounces each)

Juice of 1 medium lemon

1 teaspoon dried oregano

1/2 teaspoon garlic powder

1/4 teaspoon plus 1/8 teaspoon kosher salt

Freshly ground black pepper

1 tablespoon olive oil

1/4 cup chopped red onion

1 plum tomato, chopped

3/4 cup seeded, chopped cucumber

1/4 cup (about 11) pitted, sliced Kalamata olives

2 teaspoons finely chopped fresh oregano

Cooking spray or oil mister

4 corn tostada shells*

4 ounces feta cheese, crumbled, for serving

*Read the label to be sure this product is gluten-free.

Season the chicken with half of the lemon juice, the dried oregano, garlic powder, 1/4 teaspoon of the salt, and pepper to taste.

In a large bowl, whisk together the remaining lemon juice, the olive oil, remaining 1/8 teaspoon salt, and pepper to taste. Add the red onion, tomato, cucumber, olives, and fresh oregano and toss well.

Preheat a grill to medium (or preheat a grill pan over medium heat). Lightly rub the grates with oil (or coat the grill pan with cooking spray). Grill the chicken until a thermometer registers 165°F, 3 to 4 minutes per side. Transfer the chicken to a cutting board and let rest for 5 to 10 minutes. Cut into 1/2-inch pieces.

To serve, divide the chicken equally among the tostadas. Top each with 1/3 cup of the salad and 1 ounce feta. Serve immediately.

PER SERVING	1 tostada
CALORIES	289
FAT	16.5 g
SATURATED FAT	6.5 g
CHOLESTEROL	106 mg
CARBOHYDRATE	13 g
FIBER	2 g
PROTEIN	22 g
SUGARS	3 g
SODIUM	655 mg

TACO NIGHT

GRILLED CUMIN-RUBBED SKIRT STEAK TACOS WITH PICKLED RED ONIONS SERVES 4

Q GF DF

These tacos are piled high with everything I love—grilled skirt steak, red cabbage, and avocado—but the real star is the pickled red onions. They add a zesty tang and crunchy texture, as well as a lovely splash of pink color. I usually let them marinate longer than mentioned here (I tried to keep the recipe within 30 minutes). If you have the extra time, by all means, let them marinate for a few hours.

PICKLED RED ONIONS

1 medium red onion, cut into ¼-inch-thick slices

1 teaspoon kosher salt

Juice of 1 large lime

½ tablespoon olive oil

STEAK

1 pound skirt steak, trimmed

1 teaspoon ground cumin

1 teaspoon kosher salt

Cooking spray or oil mister

TACOS

8 corn tortillas*

2 cups shredded red cabbage

1 small Hass avocado (4 ounces), sliced

2 radishes, thinly sliced

1 lime, cut into wedges, for serving

Read the label to be sure this product is gluten-free.

For the pickled red onions: Separate the rings of the onion into a medium bowl and sprinkle with ½ teaspoon of the salt. Let sit for 5 minutes. Cover the onions with 1½ cups lukewarm water and let sit 10 more minutes.

Rinse and drain the onions. Add the lime juice, oil, and remaining ½ teaspoon salt. Mix well, cover, and refrigerate for at least 15 minutes, or overnight.

For the steak: Preheat a grill to high or a grill pan over high heat.

Season the steak with the cumin and salt. Oil the grates (or grill pan) and grill the steak about 2 minutes per side for medium-rare, or to your desired doneness. Transfer to a cutting board and let rest 5 minutes before slicing.

Grill the tortillas until the edges become charred, 30 to 60 seconds per side. Put 2 tortillas on each of 4 plates. Place ¼ cup of cabbage on each and top with the steak, avocado, pickled onions, and radishes. Serve with lime wedges.

SKINNY SCOOP The onions can be stored in a glass jar in the refrigerator for several weeks. They taste better the longer they marinate, so you may want to double the recipe.

PER SERVING	2 tacos
CALORIES	386
FAT	17.5 g
SATURATED FAT	5 g
CHOLESTEROL	73 mg
CARBOHYDRATE	33 g
FIBER	7 g
PROTEIN	29 g
SUGARS	4 g
SODIUM	534 mg

SPICY LUMP CRAB AND CHARRED CORN FLACO "TACOS" SERVES 4

Q GF DF

Charring sweet summer corn and jalapeño on the grill takes only 5 minutes, but it's time well spent because it adds so much flavor to these wonderful lettuce wraps. The delicate leaves of butter lettuce, which is usually sold in plastic clamshells to prevent the loose leaves from bruising, are perfect for these wraps. Using lettuce leaves in place of taco shells not only keeps the carbs down, but it also allows you to really taste the flavor of the crab. (Fresh crab can be pricey, so adding corn and tomatoes is also a great way to stretch your dollar.) I call these faux tacos "flaco" because the Spanish word means "skinny"!

2 medium ears yellow corn, husked

2 large fresh jalapeño peppers

1 medium tomato, chopped

¼ cup chopped red onion

Juice of 2 limes

3 tablespoons chopped fresh cilantro

1 teaspoon olive oil

¼ teaspoon kosher salt

Freshly ground black pepper

8 ounces cooked lump crabmeat, picked over for bits of shell

12 outer butter lettuce leaves

1 medium Hass avocado (5 ounces), thinly sliced

1 radish, cut into thin matchsticks

In a large pot of boiling water, cook the corn until tender, 4 to 5 minutes.

Preheat a grill to medium (or preheat a grill pan over medium heat). Grill the corn and jalapeños, turning, until charred all over, about 5 minutes. Let cool. Cut the kernels off each cob and place in a large bowl. Discard the skin, stems, and seeds of the jalapeños and chop the flesh. Add the jalapeño to the bowl of corn. Add the tomato, red onion, lime juice, cilantro, olive oil, salt, and pepper to taste. Add the crabmeat and toss gently.

To assemble, put 3 lettuce leaves on each of 4 plates. Place about ⅓ cup of the crab mixture on each lettuce leaf and top with sliced avocado and radish.

SKINNY SCOOP I prefer to buy locally caught crab from my fishmonger, who sells it cooked, shelled, and ready to go. If you don't have access to fresh, use canned lump crabmeat. Cooked shrimp would also be great here.

PER SERVING	3 "tacos"
CALORIES	178
FAT	6.5 g
SATURATED FAT	1 g
CHOLESTEROL	56 mg
CARBOHYDRATE	18 g
FIBER	4.5 g
PROTEIN	15 g
SUGARS	5 g
SODIUM	426 mg

AHI TUNA POKE JICAMA TACOS   SERVES 4

Q GF DF

When you take ahi poke (Hawaiian-style marinated sushi-grade raw tuna) and turn it into tacos, you get . . . *the best fish tacos ever!* Super light and fresh, these tacos are ridiculously tasty. Everything in this recipe is raw, including the "tortillas," which are thin slices of jicama. An intimidating-looking tuber, jicama is delicious and a surprisingly perfect low-carb tortilla substitute. It tastes like a savory apple—crunchy, sweet, and juicy.

1 pound sushi-grade ahi tuna, cut into ½-inch cubes

¼ cup reduced-sodium soy sauce*

1 teaspoon toasted sesame oil

1 teaspoon grated fresh ginger

1 garlic clove, crushed

1 medium jicama (4 inches in diameter)

TOPPINGS

1½ cups shredded romaine lettuce

1 medium Hass avocado (5 ounces), cut into 24 thin strips

2 tablespoons sliced scallions

1 teaspoon black and white sesame seeds

Sriracha sauce (optional)

Read the label to be sure this product is gluten-free.

In a medium bowl, combine the tuna, soy sauce, sesame oil, ginger, and garlic. Refrigerate for 20 minutes.

Meanwhile, peel the jicama and slice off the ends, so you have the middle third exposed. Using a mandoline or a sharp knife, cut the jicama into twelve ⅛-inch-thick slices to create your "tortillas." Set aside and refrigerate the remaining jicama for another use.

To assemble the tacos, put 3 jicama slices on each of 4 plates. Top each jicama slice with 2 tablespoons shredded lettuce, 3 tablespoons tuna, 2 slices avocado, scallions, sesame seeds, and Sriracha (if using).

PERFECT PAIRINGS Use the leftover jicama to make my Pineapple Jicama Slaw on page 269.

PER SERVING	3 "tacos"
CALORIES	226
FAT	8 g
SATURATED FAT	1.5 g
CHOLESTEROL	51 mg
CARBOHYDRATE	10 g
FIBER	5.5 g
PROTEIN	29 g
SUGARS	2 g
SODIUM	580 mg

CAULIFLOWER-POTATO TACOS WITH LIME-CILANTRO CHUTNEY

SERVES 4

(Q) (V) (GF)

Indian food and tacos—two of my favorite things—are now in one dish! Some of you may be thinking, "Gina, have you lost your mind?" Well, all I have to say is it works. I'm borderline obsessed with the Indian street food kati rolls, which are a spicy mixture of meat or vegetables rolled up in a flatbread. My favorite is the *aloo gobi* (cauliflower-potato) kati roll, which I've re-created, only served on tortillas for a twist. Give it a try and you'll probably become a member of the fan club, too!

FILLING

3½ cups (8 ounces) cauliflower florets, cut into 1-inch pieces

1 medium russet potato (8 ounces), peeled and cut into ⅓-inch cubes

2 garlic cloves, smashed

2 tablespoons olive oil

¾ teaspoon ground turmeric

¾ teaspoon ground cumin

⅛ teaspoon crushed red pepper flakes

1 teaspoon kosher salt

CHUTNEY

½ cup chopped fresh cilantro

½ fresh jalapeño or serrano pepper, chopped

1½ tablespoons fresh lime juice

¼ teaspoon kosher salt

TACOS

8 white corn tortillas*

¼ cup 0% Greek yogurt

¼ small red onion, thinly sliced

*Read the label to be sure this product is gluten-free.

Preheat the oven to 450°F.

For the filling: In a large bowl, combine the cauliflower, potato, garlic, and olive oil. In a small bowl, combine the turmeric, cumin, pepper flakes, and salt. Sprinkle the spice mixture over the vegetables and toss well to coat. Transfer to a large rimmed baking sheet.

Bake, stirring halfway, until browned, 25 to 30 minutes.

For the chutney: In a mini chopper, combine the cilantro, jalapeño, lime juice, and salt. Process until well chopped, adding a little water if it's too thick.

For the tacos: Heat the tortillas over the flame of a gas stovetop until blistered, 30 to 60 seconds per side (or microwave them). Place 2 tortillas on each of 4 plates. Top each tortilla with ⅓ cup of the filling and ½ tablespoon chutney. Divide the yogurt and sliced red onion among the tacos.

PER SERVING	2 tacos
CALORIES	243
FAT	8.5 g
SATURATED FAT	1 g
CHOLESTEROL	1 mg
CARBOHYDRATE	38 g
FIBER	5.5 g
PROTEIN	7 g
SUGARS	3 g
SODIUM	400 mg

TACO NIGHT

SLOW COOKER SALSA VERDE CHICKEN TAQUITOS SERVES 6

SC GF

Fast meets slow in this delicious dish, which starts in the slow cooker and finishes in the oven. The chicken is really simple to make, and it can also be used as a filling for enchiladas, tacos, tostadas, or even a salad. Taquitos can be served as an appetizer with salsa for dipping or as a main course topped with shredded lettuce, red cabbage, tomatoes, and anything else that strikes your fancy.

1 pound boneless, skinless chicken breasts

½ teaspoon seasoning salt, such as adobo seasoning*

1¼ teaspoons ground cumin

2 cups jarred salsa verde (I like Stonewall Kitchen)

¾ cup shredded pepper Jack cheese*

½ teaspoon chili powder*

¼ teaspoon kosher salt

Olive oil spray (such as Bertolli) or a mister

18 corn tortillas*

*Read the labels to be sure these products are gluten-free.

Season the chicken with the seasoning salt and ¾ teaspoon of the cumin, then place in a slow cooker. Top with ½ cup of the salsa verde.

Cover and cook on low for 4 hours. Transfer the chicken to a large plate and discard the liquid. Using 2 forks, shred the chicken. Transfer to a medium bowl and add the pepper Jack, the chili powder, salt, and remaining ½ teaspoon cumin. Stir well.

Preheat the oven to 400°F. Line 2 large nonstick baking sheets with foil and spray with oil.

Working in batches, place 3 or 4 tortillas between 2 paper towels and microwave 30 seconds until they are warm and pliable. Place a tortilla on a clean, dry work surface and scoop 2 heaping tablespoons of chicken filling onto the bottom third of the tortilla. Starting at the bottom, roll the tortilla up into a tube and put it on the prepared baking sheet, seam side down. Repeat with the remaining tortillas and chicken. Spray the tops of the rolled-up tortillas with oil.

Bake until the tortillas start to turn golden and crispy, about 15 minutes. Serve with the remaining 1½ cups salsa verde on the side.

SKINNY SCOOP To keep the tortillas from cracking as you're rolling them, fill them while they are warm and pliable. For this reason, I prefer to work in small batches.

PER SERVING	3 taquitos
CALORIES	325
FAT	8.5 g
SATURATED FAT	3.5 g
CHOLESTEROL	61 mg
CARBOHYDRATE	38 g
FIBER	7.5 g
PROTEIN	24 g
SUGARS	3 g
SODIUM	724 mg

MADISON'S FAVORITE BEEF TACOS   SERVES 8

(SC) (GF) (FF)

Have a picky kid? Then I have the dish for you! Madison's idea of the perfect taco is ground beef that's mild in heat and served in a crunchy shell topped with lettuce, cheese, and tomatoes. I serve some homemade guacamole on the side for the rest of us, and everyone's happy. The slow cooker is a great way to make taco meat because the leaner ground beef, which benefits from the slow, low heat, comes out very tender. This recipe also works well with ground turkey, if you prefer.

2 pounds 93% lean ground beef

1 small onion, finely chopped

¼ cup finely chopped red bell pepper

2 garlic cloves, crushed

3 teaspoons ground cumin

2 teaspoons chili powder*

2 teaspoons sweet paprika

1 teaspoon dried oregano

2 teaspoons kosher salt

1 cup tomato sauce

1 bay leaf

16 hard taco shells*

2 cups shredded romaine lettuce

2 plum tomatoes, chopped

1 cup shredded cheddar cheese*

*Read the labels to be sure these products are gluten-free.

In a large nonstick skillet, cook the beef over high heat, using a wooden spoon to break the meat into small pieces as it browns, 4 to 5 minutes. Add the onion, bell pepper, garlic, 2 teaspoons of the cumin, the chili powder, paprika, oregano, and salt. Cook, stirring, until the vegetables soften, 2 to 3 minutes. Transfer to a slow cooker and add ½ cup water, the tomato sauce, and bay leaf.

Cover and cook on high for 3 hours or on low for 6 to 8. Discard the bay leaf and add the remaining 1 teaspoon cumin.

Heat the taco shells according to the package directions. To assemble, put ¼ cup of the beef mixture into each shell and divide the lettuce and tomatoes evenly among the tacos. Top each with 1 tablespoon cheddar and serve.

SKINNY SCOOP This recipe makes enough taco filling for two meals for my family. Refrigerate the leftovers in an airtight container for up to 4 days, or freeze for another night.

PER SERVING	2 tacos
CALORIES	382
FAT	20 g
SATURATED FAT	7.5 g
CHOLESTEROL	86 mg
CARBOHYDRATE	24 g
FIBER	8 g
PROTEIN	31 g
SUGARS	4 g
SODIUM	744 mg

SLOW COOKER KOREAN-STYLE BEEF TACOS SERVES 6

SC GF DF

Tommy thinks I could open up my own Korean taco truck with this recipe—it's that good! Madison and Karina also love this dish, though they prefer theirs as rice bowls. I switch it up each time I make it. For best results, I marinate the meat overnight. If I'm making it for the kids, I use only ¼ teaspoon crushed red pepper flakes.

STEAK

1¼ pounds flank steak, trimmed and cut across the grain into 4 pieces

¼ cup reduced-sodium soy sauce*

1 teaspoon toasted sesame oil

¼ cup chopped yellow onion

3 garlic cloves, crushed

1 tablespoon light brown sugar

½ tablespoon grated fresh ginger

½ teaspoon crushed red pepper flakes

SLAW

2 cups cucumber matchsticks

1 cup shredded carrots

1½ tablespoons rice vinegar

1 teaspoon toasted sesame oil

¼ teaspoon kosher salt

TACOS

12 corn tortillas*

2 tablespoons *gochujang* (see Skinny Scoop)

1 cup chopped green leaf or romaine lettuce

1 scallion, sliced

12 lime wedges, for serving

Read the labels to be sure these products are gluten-free.

For the steak: Place the beef in a large container. In a small bowl, combine the soy sauce, sesame oil, onion, garlic, brown sugar, ginger, and pepper flakes. Pour the marinade over the beef and refrigerate overnight for best results.

Transfer the beef and marinade to a slow cooker. Cover and cook on low for 8 hours, until the meat is very tender and easily shreds with 2 forks. Reserve ¼ cup of the liquid from the slow cooker and discard the rest. Transfer the meat to a cutting board, shred with 2 forks, and return it to the slow cooker with the reserved liquid.

For the slaw: In a medium bowl, combine the cucumber, carrots, vinegar, sesame oil, and salt.

For the tacos: Heat the tortillas by putting them over a gas flame for 30 to 60 seconds per side (or microwave them). Place 2 tortillas on each of 6 plates. Divide the lettuce among the tortillas and top each with ¼ cup beef, ½ teaspoon *gochujang*, and ¼ cup slaw. Divide the scallion among the tacos and serve with lime wedges on the side.

PER SERVING	2 tacos
CALORIES	302
FAT	8 g
SATURATED FAT	2.5 g
CHOLESTEROL	57 mg
CARBOHYDRATE	34 g
FIBER	5 g
PROTEIN	25 g
SUGARS	8 g
SODIUM	569 mg

SKINNY SCOOP *Gochujang* is a savory, sweet, and spicy red chile sauce that is a must-have in Korean cuisine. It's thick, so it usually needs to be thinned out to make a sauce. Annie Chun's makes a ready-made version; look for it in the Asian aisle in most supermarkets. If you can't find it, substitute with Sriracha sauce.

SLOW COOKER HAWAIIAN PORK TACOS WITH CHARRED PINEAPPLE SALSA SERVES 8

SC GF DF

Kālua pig, a popular dish at Hawaiian luaus, is a whole pig smoked all day in a sand pit with sea salt, banana leaves, and koa wood. Delicious, but definitely a bit of work. This simple slow cooker dish mimics the smoked flavor with natural liquid smoke and sea salt. I like to wrap it in a banana leaf, which you can find at any Asian or Latin American supermarket, just before cooking to really give it an authentic taste. This step is totally optional, but worth it if you can find the leaves. I often serve it over rice, but nothing beats the convenience of heating up some tortillas and serving them with a delicious charred pineapple salsa to make it a taco night! Check out the photo on page 4—they're pretty and delicious!

PORK

2½ pounds boneless pork shoulder blade roast, trimmed

2½ teaspoons coarse red Hawaiian sea salt, or any coarse salt

1 tablespoon liquid mesquite smoke

1 large banana leaf (optional)

SALSA

½ fresh pineapple, peeled, cored, and sliced into ½-inch-thick rings

¼ teaspoon chili powder*

Cooking spray or oil mister

¼ cup finely chopped red onion

Juice of 2 limes

¼ teaspoon kosher salt

1 fresh jalapeño pepper, seeded and chopped

3 tablespoons chopped fresh cilantro

TACOS

1 cup finely shredded green cabbage

1 cup finely shredded red cabbage

1 teaspoon olive oil

1 teaspoon white wine vinegar

¼ teaspoon kosher salt

16 corn tortillas*

SKINNY SCOOP Pork shoulder is often sold on the bone. To save time, I ask my butcher to remove the bone for me. If you prefer to leave the bone in, it will still work fine, although you may need to increase the cooking time.

Read the labels to be sure these products are gluten-free.

For the pork: Pierce the pork all over with the tip of a knife. Rub the salt all over the pork, drizzle with the liquid smoke, and then wrap it in the banana leaf (if using). Transfer the pork to a 6-quart slow cooker.

Cover and cook on low for 10 to 12 hours, until the pork is tender and easily shreds with 2 forks. Transfer the pork to a large platter or cutting board. Remove any additional fat you may have missed and shred the pork with 2 forks. Reserve about ¾ cup of the liquid from the slow cooker and discard the rest. Return the shredded pork to the slow cooker with the reserved liquid and keep warm until ready to serve.

For the salsa: Sprinkle the pineapple with the chili powder.

Preheat a grill to high (or preheat a grill pan over high heat). Lightly rub the grill grates with oil (or coat the grill pan with cooking spray). Grill the pineapple until slightly charred, 2 to 3 minutes per side. Transfer to a cutting board and let cool. Cut into ½-inch cubes.

In a medium bowl, combine the red onion, lime juice, and salt. Let sit for at least 5 minutes to mellow the flavor of the onion. Add the pineapple, jalapeño, and cilantro.

For the tacos: In another bowl, toss the green and red cabbage with the olive oil, vinegar, and salt.

Heat the corn tortillas on the grill or grill pan over high heat until slightly charred, 30 to 60 seconds per side. Put 2 tortillas on each of 8 plates. Place 1½ ounces of the shredded pork on each tortilla and top each with 2 tablespoons cabbage and 2 tablespoons pineapple salsa. Serve.

PER SERVING	2 tacos
CALORIES	337
FAT	10 g
SATURATED FAT	3 g
CHOLESTEROL	85 mg
CARBOHYDRATE	32 g
FIBER	4.5 g
PROTEIN	30 g
SUGARS	7 g
SODIUM	803 mg

SLOW COOKER VEGETARIAN BLACK BEAN TACOS SERVES 4

SC V GF FF

Say mmmm . . . meatless! Slow-cooked black beans on tortillas with a pile of crunchy, fresh toppings make for an utterly satisfying vegetarian dinner. Using dried beans will save you cash and some effort, but keep in mind you must let the beans soak overnight. I wanted the beans on the drier side so the filling wouldn't spill out of the tortillas, but if you prefer them to be soupier to serve over rice, add ¼ cup more broth.

BEANS

⅓ pound (5.3 ounces) dried black beans

1 cup plus 2 tablespoons vegetable broth

½ cup chopped onions

1 fresh jalapeño pepper, chopped

1 teaspoon ground cumin

1 bay leaf

½ tablespoon fresh lime juice

¼ teaspoon kosher salt

1 teaspoon olive oil

3 garlic cloves, crushed

TACOS

2 cups shredded red cabbage

½ tablespoon olive oil

2 teaspoons fresh lime juice, plus 1 lime cut into 8 wedges

¼ teaspoon kosher salt

8 corn tortillas*

2 ounces Cotija cheese or queso blanco, crumbled

¼ cup fresh cilantro leaves

1 fresh jalapeño pepper, sliced into thin rings

Read the label to be sure this product is gluten-free.

For the beans: Rinse the beans and place them in a medium bowl. Cover with water to 2 inches above the beans and let soak for 8 hours or overnight. Drain.

In a slow cooker, combine the beans, broth, onions, jalapeño, cumin, and bay leaf. Cover and cook on low for 10 hours, until the beans are tender. Discard the bay leaf and stir in the lime juice and salt.

In a small nonstick skillet, heat the oil over medium heat. Add the garlic and cook, stirring, until golden, 30 seconds. Stir into the beans.

For the tacos: In a medium bowl, combine the cabbage, olive oil, lime juice, and salt.

Heat the tortillas in a large skillet over high heat until slightly charred, about 1 minute per side. Put 2 tortillas on each of 4 plates. Place ¼ cup beans on each tortilla, then top with ¼ cup cabbage and ¼ ounce cheese. Divide the cilantro and jalapeño slices among the tacos, and serve with lime wedges.

PER SERVING	2 tacos
CALORIES	346
FAT	8.5 g
SATURATED FAT	3 g
CHOLESTEROL	15 mg
CARBOHYDRATE	55 g
FIBER	14 g
PROTEIN	16 g
SUGARS	5 g
SODIUM	640 mg

FAST

Q Asiago-Crusted Chicken Breasts **148**

Q **GF** **DF** Korean-Inspired Chicken Lettuce Wraps **151**

Q **GF** Chicken Scaloppine with Broccoli and Melted Mozzarella **152**

Q Santa Fe Turkey Egg Rolls with Avocado Ranch Sauce **154**

Q Pizza-Stuffed Chicken Roll-Ups **157**

Q **GF** Greek Chicken Sheet Pan Dinner **158**

Q **PC** **GF** **DF** Pressure Cooker Three-Cup Chicken **160**

SLOW

SC **GF** **FF** Slow Cooker Chicken Tikka Masala **161**

SC **GF** **DF** Slow Cooker Adobo Chicken with Sriracha, Ginger, and Scallions **163**

SC **GF** **FF** Slow Cooker Indian Chicken and Peas **164**

SC **GF** **DF** Slow Cooker Maple-Dijon Chicken Drumsticks **167**

SC **GF** **DF** **FF** Slow Cooker BBQ Pulled Chicken **168**

SC **GF** **FF** Slow Cooker Czech Chicken Paprikash **171**

SC **GF** **FF** Slow Cooker Buffalo Chicken Lettuce Wraps **172**

SC **GF** **DF** Slow Cooker Stuffed Turkey Tenderloins with Gravy **174**

SC **FF** Slow Cooker Turkey Meatloaf **177**

POULTRY

MAINS

ASIAGO-CRUSTED CHICKEN BREASTS   SERVES 4

Q

Baking, rather than frying, these chicken breasts offers a few advantages. Aside from the obvious fact that it cuts the fat and calories, it also saves you time because it's not as messy and requires less of your attention. So, while they bake, you can multitask by preparing side dishes to get dinner on the table in under 30 minutes. The whole family will devour these; they turn out so juicy on the inside with a crisp, golden coating. I love to serve them with Zucchini Wedges with Lemon and Fresh Oregano (page 256).

Olive oil spray (such as Bertolli) or a mister

2 (8-ounce) boneless, skinless chicken breasts

½ teaspoon kosher salt

Freshly ground black pepper

1 tablespoon olive oil

½ cup seasoned whole wheat bread crumbs

¼ cup whole wheat panko bread crumbs

¼ cup shredded Asiago cheese

½ tablespoon dried oregano

Finely chopped fresh parsley, for garnish

1 lemon, cut into wedges

Preheat the oven to 425°F. Spray a nonstick baking sheet with oil.

Halve each chicken breast horizontally to create 2 cutlets. Season both sides with the salt and pepper. Place the chicken cutlets and oil in a shallow bowl and toss to coat.

On a plate, combine the bread crumbs, panko, Asiago, and oregano. Dredge each chicken breast in the bread crumb mixture, then transfer to the prepared baking sheet. Spray the tops of the chicken with oil.

Bake until golden on the outside and a thermometer registers an internal temperature of 165°F, about 15 minutes. Divide the chicken among 4 plates and garnish with a sprinkle of chopped parsley. Serve with the lemon wedges.

PER SERVING	1 cutlet
CALORIES	241
FAT	8.5 g
SATURATED FAT	2 g
CHOLESTEROL	76 mg
CARBOHYDRATE	13 g
FIBER	2 g
PROTEIN	28 g
SUGARS	1 g
SODIUM	588 mg

KOREAN-INSPIRED CHICKEN LETTUCE WRAPS SERVES 4

Q GF DF

Don't you just love food that you can eat with your hands? These lettuce wraps were inspired by my friend John Chan. Long before Korean food became popular here in the States, John would make these incredible Korean short ribs on the grill for my family, and we'd eat them wrapped in lettuce with rice. I turned that idea into this quick weeknight meal, using ground chicken and cooking it in a skillet.

¼ cup reduced-sodium soy sauce*

1 teaspoon toasted sesame oil

2 teaspoons light brown sugar

½ teaspoon crushed red pepper flakes

Cooking spray or oil mister

1 pound ground chicken

¼ cup chopped yellow onion

2 garlic cloves, crushed

1 teaspoon grated fresh ginger

12 large outer lettuce leaves, such as green leaf or Bibb

2¼ cups cooked brown rice (see page 50)

2 tablespoons *gochujang* (see page 141)

½ tablespoon sesame seeds

2 scallions, sliced

Read the label to be sure this product is gluten-free.

In a small bowl, combine the soy sauce, sesame oil, brown sugar, and pepper flakes.

Heat a large deep nonstick skillet over high heat and coat with cooking spray. Add the chicken and cook, using a wooden spoon to break the meat into pieces as it browns, about 5 minutes. Add the onion, garlic, and ginger and cook 1 minute. Pour the soy sauce mixture over the chicken, reduce the heat to medium-low, cover, and simmer for 5 minutes.

To serve, place 3 lettuce leaves on each of 4 plates. Spoon 3 tablespoons rice into the middle of each leaf and top with 3½ tablespoons chicken. Evenly divide the *gochujang*, sesame seeds, and scallions among the leaves.

PER SERVING	3 lettuce wraps
CALORIES	346
FAT	12 g
SATURATED FAT	3 g
CHOLESTEROL	98 mg
CARBOHYDRATE	36 g
FIBER	3.5 g
PROTEIN	25 g
SUGARS	8 g
SODIUM	725 mg

CHICKEN SCALOPPINE WITH BROCCOLI AND MELTED MOZZARELLA SERVES 4

Q GF

You can never go wrong with the winning combination of chicken, broccoli, and cheese. This recipe does beautifully as a weeknight meal or a decadent dinner with friends. Inspired by a dish I love from a local Italian restaurant, my scaloppine is lightened up by reducing the coating on the chicken to just a slight dusting—enough to get good texture once it's browned. Serve it with a crisp green salad on the side.

2 broccoli spears (about 12 ounces)

3 garlic cloves, smashed

1 tablespoon plus 1½ teaspoons extra-virgin olive oil

1 teaspoon kosher salt

⅔ cup reduced-sodium chicken broth*

¼ cup all-purpose flour*

4 (4-ounce) thin chicken breast cutlets

Freshly ground black pepper

½ teaspoon unsalted butter

Juice of ½ lemon

4 ounces part-skim mozzarella cheese,* thinly sliced

Chopped fresh flat-leaf parsley, for garnish

*Read the labels to be sure these products are gluten-free.

Preheat the oven to 450°F.

Trim about 1 inch off the ends of the broccoli stems and discard. Slice each broccoli spear lengthwise into 4 pieces. Place the broccoli and the garlic on a large rimmed baking sheet and toss with 1 tablespoon of the olive oil and ¼ teaspoon of the salt.

Roast until crisp-tender, flipping halfway through, about 20 minutes.

Meanwhile, in a small bowl, whisk together the broth and 1 teaspoon of the flour.

Place the remaining flour in a shallow dish. Season the chicken with the remaining ¾ teaspoon salt and pepper to taste, then lightly dredge both sides of the chicken in the flour, shaking off any excess.

Heat a large nonstick skillet over medium-high heat. Add the butter, 1 teaspoon of the olive oil, and half of the chicken. Cook until slightly golden, 2 to 3 minutes per side, and transfer to a plate. Add the remaining ½ teaspoon olive oil and repeat with the remaining chicken.

TIME-SAVING TIP I often buy chicken breasts that have been sliced into thin cutlets, so there's no need to cut or pound them thin.

PER SERVING	1 piece of chicken
CALORIES	329
FAT	14.5 g
SATURATED FAT	5.5 g
CHOLESTEROL	89 mg
CARBOHYDRATE	14 g
FIBER	2.5 g
PROTEIN	35 g
SUGARS	2 g
SODIUM	684 mg

Reduce the heat to medium-low, whisk in the broth mixture and lemon juice, and scrape up any browned bits on the bottom of the pan as the mixture comes to a simmer. Cook, whisking, until slightly reduced, 2 to 3 minutes. Return the chicken to the skillet, then top each cutlet with 2 pieces roasted broccoli and one-fourth of the mozzarella. Cover the skillet and simmer until the cheese has melted, 3 to 4 minutes.

To serve, using a spatula, transfer the chicken to 4 serving dishes. Spoon the pan sauce over each piece and garnish with parsley.

SANTA FE TURKEY EGG ROLLS WITH AVOCADO RANCH SAUCE SERVES 12

When I have a house full of friends, I like to ditch the traditional sit-down dinner in favor of an appetizer party. These egg rolls, inspired by ones served at the popular restaurant chain Chili's, are always a hit, and they're considerably lighter than the original. You can assemble them and make the dip ahead of time, then bake when your guests arrive.

AVOCADO RANCH SAUCE

2 ounces (½ small) Hass avocado

¼ cup light mayonnaise

¼ cup low-fat buttermilk

¼ cup chopped scallions

¼ teaspoon kosher salt

⅛ teaspoon garlic powder

⅛ teaspoon onion powder

⅛ teaspoon dried parsley flakes

⅛ teaspoon dried basil

Freshly ground black pepper

EGG ROLLS

Cooking spray or oil mister

8 ounces 93% lean ground turkey

½ teaspoon kosher salt

¼ cup chopped onion

2 tablespoons chopped red bell pepper

1 garlic clove, crushed

1 (4.25-ounce) can diced green chiles

½ cup frozen spinach, thawed and drained

¼ cup frozen corn kernels, thawed

¼ cup canned black beans, rinsed and drained

¾ teaspoon ground cumin

½ teaspoon Mexican chili powder

12 egg roll wrappers (I like Nasoya)

¾ cup shredded pepper Jack cheese

In a small blender, combine the ingredients for the avocado ranch sauce and blend until smooth.

Preheat the oven to 400°F. Coat a baking sheet with cooking spray.

Heat a medium skillet over medium-high heat and coat it with cooking spray. Add the ground turkey and salt. Cook, using a wooden spoon to break the meat into small pieces as it browns, about 4 minutes. Add the onion, bell pepper, and garlic and cook, stirring, until tender, 2 to 3 minutes. Add the green chiles, spinach, corn, black beans, cumin, and chili powder and cook, stirring, until the liquid evaporates, 3 to 4 minutes.

Place an egg roll wrapper on a clean work surface with a corner facing you. Spoon ¼ cup of the turkey mixture at the bottom corner and top with 1 tablespoon Jack cheese. Fold the bottom corner over the mixture so that it covers it completely, then roll to the center of the

PER SERVING	1 roll + 1 tablespoon sauce
CALORIES	189
FAT	6.5 g
SATURATED FAT	2 g
CHOLESTEROL	25 mg
CARBOHYDRATE	23 g
FIBER	1.5 g
PROTEIN	9 g
SUGARS	1 g
SODIUM	388 mg

wrapper. Fold the left and right corners into the center to form an envelope. Roll the wrap upward one time, leaving the top corner open. Wet your index finger with a little water and moisten the corner. Fold the corner down to seal the roll. Repeat for all the rolls and place on the prepared baking sheet. Coat each roll with cooking spray.

Bake until the rolls are crisp and golden brown, 6 to 8 minutes per side.

Serve with the sauce on the side for dipping.

PIZZA-STUFFED CHICKEN ROLL-UPS SERVES 4

Q

What happens when you combine chicken cutlets with pizza toppings? Winner, winner, chicken dinner! I love making chicken roll-ups. I stuff them with just about anything I have in my refrigerator. And honestly, what can be more family-friendly than pizza toppings? Here we have the works: pepperoni, mushrooms, bell peppers, and mozzarella cheese. Feel free to mix it up with anything you like on your pizza.

Olive oil spray (such as Bertolli) or a mister

2 (8-ounce) boneless, skinless chicken breasts

¼ teaspoon kosher salt

Freshly ground black pepper

½ cup shredded part-skim mozzarella

8 slices turkey pepperoni

8 slices white button mushrooms

¼ cup seasoned whole wheat bread crumbs

2 tablespoons freshly grated Parmesan cheese

½ tablespoon olive oil

1 tablespoon fresh lemon juice

¼ cup marinara sauce, homemade (page 52) or store-bought

8 thin slices red onion

2 tablespoons finely chopped green bell pepper

Preheat the oven to 450°F. Line a rimmed baking sheet with foil or parchment and spray with oil.

Halve each chicken breast horizontally to create 2 cutlets. Cover with a piece of wax paper and lightly pound to a ¼-inch thickness. Season with the salt and pepper.

Lay the chicken cutlets on a work surface and top each piece, in the center, with 1 tablespoon mozzarella, 2 slices pepperoni, and 2 slices mushroom. Loosely roll each one up and set them seam side down.

In a bowl, combine the bread crumbs and Parmesan. In a second bowl, combine the olive oil, lemon juice, and pepper to taste. Dip a chicken roll-up into the oil mixture, then in the bread crumb mixture. Place it seam side down on the prepared baking sheet. Repeat with the remaining chicken. Lightly spray the roll-ups with oil.

Bake until the chicken is nearly done, about 20 minutes. Remove the baking sheet from the oven. Top each roll-up with 1 tablespoon marinara, 1 tablespoon mozzarella, 2 slices red onion, and 1½ teaspoons bell pepper. Bake until the cheese is melted and the sauce is hot, 4 to 5 more minutes. Serve immediately.

PERFECT PAIRINGS These are perfect with my Italian House Salad with Dijon Vinaigrette (page 252).

PER SERVING	1 chicken roll-up
CALORIES	245
FAT	9 g
SATURATED FAT	3.5 g
CHOLESTEROL	87 mg
CARBOHYDRATE	8 g
FIBER	1.5 g
PROTEIN	31 g
SUGARS	2 g
SODIUM	551 mg

GREEK CHICKEN SHEET PAN DINNER

SERVES 4

Q GF

The four keys of a successful weeknight dinner: quick, flavorful, inexpensive, and easy. This is one of those dishes, as you make the entire thing on a single baking sheet! Simply toss your chicken and vegetables with a little oil, lemon juice, and spices, spread them all on a sheet pan, and pop it in the oven. Dinner is ready in just 30 minutes total! What's more, if you use foil on your sheet pan, cleanup is a snap.

Olive oil spray (such as Bertolli) or a mister

2 lemons

4 (4-ounce) boneless, skinless chicken thighs

1 pound baby red potatoes, cut into ¼-inch-thick slices

12 small heirloom carrots (12 ounces total), trimmed

2 tablespoons olive oil

4 teaspoons fresh oregano leaves

1¼ teaspoons kosher salt

1 teaspoon garlic powder

Freshly ground black pepper

1½ ounces feta cheese, grated

1 tablespoon grated lemon zest

Adjust the oven racks in the center and bottom third and preheat the oven to 450°F. Line 2 large rimmed baking sheets with foil and spray with oil.

Slice 1 of the lemons into ¼-inch-thick rounds. Cut the second lemon in half.

In a large bowl, combine the chicken, potatoes, carrots, juice from ½ lemon, the olive oil, 3 teaspoons of the oregano, 1 teaspoon of the salt, the garlic powder, and pepper to taste and toss well, using your hands so everything is evenly coated. Spread out in a single layer along with the lemon slices, without overcrowding, onto the prepared baking sheets.

Roast until the bottoms of the potatoes are golden, about 14 minutes. Flip the potatoes and carrots, switch the baking sheets from rack to rack, and roast until the vegetables are tender, the potatoes are golden, and the chicken is cooked through, 14 more minutes.

Squeeze the remaining ½ lemon over everything, then top with grated feta, lemon zest, the remaining ¼ teaspoon salt, pepper to taste, and the remaining 1 teaspoon fresh oregano. Serve immediately.

SKINNY SCOOP For best results, I prefer to grate the feta from a block myself rather than buy it precrumbled. The taste is better and it melts beautifully over the chicken.

PER SERVING	1 thigh + ¼ of potatoes + carrots
CALORIES	343
FAT	14 g
SATURATED FAT	4 g
CHOLESTEROL	117 mg
CARBOHYDRATE	28 g
FIBER	5 g
PROTEIN	27 g
SUGARS	6 g
SODIUM	650 mg

PRESSURE COOKER THREE-CUP CHICKEN

SERVES 4

Q PC GF DF

This easy, delicious Taiwanese chicken dish is named "three-cup" because the three key ingredients—soy sauce, sesame oil, and cooking wine—are supposedly used in equal proportions, though I have yet to see a recipe that literally follows that rule. While this recipe can be made either fast or slow, for the best flavor, I prefer to use my pressure cooker (I love my Instant Pot). If you prefer to go the slow cooker route, cook it on low for 6 to 8 hours. You can even do it via stovetop; it takes 35 to 40 minutes.

2 teaspoons toasted sesame oil

6 garlic cloves, smashed slightly

1-inch piece fresh ginger, thinly sliced

2 medium scallions, cut into 1-inch pieces

4 bone-in chicken thighs (26 ounces total), skin removed

2 tablespoons reduced-sodium soy sauce*

2 tablespoons Chinese cooking wine or sherry

16 Thai basil or regular basil leaves

Read the label to be sure this product is gluten-free.

Press the sauté button if using the Instant Pot, or heat a standard pressure cooker over medium heat. Add 1 teaspoon of the sesame oil, the garlic, ginger, and scallions. Cook until fragrant, about 2 minutes. Add the chicken thighs, soy sauce, wine, and remaining 1 teaspoon oil. Stir, cover, and lock the lid.

Cook on high pressure until the chicken is tender, 15 to 20 minutes. Just before serving, stir in the basil leaves.

PER SERVING	1 thigh
CALORIES	266
FAT	10 g
SATURATED FAT	2.5 g
CHOLESTEROL	160 mg
CARBOHYDRATE	3 g
FIBER	0.5 g
PROTEIN	37 g
SUGARS	0.5 g
SODIUM	269 mg

PERFECT PAIRINGS Serve this over steamed rice or Cauliflower "Fried Rice" (page 260).

SLOW COOKER CHICKEN TIKKA MASALA   SERVES 6

SC **GF** **FF**

If there's one dish guaranteed to be on every Indian restaurant menu, it's chicken tikka masala. A mild tomato-based curry with chunks of chicken in a creamy sauce, it's one of my favorite Indian dishes—although many say it actually originated in an Indian restaurant in the UK. I've created a really easy slow cooker version that's cheaper and lighter than what you find in a restaurant. It's also great with boneless chicken breast if you prefer white meat instead; and if you want to spice it up, simply increase the cayenne pepper.

1½ pounds skinless, boneless chicken thighs, cubed

1½ teaspoons kosher salt

½ tablespoon ghee or butter

½ onion, chopped

3 garlic cloves, minced

1 teaspoon grated fresh ginger

½ teaspoon ground turmeric

½ teaspoon garam masala*

1 teaspoon ground coriander

1 teaspoon ground cumin

¼ teaspoon cayenne pepper

¼ teaspoon ground cardamom

1 (14-ounce) can petite diced tomatoes

6 tablespoons canned full-fat coconut milk

¼ cup fresh cilantro leaves, for garnish

Read the label to be sure this product is gluten-free.

Place the chicken in a slow cooker and season with 1 teaspoon of the salt.

In a medium skillet, melt the ghee over medium heat. Add the onion, garlic, ginger, turmeric, garam masala, coriander, cumin, cayenne, and cardamom. Cook, stirring, until the vegetables are soft and the spices are fragrant, about 5 minutes. Transfer to a blender along with the tomatoes and blend until smooth. Pour over the chicken in the slow cooker and add the remaining ½ teaspoon salt.

Cover and cook on low for 6 hours. Stir in the coconut milk. Serve garnished with the cilantro.

PERFECT PAIRINGS Serve this with basmati rice or garlic naan and a salad topped with chutney (see page 135) to make it a meal.

PER SERVING	3 ounces chicken + ½ cup sauce
CALORIES	196
FAT	8.5 g
SATURATED FAT	4 g
CHOLESTEROL	110 mg
CARBOHYDRATE	6 g
FIBER	1.5 g
PROTEIN	23 g
SUGARS	2 g
SODIUM	507 mg

SLOW COOKER ADOBO CHICKEN WITH SRIRACHA, GINGER, AND SCALLIONS SERVES 4

SC GF DF

My friend Liren introduced me to Filipino chicken a few years ago, and it quickly became a once-a-month staple in my house. I've adapted it for the slow cooker—and cook it long and slow so that it literally falls off the bone. To boost the flavor otherwise lost due to the long cooking time, I add fresh ginger to the marinade and sprinkle with chopped scallions at the end.

¼ cup reduced-sodium soy sauce*

3 tablespoons red wine vinegar

1 tablespoon Sriracha sauce

1 tablespoon dark brown sugar

8 garlic cloves, crushed

1 tablespoon grated fresh ginger

Freshly ground black pepper

8 skinless chicken drumsticks (1¾ pounds total)

6 bay leaves

1 scallion, chopped, for garnish

Read the label to be sure this product is gluten-free.

In a medium bowl, combine the soy sauce, vinegar, Sriracha, brown sugar, garlic, ginger, and pepper to taste.

Arrange the chicken in an even layer in the bottom of a slow cooker. Add the bay leaves and pour the sauce over the chicken.

Cover and cook on high for 2 to 3 hours or on low for 4 to 6 hours, until the chicken is cooked through and falling off the bone. Discard the bay leaves. Serve garnished with scallions.

PERFECT PAIRINGS Serve this over cooked brown rice with sliced cucumber wedges on the side.

PER SERVING	**2 drumsticks**
CALORIES	**276**
FAT	**8 g**
SATURATED FAT	**2 g**
CHOLESTEROL	**179 mg**
CARBOHYDRATE	**10 g**
FIBER	**1 g**
PROTEIN	**39 g**
SUGARS	**5 g**
SODIUM	**833 mg**

SLOW COOKER INDIAN CHICKEN and PEAS SERVES 6

SC **GF** **FF**

When I worked full time in New York City, I had Indian food for lunch at least once a week from a small family restaurant a few blocks away from my office. Each week I would try something new, but one of my favorites was kheema, which is made with lamb or chicken. It instantly felt like comfort food to me because it reminded me so much of picadillo, a Cuban dish I grew up eating. It's very mild in heat, so it's a great dish to try if you're new to Indian food.

2 teaspoons ghee or unsalted butter

1 medium onion, finely chopped

3 garlic cloves, minced

1 teaspoon grated fresh ginger

1 pound ground chicken

1 teaspoon kosher salt

¾ cup canned tomato sauce

4 tablespoons chopped fresh cilantro

1 fresh jalapeño or other chile pepper, seeded and finely chopped

¾ teaspoon ground coriander

¾ teaspoon ground cumin

¾ teaspoon chili powder*

¾ teaspoon ground turmeric

¾ teaspoon garam masala*

¾ teaspoon ground cinnamon

1 bay leaf

¾ cup frozen peas

Read the labels to be sure these products are gluten-free.

In a large nonstick skillet, melt the ghee over medium heat. Add the onion and cook, stirring, until golden, 6 to 8 minutes. Add the garlic and ginger and cook until fragrant, about 2 minutes. Add the ground chicken and salt and cook, breaking the meat up with a wooden spoon as it cooks, 5 to 6 minutes.

Transfer to a slow cooker and add the tomato sauce, ¼ cup water, 2 tablespoons of the cilantro, the jalapeño, coriander, cumin, chili powder, turmeric, garam masala, cinnamon, and bay leaf. Stir well.

Cover and cook on high 3 to 4 hours or on low for 6 to 8 hours, adding the peas during the last 30 minutes of cooking time. Discard the bay leaf, add the remaining 2 tablespoons cilantro, and serve.

PER SERVING	½ cup
CALORIES	177
FAT	8.5 g
SATURATED FAT	3 g
CHOLESTEROL	69 mg
CARBOHYDRATE	10 g
FIBER	2.5 g
PROTEIN	15 g
SUGARS	5 g
SODIUM	384 mg

PERFECT PAIRINGS There are so many ways to serve this dish. My favorite is over brown rice, but Tommy loves it with naan or roti. If you want to get creative, whip up some mashed potatoes and make an Indian-inspired shepherd's pie, or serve it on a roll for an Indian sloppy joe.

SLOW COOKER MAPLE-DIJON CHICKEN DRUMSTICKS   SERVES 4

SC GF DF

This simple slow cooker dish is made with only six ingredients—including salt and pepper! It's very family friendly, especially if you have picky kids at home. The chicken literally falls off the bone and is absolutely delicious. I like to leave it in my slow cooker on warm for a few hours after the cooking time has elapsed to get the chicken slightly browned—but that's totally optional.

8 skinless chicken drumsticks (28 ounces total)

¾ teaspoon garlic salt

Freshly ground black pepper

¼ cup pure maple syrup

¼ cup Dijon mustard

2 tablespoons balsamic vinegar

Season the chicken with the garlic salt and pepper to taste. Place in a slow cooker.

In a small bowl, whisk together the maple syrup, mustard, and vinegar. Pour the mixture over the chicken legs, making sure the chicken is covered.

Cover and cook on high for 4 hours, or until cooked through and tender. Serve warm. If you'd like to get a little brown color on the chicken, set the slow cooker to warm and leave the chicken alone for 3 to 4 hours.

PERFECT PAIRINGS This is great with sautéed shredded Brussels sprouts. Sauté garlic and shallots in a little oil over high heat. Add shredded Brussels sprouts and season with salt and pepper. Cook, stirring, until slightly browned and crisp-tender, 8 to 10 minutes.

PER SERVING	2 drumsticks
CALORIES	354
FAT	9.5 g
SATURATED FAT	2.5 g
CHOLESTEROL	220 mg
CARBOHYDRATE	15 g
FIBER	0 g
PROTEIN	46 g
SUGARS	13 g
SODIUM	847 mg

POULTRY MAINS

SLOW COOKER BBQ PULLED CHICKEN   SERVES 6

SC GF DF FF

Thanks to the slow cooker, you can enjoy this easy, flavorful pulled chicken, which is simmered in a simple 20-minute homemade BBQ sauce, any night of the week. I prefer to use chicken thighs rather than breasts, which I find a bit dry, but really, either will work. To freeze leftovers, let them cool and transfer to freezer-safe containers.

1½ pounds boneless, skinless chicken thighs, trimmed

1 teaspoon kosher salt

½ teaspoon garlic powder

Freshly ground black pepper

¾ cup Homemade BBQ Sauce (recipe follows)

Season the chicken with the salt, garlic powder, and pepper to taste. Place it in a slow cooker and pour the BBQ sauce over the chicken.

Cover and cook on low for 6 hours, or until the chicken is falling apart. Shred the chicken with 2 forks and serve.

PERFECT PAIRINGS Serve the pulled chicken on whole wheat buns with coleslaw, over greens to make a salad, or with corn on the cob and baked beans.

PER SERVING	½ cup
CALORIES	159
FAT	4.5 g
SATURATED FAT	1 g
CHOLESTEROL	108 mg
CARBOHYDRATE	5 g
FIBER	0.5 g
PROTEIN	22 g
SUGARS	4 g
SODIUM	389 mg

HOMEMADE BBQ SAUCE   MAKES ABOUT 2 CUPS

1 (8-ounce) can tomato sauce

1/2 cup apple cider vinegar

1/4 cup tomato paste

1/4 cup honey

3 tablespoons molasses

2 teaspoons liquid hickory smoke (I like Colgin)

1/2 teaspoon kosher salt

1/2 teaspoon smoked paprika

1/4 teaspoon garlic powder

1/4 teaspoon onion powder

1/8 teaspoon ground cinnamon

1/8 teaspoon chili powder*

*Read the label to be sure this product is gluten-free.

In a large saucepan, combine the tomato sauce, vinegar, tomato paste, honey, molasses, liquid smoke, salt, smoked paprika, garlic powder, onion powder, cinnamon, and chili powder. Bring to a simmer over low heat and cook, stirring occasionally, until thickened, 15 to 20 minutes. The sauce will keep in an airtight container in the refrigerator for up to 1 month.

PER SERVING	2 tablespoons
CALORIES	23
FAT	0 g
SATURATED FAT	0 g
CHOLESTEROL	0 mg
CARBOHYDRATE	5 g
FIBER	0.5 g
PROTEIN	0 g
SUGARS	4 g
SODIUM	51 mg

SLOW COOKER CZECH CHICKEN PAPRIKASH   SERVES 4

SC **GF** **FF**

Czech cuisine is very similar to Hungarian and Russian. But with lots of hearty soups, stews, and meat dishes in creamy gravy, it's not exactly synonymous with healthy cooking. Fortunately, with some minor tweaking, I've found a way to make it work. This recipe is based on one of my favorite Czech dishes that my family ate while I was growing up: braised chicken legs in a creamy paprika sauce. It's comfort food through and through. Using Hungarian paprika is an absolute must, because it has a richer, more pungent sweet red pepper flavor than regular paprika.

8 skinless chicken drumsticks (28 ounces total)

¾ teaspoon kosher salt

½ teaspoon olive oil

⅓ cup chopped onion

2 teaspoons Hungarian paprika

Olive oil spray (such as Bertolli) or a mister

1 cup fat-free milk

⅓ cup all-purpose flour, wheat or gluten-free

1 tablespoon chicken bouillon* (I like Better Than Bouillon)

Chopped fresh parsley, for garnish

Read the label to be sure this product is gluten-free.

Season the chicken with the salt.

Heat a large nonstick skillet over medium heat. Add the oil, onion, and 1 teaspoon of the paprika. Cook, stirring, until the onion is soft, 3 to 4 minutes. Transfer to a slow cooker.

Increase the heat under the skillet to high, spray the pan with oil, and add the drumsticks. Cook until browned on all sides, 2 to 3 minutes total. Transfer to the slow cooker.

In a blender, combine the milk, 1 cup water, the flour, bouillon, and remaining 1 teaspoon paprika and blend until smooth. Pour the mixture over the chicken.

Cover and cook on low for 6 hours, or until the chicken is tender and the gravy is thick, stirring once if needed to prevent the gravy from clumping. Serve garnished with parsley.

PERFECT PAIRINGS My parents always served this with dumplings, but it's also great with noodles, roasted potatoes, or gnocchi to soak up all the gravy.

PER SERVING	2 drumsticks + ⅔ cup sauce
CALORIES	300
FAT	8.5 g
SATURATED FAT	2 g
CHOLESTEROL	180 mg
CARBOHYDRATE	14 g
FIBER	1 g
PROTEIN	42 g
SUGARS	4 g
SODIUM	985 mg

POULTRY MAINS

SLOW COOKER BUFFALO CHICKEN LETTUCE WRAPS

SERVES 6

(SC) (GF) (FF)

All the flavors you love from Buffalo wings, without all those darn calories—it's time to get your fingers dirty! I love making shredded Buffalo chicken in the slow cooker because it's super easy and so versatile. I use leftovers on sandwiches, over salads, as tacos, and in just about anything I can think up.

CHICKEN

1½ pounds boneless, skinless chicken breasts

1 medium celery stalk

½ medium onion, chopped

1 garlic clove

2 cups low-sodium chicken broth*

½ cup cayenne pepper sauce (I like Frank's RedHot Original), plus more for serving

BLUE CHEESE DRESSING

6 tablespoons low-fat buttermilk

¼ cup light mayonnaise

5 tablespoons crumbled blue cheese

2 tablespoons chopped scallion, white parts only

⅛ teaspoon garlic powder

⅛ teaspoon onion powder

⅛ teaspoon dried parsley flakes

⅛ teaspoon kosher salt

Freshly ground black pepper

12 outer lettuce leaves, such as green leaf, red leaf, or iceberg

¾ cup shredded carrots

¾ cup 2-inch-long celery matchsticks (from 2 large stalks)

Read the label to be sure this product is gluten-free.

For the chicken: In a slow cooker, arrange the chicken, celery, onion, and garlic. Pour in enough broth to cover the chicken (add water if the broth isn't enough).

Cover and cook on high for 2 hours or on low for 4 hours, until the chicken is cooked through.

Remove the chicken from the slow cooker and discard the liquid and vegetables. Shred the chicken with 2 forks and return it to the slow cooker. Add the hot sauce and cook on high for 30 minutes.

For the blue cheese dressing: In a blender, combine the buttermilk, mayonnaise, 2 tablespoons of the blue cheese, the scallion whites, garlic powder, onion powder, parsley, salt, and pepper to taste. Blend until smooth. Stir in the remaining 3 tablespoons blue cheese.

To serve, put 2 lettuce leaves on each of 6 plates. Place a generous ¼ cup chicken on each leaf, top each with 1 tablespoon shredded carrots, 1 tablespoon celery, and 1 tablespoon of the dressing.

PER SERVING	2 wraps
CALORIES	210
FAT	8.5 g
SATURATED FAT	2.5 g
CHOLESTEROL	82 mg
CARBOHYDRATE	5 g
FIBER	1.5 g
PROTEIN	27 g
SUGARS	3 g
SODIUM	1,140 mg

SLOW COOKER STUFFED TURKEY TENDERLOINS WITH GRAVY SERVES 4

SC GF DF

These turkey tenderloins, stuffed with butternut squash, cranberries, and pears, are like a mini Thanksgiving feast—from your slow cooker! They're perfect any time of year when you're craving a taste of the holidays. They're also great for smaller Turkey Day gatherings, when a whole bird is too much. You and your guests will, um, gobble them up!

½ tablespoon olive oil

⅓ cup chopped shallots

2 garlic cloves, chopped

1 cup (5 ounces) chopped (½-inch) butternut squash

½ cup fresh or frozen cranberries

2 tablespoons pure maple syrup

1 small pear, peeled, cored, and chopped

¾ cup chopped baby spinach

2 tablespoons chopped pecans

3 fresh sage leaves, chopped

1½ teaspoons kosher salt

Freshly ground black pepper

2 large boneless turkey tenderloins (1½ pounds total)

8 (12-inch) pieces of kitchen string

Olive oil spray (such as Bertolli) or a mister

GRAVY

¼ cup all-purpose flour* (I like Bob's Red Mill)

2 teaspoons chicken or turkey bouillon* (I like Better Than Bouillon)

4 fresh sage leaves

2 bay leaves

*Read the labels to be sure these products are gluten-free.

In a large skillet, heat the oil over medium-low heat. Add the shallots and garlic and cook, stirring, until golden, 4 to 5 minutes. Add the butternut squash, cranberries, maple syrup, and 1 tablespoon water. Cover, reduce the heat to low, and cook until tender, about 8 minutes. Remove the pan from the heat and stir in the pear, spinach, pecans, sage, ¼ teaspoon of the salt, and pepper to taste.

Cut a slit into the sides of the tenderloins, being careful not to cut all the way through. Season the inside and outside of the tenderloins with the remaining 1¼ teaspoons salt and pepper to taste. Stuff each turkey breast with about 1 cup of the squash mixture. Tie each tenderloin closed with 4 pieces of kitchen string, cutting off the extra string.

Wipe the skillet clean and set it over medium-high heat. Spray with oil and carefully sear each turkey breast until browned, 2 to 3 minutes per side. Transfer to a slow cooker.

PER SERVING	½ tenderloin + generous ⅓ cup gravy
CALORIES	351
FAT	6 g
SATURATED FAT	0.5 g
CHOLESTEROL	119 mg
CARBOHYDRATE	28 g
FIBER	3.5 g
PROTEIN	50 g
SUGARS	12 g
SODIUM	934 mg

For the gravy: In a blender, combine 1½ cups water, the flour, and bouillon and blend until smooth. Pour over the turkey and add the sage and bay leaves.

Cover and cook on low for 4 hours, or until the turkey is tender and the gravy is thickened.

To serve, discard the bay leaves and sage and remove the twine from the tenderloins. Cut each tenderloin in half and serve each piece with ⅓ cup gravy.

PERFECT PAIRINGS Serve this with roasted vegetables such as Burnt Broccoli (page 255) or Roasted Acorn Squash with Parmesan (page 263) and Italian House Salad with Dijon Vinaigrette (page 252).

SLOW COOKER TURKEY MEATLOAF

SERVES 6

SC FF

I took one of my favorite childhood dinners—an all-American weeknight classic—and made it lighter by replacing ground beef with a combo of ground turkey and mushrooms. The result: a moist, flavorful loaf my family loves—especially Madison! This is perfect to prepare on those nights you know you'll be running around.

MEATLOAF

1 teaspoon canola oil

1 large shallot, minced

1½ pounds 93% lean ground turkey

⅔ cup Italian seasoned bread crumbs

½ cup chopped cremini mushrooms

¼ cup ketchup

1 large egg, beaten

1 large egg white

1 teaspoon dried marjoram

1 teaspoon kosher salt

SAUCE

2 tablespoons ketchup

2 teaspoons Worcestershire sauce

1 teaspoon Dijon mustard

1 teaspoon light brown sugar

For the meatloaf: Cut a 15 x 8-inch piece of parchment paper and place it in a 5-quart slow cooker, allowing the edges to come up the sides (this will make it easier to take the loaf out after it's cooked).

In a small nonstick skillet, heat the oil over medium heat. Add the shallot and cook, stirring, until golden, 2 to 3 minutes. Transfer to a large bowl. Add the turkey, bread crumbs, mushrooms, ketchup, whole egg, egg white, marjoram, and salt. Mix well and shape into an oval loaf. Place in the slow cooker.

For the sauce: In a small bowl, whisk together the ketchup, Worcestershire sauce, mustard, and brown sugar. Brush half of the sauce over the loaf and refrigerate the remaining sauce.

Cover and cook on low for 6 hours, until a thermometer registers 165°F.

Preheat the broiler. Line a baking sheet with foil.

Transfer the meatloaf to the lined baking sheet. Brush with the reserved sauce. Broil until a crust forms, 1 to 2 minutes. Cut into 12 slices, divide among 6 serving plates, and serve.

PER SERVING	2 slices
CALORIES	**270**
FAT	**12 g**
SATURATED FAT	**3 g**
CHOLESTEROL	**115 mg**
CARBOHYDRATE	**16 g**
FIBER	**1 g**
PROTEIN	**25 g**
SUGARS	**6 g**
SODIUM	**728 mg**

FAST

Q **GF** Fork-and-Knife Cheeseburgers **181**

Q **GF** **DF** Steak and Onions **182**

Q **GF** **DF** **FF** Brazilian Black Beans with Collard Greens **185**

Q Grilled Veal Chop Milanese with Arugula Salad **187**

Q **GF** Skillet Pork Chops with Braised Fennel and Shallots **188**

Q **GF** **DF** Pork Tenderloin with Potatoes and Caraway Seeds **191**

SLOW

SC **GF** **DF** **FF** Slow Cooker Brisket with Onions **192**

SC **GF** **DF** **FF** Slow Cooker Carne Desmechada **195**

SC **GF** **DF** Perfect Medium-Rare Roast Beef in the Slow Cooker **196**

SC **GF** **DF** **FF** Slow Cooker Osso Buco **199**

SC **GF** **DF** **FF** Slow Cooker Stuffed Cabbage Rolls **200**

SC **GF** **FF** Slow Cooker Goulash with Sauerkraut **202**

SC **GF** **DF** **FF** Slow Cooker Pernil **203**

SC **DF** **FF** Slow Cooker Asian Pork with Mushrooms **205**

MEAT
LOVER
MAINS

SKINNY SCOOP Buy firm, plump portobello mushroom caps that are the size of a burger bun. Before cooking, lightly wipe the dirt off of the mushrooms or gently rinse them under a trickle of cold water, and pat dry with a paper towel. Never soak them or put them under water for too long, as they are porous and soak up liquid quickly.

FORK-AND-KNIFE CHEESEBURGERS

SERVES 4

Q GF

Say buh-bye, buns! These burgers are sandwiched in roasted portobello mushroom caps instead of bread, so you'll need a fork and a knife to eat them. This simple swap not only helps you cut calories and carbs, but it also gives you a dose of nutrients (like the B vitamin niacin, which is good for the skin and digestive system, as well as selenium, a mineral that helps prevent cell damage). I like traditional burger add-ons, such as cheddar, lettuce, red onion, and ketchup, while Tommy likes Swiss and bacon. Feel free to experiment with your toppings.

8 medium portobello mushroom caps, about 4 inches in diameter

Cooking spray or oil mister

1 teaspoon kosher salt

1 pound 93% lean ground beef

4 slices (3 ounces) cheddar cheese

4 slices red onion

4 leaves iceberg or romaine lettuce

4 slices tomato

Condiments, such as ketchup, mustard, or BBQ sauce (optional)

1 teaspoon sesame seeds (optional)

4 cornichons

Preheat the oven to 450°F.

Gently remove the stems from the mushrooms, then scrape out the gills with a spoon. Lightly coat both sides with cooking spray, sprinkle them with ¼ teaspoon of the salt, and arrange on a large baking sheet in one layer, gill side up. Bake until cooked through and tender, 7 to 8 minutes per side.

Meanwhile, gently form the meat into 4 patties. Season both sides with the remaining ¾ teaspoon salt.

Heat a cast iron skillet over medium-high heat until it smokes slightly, about 2 minutes. Coat with cooking spray, add the patties, and cook, flipping once, until browned and cooked through, about 4 minutes total for medium. Place a slice of cheddar on top of each patty, cover, and cook until the cheese has melted, 20 to 30 seconds. Quickly transfer to a plate.

Place the patties on 4 of the mushroom caps. Top with red onion, lettuce, tomato, and the condiments of your choice, then top with the remaining mushroom caps. Sprinkle the "buns" with sesame seeds, if desired, and secure a cornichon to the top with a toothpick.

PER SERVING	1 burger
CALORIES	301
FAT	15.5 g
SATURATED FAT	7.5 g
CHOLESTEROL	93 mg
CARBOHYDRATE	9 g
FIBER	2.5 g
PROTEIN	33 g
SUGARS	6 g
SODIUM	519 mg

STEAK and ONIONS SERVES 4

Q GF DF

Living in a multicultural home means I end up with quite an eclectic roster of dinner dishes. One day, we'll have arroz con pollo, and the next day it's chicken Parmesan. Our meals are never boring! One of my absolute favorite cuisines is Puerto Rican, because the food is flavorful and simple. Tommy's mom is Puerto Rican, and he grew up eating this dish, which they call *bistec encebollado*. His mom uses cubed steak, but I prefer sirloin, which cooks faster. Don't forget the vinegar—it really makes this dish sing!

1 pound petite sirloin, cut into ¼-inch-thick strips

1 teaspoon kosher salt

½ teaspoon garlic powder

¼ teaspoon onion powder

¼ teaspoon ground cumin

¼ teaspoons dried oregano

⅛ teaspoon freshly ground black pepper

1½ tablespoons red wine vinegar

3 teaspoons olive oil

1 medium white onion, cut into ¼-inch-thick slices

1 cup reduced-sodium beef broth*

⅓ cup canned tomato sauce

8 Manzanilla olives

2 tablespoons Sofrito (recipe follows)

1 tablespoon chopped fresh cilantro, for garnish

Read the label to be sure this product is gluten-free.

Put the steak in a bowl and season it with the salt, garlic powder, onion powder, cumin, oregano, pepper, and ½ tablespoon of the vinegar.

In a large nonstick skillet, heat 1 teaspoon of the oil over high heat. Add half of the steak and cook until browned, 1 minute per side. Transfer to a plate. Add another 1 teaspoon oil and cook the remaining steak. Transfer to the plate with the rest of the meat.

Reduce the heat to medium, add the remaining 1 teaspoon oil and the onion and cook, stirring, for 2 minutes. Add the broth, tomato sauce, olives, sofrito, and remaining 1 tablespoon vinegar. Bring to a simmer and cook until the onions soften, 2 to 3 minutes. Return the meat to the pan, cover, reduce the heat to low, and cook another 5 minutes. Serve garnished with cilantro.

PERFECT PAIRINGS Serve this over rice with sliced tomatoes and avocado. It's also great with Baked Sweet Plantains with Cheese (page 259).

PER SERVING	generous ¾ cup
CALORIES	220
FAT	9 g
SATURATED FAT	2.5 g
CHOLESTEROL	76 mg
CARBOHYDRATE	7 g
FIBER	1.5 g
PROTEIN	28 g
SUGARS	4 g
SODIUM	653 mg

SOFRITO MAKES 28 SERVINGS

(V) (GF) (DF) (FF)

These small green cubes are my secret ingredient for quickly infusing *sabor* (flavor) into just about any dish. I keep my freezer stocked with these instant flavor boosters, so I can easily add them to dishes like Steak and Onions (page 182), beans, stews, and rice, to name just a few ideas. I simply melt and sauté them into whatever I'm cooking. Simple and scrumptious!

1 medium yellow onion

1 medium red bell pepper

1 medium green bell pepper

1 cubanelle pepper

10 garlic cloves, peeled

1 tablespoon extra-virgin olive oil

10 ounces (2 to 3 bunches) fresh cilantro, chopped

2 tablespoons capers with brine

½ tablespoon dried oregano

Roughly chop the onion, bell peppers, cubanelle pepper, and garlic and place in a large bowl. Add the oil, cilantro, capers, and oregano. Working in batches (you'll probably have to do this in 4 or 5 batches), pulse the mixture in a blender until well chopped, but don't overblend it into a puree. You may have to stop and use a spatula to mix things around to get them to blend evenly. If you must, you can add a few teaspoons of water to each batch to help it blend.

To freeze, pour 2 tablespoons of the sofrito into each section of two 14-cube ice cube trays (you'll completely fill both) and freeze overnight. The next day, pop them out of the tray and transfer to a zip-top plastic bag to keep handy in the freezer.

PER SERVING	2 tablespoons or 1 cube
CALORIES	15
FAT	0.5 g
SATURATED FAT	0 g
CHOLESTEROL	0 mg
CARBOHYDRATE	2 g
FIBER	0.5 g
PROTEIN	0.5 g
SUGARS	1 g
SODIUM	25 mg

BRAZILIAN BLACK BEANS WITH COLLARD GREENS SERVES 6

(Q) (GF) (DF) (FF)

This quick, trimmed-down version of Brazil's national dish—feijoada—is a favorite in my home. My cousin Katia, who's Brazilian, taught me how to make this dish, and with her help, we trimmed the fat and created a streamlined version of the classic that's ready in a fraction of the time.

BEANS

½ tablespoon olive oil

1 large onion, chopped

6 ounces lean ham steak, diced

6 ounces boneless pork loin chop, trimmed and diced

2 garlic cloves, minced

2 (15.5-ounce) cans low-sodium black beans*

¼ cup chopped fresh flat-leaf parsley

1 teaspoon ground cumin

¼ teaspoon kosher salt

Pinch of crushed red pepper flakes

2 bay leaves

COLLARD GREENS

1 large bunch collard greens, washed and dried

2 slices center-cut bacon, chopped

½ tablespoon olive oil

3 garlic cloves, chopped

½ teaspoon kosher salt

4½ cups cooked brown rice (see page 50)

1 medium orange, halved and sliced, for garnish

*Read the label to be sure this product is gluten-free.

For the beans: In a medium pot, heat the oil over medium-high heat. Add the onion, ham, and pork and cook, stirring, until the onion is golden, about 5 minutes. Add the garlic and cook, stirring, for 2 minutes. Add the beans, 1 cup water, the parsley, cumin, salt, pepper flakes, and bay leaves. Stir, reduce the heat to medium-low, cover, and simmer until the beans thicken, about 20 minutes. Discard the bay leaves.

For the collard greens: Cut out the tough center ribs from the leaves and discard. Slice the leaves crosswise into thin strips.

Heat a large nonstick skillet over medium-low heat. Cook the bacon until the fat renders, 2 to 3 minutes. Add the oil and the garlic and cook, stirring, until fragrant, 1 minute. Add the greens and salt, cover, and simmer, stirring occasionally, until tender, 10 minutes.

To serve, put ¾ cup rice in each of 6 bowls. Top with 1 cup beans and ⅓ cup greens. Serve with orange slices on the side.

SKINNY SCOOP Double the beans for freezer-friendly meals. The beans can be refrigerated in an airtight container for up to 3 days or frozen for up to 1 month.

PER SERVING	¾ cup brown rice + 1 cup beans + ⅓ cup greens
CALORIES	456
FAT	9 g
SATURATED FAT	2 g
CHOLESTEROL	29 mg
CARBOHYDRATE	69 g
FIBER	11.5 g
PROTEIN	27 g
SUGARS	9 g
SODIUM	731 mg

GRILLED VEAL CHOP MILANESE WITH ARUGULA SALAD SERVES 4

Q

This slimmed-down spin on one of my all-time favorite restaurant dishes replaces the standard pan-fried version with grilled (yes, grilled!). The first time I grilled breaded veal chops, it was by accident. I was barbecuing some veal chops for dinner and my husband asked me if I could bread his. It was summer and I had no intention of cooking them indoors, so I threw them on the grill. The results were wonderful! If some of the crumbs fall off, don't worry; it adds a little bit of a rustic charm to the dish.

VEAL

4 (8-ounce) bone-in veal chops, fat trimmed

2 tablespoons fresh lemon juice

2 teaspoons olive oil

2 garlic cloves, crushed

1 teaspoon kosher salt

Freshly ground black pepper

2/3 cup seasoned whole wheat bread crumbs

Cooking spray or oil mister

SALAD

4½ cups baby arugula

3 tablespoons chopped red onion

1 medium vine tomato, finely chopped

6 fresh basil leaves, chopped

1 teaspoon olive oil

1 lemon, halved

¼ teaspoon kosher salt

Freshly ground black pepper

For the veal: Place each chop between 2 sheets of wax paper and, using a meat pounder, pound until the chops are about ¼ inch thick.

In a small bowl, combine the lemon juice, olive oil, and garlic. Season the veal with the salt and pepper to taste, and place it in a shallow dish. Pour the lemon mixture over the chops. Let sit for 15 minutes.

Place the bread crumbs on a large plate. Bread the veal chops, then lightly coat both sides with cooking spray.

For the salad: In a large bowl, combine the arugula, red onion, tomato, basil, olive oil, and the juice from half of the lemon. Season with the salt and pepper to taste.

Preheat the grill (or preheat a grill pan) over medium heat. Oil the grates with oil or spray a grill pan with nonstick cooking spray. Grill the chops until the crumbs are golden and the veal is no longer pink in the center, about 3 minutes per side.

Put a chop on each of 4 plates, and top each with 1 cup of the salad. Slice the remaining half lemon into wedges and serve on the side.

SKINNY SCOOP If you don't eat veal, a pork chop would work great here, too.

PER SERVING	1 chop + 1 cup salad
CALORIES	364
FAT	12 g
SATURATED FAT	3 g
CHOLESTEROL	204 mg
CARBOHYDRATE	15 g
FIBER	3 g
PROTEIN	48 g
SUGARS	3 g
SODIUM	884 mg

SKILLET PORK CHOPS WITH BRAISED FENNEL AND SHALLOTS   SERVES 4

Q **GF**

I fell in love with fennel a few years ago at a fancy gala dinner in San Francisco, where I tried a scallop dish that was topped with a delicious braised fennel sauce. Before that moment, I had only eaten fennel raw, and was not a fan of its strong licorice-like taste. But when braised, it mellows nicely, and it's a perfect complement to these thick, juicy pork chops.

4 bone-in center-cut pork loin chops, 1 inch thick, trimmed (about 20 ounces trimmed)

1 tablespoon garlic powder

1 tablespoon herbes de Provence

1¼ teaspoons plus ⅛ teaspoon kosher salt

Freshly ground black pepper

¾ cup reduced-sodium chicken broth*

1 tablespoon Dijon mustard

1 fennel bulb (14 ounces), stalks cut off

1 teaspoon salted butter

2 teaspoons olive oil

1 large shallot, cut into ½-inch-thick wedges

Read the label to be sure this product is gluten-free.

Season the pork chops with the garlic powder, herbes de Provence, 1¼ teaspoons of the salt, and pepper to taste. In a small bowl, combine the broth and mustard.

Chop 1 tablespoon of the fronds and set aside. Halve the fennel bulbs lengthwise. Slice each half lengthwise into quarters so you get 8 pieces total, leaving the core intact so they don't fall apart.

In a 12-inch cast iron or heavy skillet, melt the butter over medium heat. Add the pork chops and cook until browned and cooked through and a thermometer inserted into the center registers 140°F, 7 to 8 minutes per side. Transfer to a platter and tent with foil.

Turn the heat under the skillet to medium-low and add the olive oil, fennel, and shallots. Cook, undisturbed, until browned, 2 minutes. Turn the vegetables, season with the remaining ⅛ teaspoon salt and a pinch of pepper, and cook until browned, 2 minutes. Reduce the heat to low and add the broth-mustard mixture, scraping up any browned bits from the bottom of the pan. Cover and simmer until the fennel is tender, 10 to 12 minutes. Increase the heat to medium, uncover, and simmer until the liquid reduces, 3 minutes. Transfer to the platter with the pork and pour the sauce over the pork. Garnish with the reserved chopped fennel fronds.

SKINNY SCOOP Fresh fennel bulbs usually come with the stalks and dill-like fronds attached. I use the fronds as a garnish in this dish, so be sure not to toss them out.

PER SERVING	1 chop + 2 pieces fennel + shallots
CALORIES	277
FAT	10.5 g
SATURATED FAT	3 g
CHOLESTEROL	82 mg
CARBOHYDRATE	11 g
FIBER	3.5 g
PROTEIN	33 g
SUGARS	1 g
SODIUM	733 mg

PORK TENDERLOIN WITH POTATOES AND CARAWAY SEEDS   SERVES 4

(Q) (GF) (DF)

When I was growing up, my dad always cooked on Sundays, which meant we were having one of his Czech specialties. We would have roasted pork with caraway seeds at least once a month, and he usually served it with dumplings and braised red cabbage or sauerkraut. I created a quicker, leaner version that uses pork tenderloin and baby potatoes—and the whole thing is made all in one pan. Fuss-free and flavorful—my kind of meal!

PORK

1¼ pounds pork tenderloin

½ tablespoon apple cider vinegar

½ teaspoon garlic powder

¾ teaspoon kosher salt

½ teaspoon caraway seeds

Olive oil spray (such as Bertolli) or a mister

POTATOES

12 baby gold or red potatoes (1 pound total), halved

1 tablespoon olive oil

¾ teaspoon salt

½ teaspoon garlic powder

Freshly ground black pepper

Preheat the oven to 425°F.

For the pork: Place the pork in a large bowl, rub it with the vinegar, then season with the garlic powder, salt, and caraway seeds.

Heat a 12-inch cast iron skillet or enameled cast iron braising pan over high heat and spray it with oil. Add the pork and sear both sides until browned, about 3 minutes total. Transfer to a cutting board and insert an oven-safe thermometer into the thickest part of the pork.

For the potatoes: In the same bowl the pork was in, combine the potatoes, oil, salt, garlic powder, and pepper to taste. Return the pork to the skillet and add the potatoes.

Roast until the thermometer registers 145°F, 15 to 20 minutes. Keeping the potatoes in the pan, use tongs to transfer the pork to a cutting board, tenting with foil and letting rest for 10 minutes before slicing. Stir the potatoes, return to the oven, and roast until a knife inserts easily and the potatoes are browned on the edges, 10 more minutes.

Thinly slice the pork and divide evenly among 4 serving plates. Spoon the drippings over the top. Divide the potatoes among the plates and serve.

PERFECT PAIRINGS My Braised Red Cabbage with Vinegar recipe (page 265) is a must to make this a complete and satisfying meal.

PER SERVING	4 ounces pork + 3 potatoes
CALORIES	283
FAT	8.5 g
SATURATED FAT	2 g
CHOLESTEROL	92 mg
CARBOHYDRATE	19 g
FIBER	2 g
PROTEIN	32 g
SUGARS	1 g
SODIUM	515 mg

SLOW COOKER BRISKET WITH ONIONS   SERVES 8

SC **GF** **DF** **FF**

This is my absolute favorite way to make brisket. The meat is braised slowly all day with caramelized onions and garlic. Then, just before it's ready, I thinly slice the meat and place it back in the slow cooker for a little longer while I prep my side dishes. The results are incredible! The meat is deliciously moist and tender, with juices seeping into every flavorful bite, and the onions melt into the savory sauce. It tastes even better the next day and also freezes beautifully.

2½ pounds lean (first-cut) beef brisket, trimmed

1 teaspoon kosher salt

Freshly ground black pepper

½ tablespoon all-purpose flour*

2 teaspoons olive oil

1 tablespoon Worcestershire sauce*

2 large onions, sliced

1²/₃ cups reduced-sodium beef broth*

2 tablespoons tomato paste

3 garlic cloves, quartered

1 tablespoon chopped fresh parsley, for garnish

Read the labels to be sure these products are gluten-free.

Season the brisket with ¾ teaspoon of the salt and pepper to taste, then dust with the flour.

Heat a large skillet over medium-high heat. Add 1 teaspoon of the oil and the brisket and cook until browned, about 5 minutes per side. Transfer the meat to a slow cooker. Top the brisket with the Worcestershire sauce.

Reduce the heat under the skillet to medium-low and add the remaining 1 teaspoon oil and the onions. Cook, stirring, until soft and golden, about 15 minutes. Place the onions over the brisket and sprinkle with the remaining ¼ teaspoon salt and pepper to taste. Add the broth, tomato paste, and garlic to the slow cooker.

Cover and cook on low for 9 to 10 hours, until the meat is very tender. About 30 minutes before your timer goes off, transfer the brisket to a cutting board. Using a sharp knife, slice the meat across the grain into ⅛-inch-thick slices. Return the sliced meat to the slow cooker, submerging the meat under the gravy and onions. Cook for 30 more minutes. Keep warm until ready to serve. Divide the meat, gravy, and onions among 8 serving plates. Serve garnished with the parsley.

SKINNY SCOOP An oval-shaped 6-quart slow cooker is best for this recipe.

PER SERVING	3 ounces meat + ½ cup onions and gravy
CALORIES	224
FAT	8.5 g
SATURATED FAT	3 g
CHOLESTEROL	95 mg
CARBOHYDRATE	6 g
FIBER	1 g
PROTEIN	32 g
SUGARS	3 g
SODIUM	370 mg

PERFECT PAIRINGS
Serve this with Whipped Parmesan Cauliflower Puree (page 264) and roasted vegetables).

SLOW COOKER CARNE DESMECHADA   SERVES 8

SC GF DF FF

My mom is Colombian, so I grew up eating this flavorful shredded beef stew, which is also popular in Venezuela. It's pretty similar to a Cuban *ropa vieja*, and not spicy at all, which makes it very family friendly. We typically serve it over rice with sliced avocado, cabbage salad, or Baked Sweet Plantains with Cheese (page 259) on the side. But it's so versatile, you can easily give this a Mexican flair by adding fresh jalapeños and serving it over tortillas with a shredded slaw on top.

1 teaspoon olive oil

⅓ cup chopped scallions

½ cup chopped red bell pepper

3 garlic cloves, chopped

2 plum tomatoes, chopped

1½ teaspoons kosher salt

1½ teaspoons ground cumin

¼ teaspoon garlic powder

½ cup reduced-sodium beef broth*

1½ cups canned tomato sauce

1½ pounds flank steak, fat trimmed

2 bay leaves

*Read the label to be sure this product is gluten-free.

Heat a medium nonstick skillet over medium heat. Add the oil, scallions, bell pepper, and garlic and cook, stirring, until tender, 2 to 3 minutes. Add the tomatoes, ½ teaspoon of the salt, ½ teaspoon of the cumin, and the garlic powder and cook until the tomatoes soften and begin to break up, 4 to 5 minutes more. Transfer to a slow cooker. Add the broth and tomato sauce and stir well.

Season the meat with the remaining 1 teaspoon salt and 1 teaspoon cumin, and place in the slow cooker, making sure the liquid covers the meat. If it does not, add a little more broth. Add the bay leaves.

Cover and cook on high for 4 hours or on low for 8 hours, until the meat is tender and easily shreds. Discard the bay leaves. Carefully transfer the meat to a plate and shred with 2 forks. Return the meat to the slow cooker and keep warm until ready to serve.

SKINNY SCOOP To make a simple cabbage salad, thinly shred red or green cabbage with a knife, then toss with olive oil, vinegar, salt, and pepper.

PER SERVING	generous ½ cup
CALORIES	176
FAT	6 g
SATURATED FAT	2 g
CHOLESTEROL	52 mg
CARBOHYDRATE	9 g
FIBER	2 g
PROTEIN	20 g
SUGARS	5 g
SODIUM	473 mg

PERFECT MEDIUM-RARE ROAST BEEF IN THE SLOW COOKER SERVES 10

SC GF DF

Slow cookers are best known for slow braises and stewed roasts. But did you know that you can use your slow cooker to make perfectly sliceable, medium-rare roast beef that tastes like it just came out of the oven? It really works! The trick is to give the roast a good sear on all sides before placing it in the slow cooker to give it good flavor. Then all you need is a slow cooker large enough to hold the roast (6 quarts is perfect) and a meat thermometer so you know when it's done. We like our roast beef medium-rare; if you prefer yours a bit less pink, adjust the cooking time and final temperature accordingly.

BEEF

Cooking spray

2½ pounds beef roast, such as top sirloin roast or round roast, fat trimmed

1½ teaspoons kosher salt

½ teaspoon freshly ground black pepper

GRAVY

2 cups beef broth*

2 tablespoons all-purpose flour*

Freshly ground black pepper (optional)

Read the labels to be sure these products are gluten-free.

For the beef: Heat a large nonstick skillet over high heat and coat it with cooking spray. Season the roast with the salt and pepper. Add the meat to the pan and sear until browned on all sides, 3 to 4 minutes per side. Transfer the beef to a slow cooker. Insert an oven-safe meat thermometer into the thickest part of the roast.

Cover and cook on low until the internal temperature reaches 135°F for medium-rare, about 1½ hours depending on the size of the roast, or until 140°F for medium. Transfer the roast to a cutting board, tent it with foil, and let it rest for 20 to 30 minutes. Thinly slice the roast across the grain.

For the gravy: In a small saucepan, whisk together the broth and flour over medium heat until it comes to a boil. Simmer, stirring occasionally, until the mixture thickens, about 1 minute. Strain the drippings from the slow cooker into a bowl, then pour them into the gravy. Cook, whisking, for another minute. Season with pepper to taste, if desired.

PER SERVING	3 ounces beef + 3½ tablespoons gravy
CALORIES	227
FAT	13 g
SATURATED FAT	5 g
CHOLESTEROL	83 mg
CARBOHYDRATE	1 g
FIBER	0 g
PROTEIN	24 g
SUGARS	0 g
SODIUM	332 mg

PERFECT PAIRINGS This is great with Whipped Parmesan Cauliflower Puree (page 264) and a roasted vegetable such as Burnt Broccoli (page 255) or Roasted Acorn Squash with Parmesan (page 263). Also wonderful with an Italian House Salad with Dijon Vinaigrette (page 252).

PERFECT PAIRINGS This is great over noodles, polenta, or even a simple root vegetable puree, like my Whipped Parmesan Cauliflower Puree (page 264) pictured here.

SLOW COOKER OSSO BUCO

SERVES 4

SC GF DF FF

One of my favorite restaurant dishes—braised veal shanks, or osso buco—is easy to make at home, and comes out meltingly tender when made in the slow cooker. As it cooks over the course of the day, the house becomes filled with a savory "welcome home" aroma. This recipe is easy to whip up any night of the week, but because of the price of veal, I usually save it for special occasions.

1 teaspoon olive oil

⅓ cup chopped onion

⅓ cup chopped carrots

⅓ cup chopped celery

2 garlic cloves, chopped

1 teaspoon kosher salt

1 tablespoon tomato paste

1¼ cups canned crushed tomatoes

¾ cup beef broth*

Freshly ground black pepper

4 pieces veal shank, each 1¼ inches thick (about 2 pounds total)

3 sprigs of fresh thyme

1 large sprig of fresh rosemary

Chopped fresh flat-leaf parsley, for garnish

Read the label to be sure this product is gluten-free.

Heat a medium nonstick skillet over medium heat. Add the oil, onion, carrots, celery, garlic, and ¼ teaspoon of the salt. Cook, stirring, until soft, 8 to 10 minutes. Add the tomato paste, stir, and cook 1 minute before transferring to a slow cooker.

Add the crushed tomatoes, broth, ¼ teaspoon of the salt, and pepper to taste to the slow cooker. Stir well.

Wipe out the skillet and set it over medium-high heat. Season the veal shanks with the remaining ½ teaspoon salt and pepper to taste. Add to the skillet and cook until browned on all sides, 3 to 4 minutes per side. Nestle the shanks into the sauce and vegetables in the slow cooker and add the thyme and rosemary.

Cover and cook on high for 4 hours or on low for 8 hours. Discard the thyme and rosemary sprigs. Serve garnished with the parsley.

SKINNY SCOOP This fits best in a 6-quart slow cooker. You can swap the lamb shanks for veal, although, because they are larger, use three lamb shanks instead of four; it will still be more than enough for four people.

PER SERVING	1 shank + ⅓ cup sauce
CALORIES	**312**
FAT	**9 g**
SATURATED FAT	**2.5 g**
CHOLESTEROL	**170 mg**
CARBOHYDRATE	**9 g**
FIBER	**2 g**
PROTEIN	**46 g**
SUGARS	**6 g**
SODIUM	**747 mg**

SLOW COOKER STUFFED CABBAGE ROLLS SERVES 8

SC GF DF FF

Stuffed cabbage, a hearty Eastern European comfort food, is known by many names. In the Czech Republic, where my dad is from, it's called *holubky* and traditionally features ground beef and white rice cooked in a tomato sauce. I took some liberties with my parents' recipe to make it lighter: swapping half the ground beef with turkey, using brown rice instead of white, and adapting it for the slow cooker.

1 medium head cabbage, cored

½ teaspoon olive oil

1 cup chopped onion

¾ teaspoon Hungarian paprika

¼ teaspoon kosher salt

1 (16-ounce) can tomato sauce

1½ cups reduced-sodium beef broth*

2 tablespoons raisins

Freshly ground black pepper

FILLING

10 ounces 93% lean ground beef

10 ounces 93% lean ground turkey

1 cup cooked brown rice (see page 50)

1 garlic clove, minced

1 large egg, beaten

1 tablespoon dried marjoram

1¼ teaspoons kosher salt

⅛ teaspoon freshly ground black pepper

Read the label to be sure this product is gluten-free.

Bring a large pot of water to a boil over high heat. Immerse the whole cabbage in the boiling water for a few minutes, peeling off each leaf with tongs as soon as it becomes flexible, about 3 minutes. Set the leaves aside to dry and cool. You will need 8 outer leaves. Shave or trim the thick ribs with a knife to make them easy to roll.

Heat a medium pot over medium heat. Add the oil, onion, paprika, and salt and cook, stirring, until soft, 5 minutes. Set ¼ cup aside for the filling. To the pot, add the tomato sauce, broth, raisins, and pepper. Simmer for 5 minutes. Scoop 1 cup of the sauce into the slow cooker.

For the filling: Put the reserved ¼ cup onion in a large bowl and add the ground beef, ground turkey, rice, garlic, egg, marjoram, salt, and pepper. Add ⅓ cup of the sauce and mix well. Scoop about ½ cup of the filling into the center of each cabbage leaf. Roll up the leaves, tucking in the ends. Transfer seam side down to the slow cooker. Top with the remaining sauce.

Cover and cook on high for 4 hours or on low for 8 hours.

SKINNY SCOOP The eight rolls fit in my 6-quart slow cooker; if your cooker is smaller, stack them on top of one another.

PER SERVING	1 roll + ⅓ cup sauce
CALORIES	241
FAT	8 g
SATURATED FAT	2.5 g
CHOLESTEROL	73 mg
CARBOHYDRATE	24 g
FIBER	5.5 g
PROTEIN	19 g
SUGARS	11 g
SODIUM	598 mg

SLOW COOKER GOULASH WITH SAUERKRAUT   SERVES 6

SC GF FF

Many of my dad's Czech dishes that I grew up eating work wonderfully in the slow cooker. This amazing, creamy Czech/Slovakian stew, called *Segedin goulash*, is the perfect example. It's a bit different from Hungarian goulash because it contains sauerkraut—and even if you're not a kraut fan, you'll be surprised by how delicious this is. It's commonly made with pork, but you can also use veal, venison, or any meat you like.

1½ pounds pork shoulder, cubed

1½ teaspoons kosher salt

¼ teaspoon Hungarian paprika

Cooking spray

1 teaspoon olive oil

1 medium onion, chopped

½ pound sauerkraut, drained

1 cup light sour cream

2 tablespoons all-purpose flour*

½ teaspoon caraway seeds

*Read the label to be sure this product is gluten-free.

Season the pork with the salt and paprika.

Heat a large skillet over high heat and coat it with cooking spray. Add the meat and cook until browned on all sides, about 3 minutes. Transfer to a slow cooker.

Add the oil to the skillet and reduce the heat to medium. Add the onion and cook, stirring, until golden, about 5 minutes. Transfer to the slow cooker along with the sauerkraut.

In a blender, combine 1 cup water, the sour cream, flour, and caraway seeds. Blend until smooth and pour over the meat.

Cover and cook on low for 8 hours.

PERFECT PAIRINGS Though this dish is traditionally served over dumplings to soak up the juice, I prefer to serve it with roasted vegetables, which balance out the richness of the dish.

PER SERVING	generous ¾ cup
CALORIES	237
FAT	11.5 g
SATURATED FAT	5 g
CHOLESTEROL	83 mg
CARBOHYDRATE	8 g
FIBER	1.5 g
PROTEIN	24 g
SUGARS	2 g
SODIUM	634 mg

SLOW COOKER PERNIL   SERVES 10

SC GF DF FF

This succulent pork roast is a staple in Latin homes around the holidays or any time there's something to celebrate. It's an inexpensive crowd-pleaser that marinates overnight with citrus, garlic, and spices. I've lightened this dish by removing the pork's fatty skin and transformed it into an everyday meal by making it in the slow cooker—it turns out wonderfully juicy.

4½ pounds trimmed, skinless bone-in pork shoulder

5 garlic cloves, crushed

½ cup fresh orange juice (from 1 large navel orange)

Juice of 2 limes

1 tablespoon kosher salt

½ tablespoon ground cumin

½ teaspoon dried oregano

¼ teaspoon freshly ground black pepper

Using a sharp knife, cut slits into the pork about 1 inch deep and stuff the holes with half the garlic. Place the pork in a large bowl.

In a medium bowl, combine the orange and lime juices, the salt, cumin, oregano, pepper, and remaining garlic. Pour the marinade over the pork. Refrigerate overnight, turning occasionally so the marinade covers all of the pork.

Transfer the pork and marinade to a slow cooker, cover, and cook on low for 10 to 12 hours.

Transfer the pork to a cutting board and, using 2 forks, shred the meat. Discard all but 1 cup of the liquid in the slow cooker. Return the pork to the slow cooker with the reserved liquid. Cover and cook on low for 30 more minutes, to allow the flavors to meld.

SKINNY SCOOP If your market sells pork shoulder with the skin on, ask the butcher to trim it off along with any fat. For the best flavor I prefer a bone-in shoulder; the meat will fall off the bone easily once it's cooked.

PER SERVING	generous 3 ounces pork
CALORIES	313
FAT	14.5 g
SATURATED FAT	5 g
CHOLESTEROL	137 mg
CARBOHYDRATE	3 g
FIBER	0 g
PROTEIN	40 g
SUGARS	1 g
SODIUM	492 mg

SLOW COOKER ASIAN PORK WITH MUSHROOMS SERVES 8

SC DF FF

Love Asian food? Then mushroom soy sauce, a key ingredient in this recipe, is a must-have. The thick, dark, and savory sauce imparts a robust flavor to anything you make. I buy a big bottle at my local Asian supermarket (you can also find it on Amazon.com)—it's cheap and it lasts forever.

¼ cup dark mushroom soy sauce (I like Pearl River Bridge)

3 tablespoons honey

1 teaspoon toasted sesame oil

1 tablespoon minced garlic

2 teaspoons grated fresh ginger

2¼ pounds boneless pork shoulder, trimmed

5 ounces sliced shiitake mushrooms

2 medium scallions, sliced, for garnish

In a small bowl, whisk together the soy sauce, honey, oil, garlic, and ginger. Pour into a large zip-top plastic bag. Add the pork to the bag and seal. Marinate in the refrigerator for at least 2 hours, turning occasionally.

Place the pork and marinade in a slow cooker, along with the shiitakes. Cover and cook on low for 8 hours. Transfer the pork to a cutting board and shred with 2 forks. Serve with the sauce and garnish with the scallions.

SKINNY SCOOP Inexpensive, tougher cuts of meat, such as pork shoulder, are my favorite types to make in the slow cooker. They always turn out moist and tender after slow cooking all day. If you use a pork shoulder with the bone in, increase the cooking time to 10 to 12 hours.

PER SERVING	3 ounces pork + ¼ cup sauce
CALORIES	204
FAT	7.5 g
SATURATED FAT	2.5 g
CHOLESTEROL	75 mg
CARBOHYDRATE	11 g
FIBER	0.5 g
PROTEIN	24 g
SUGARS	8 g
SODIUM	863 mg

FISH AND SEAFOOD MAINS

FAST

Q GF DF Zesty Lime Shrimp and Avocado Salad **208**

Q GF DF Sweet 'n' Spicy Salmon with Stir-Fried Veggies **211**

Q GF Baked Fish and Chips **212**

Q GF Veggie-Stuffed Flounder Sheet Pan Dinner **215**

Q GF DF Roasted Asian Striped Bass **216**

Q GF DF Broiled Whole Porgies **219**

SLOW

SC GF DF Slow Cooker Shrimp à la Criolla **220**

SC GF DF Slow Cooker Poached Salmon with Meyer Lemon, Capers, and Parsley **222**

ZESTY LIME SHRIMP AND AVOCADO SALAD

SERVES 4

Q GF DF

Lime juice and cilantro are the star ingredients in this light and tasty salad that you'll want to make all summer long. It's very quick and easy to toss together, and using precooked shrimp makes it even speedier! You can easily double this salad for a crowd, and it also works great as an appetizer that's a guaranteed hit at parties.

¼ cup chopped red onion

Juice of 2 small limes

1 teaspoon olive oil

¼ teaspoon kosher salt

Freshly ground black pepper

1 pound peeled and cooked jumbo shrimp, cut into bite-size pieces

1 medium Hass avocado (5 ounces), chopped

1 medium tomato, chopped

1 fresh jalapeño pepper, seeded and finely chopped

1 tablespoon chopped fresh cilantro

In a small bowl, combine the onion, lime juice, olive oil, salt, and pepper to taste. Let sit for at least 5 minutes.

In a large bowl, combine the shrimp, avocado, tomato, and jalapeño. Add the onion mixture and the cilantro, and toss gently. Season with pepper, if desired.

SKINNY SCOOP You can make this salad ahead of time by combining all the ingredients except for the avocado and cilantro and refrigerating it. Toss in the two reserved ingredients just before serving.

PER SERVING	about 1 cup
CALORIES	252
FAT	9 g
SATURATED FAT	1.5 g
CHOLESTEROL	234 mg
CARBOHYDRATE	11 g
FIBER	4 g
PROTEIN	33 g
SUGARS	3 g
SODIUM	771 mg

SWEET 'N' SPICY SALMON WITH STIR-FRIED VEGGIES   SERVES 4

Q GF DF

I try to eat salmon at least once a week because it's rich in omega-3 fats, which are great for your health. I also happen to love the taste, and, luckily, so do my kids. To accommodate Madison's more sensitive palate, I make hers without the spicy Sriracha. Start to finish, the whole dish takes less than 15 minutes to make. You can use any mix of veggies you like, but try to vary the colors.

1 pound wild salmon fillet, skinned

¾ teaspoon kosher salt

¼ cup Thai sweet chili sauce

2 teaspoons Sriracha sauce

2 teaspoons canola oil

2 garlic cloves, minced

1 teaspoon grated fresh ginger

5 baby bok choy (about 6½ ounces), quartered

4 ounces sliced shiitake mushrooms

1 medium red bell pepper, cut into strips

1 medium yellow bell pepper, cut into strips

Preheat the oven to 400°F. Line a baking sheet with foil.

Cut the salmon into 4 pieces and season them with ¼ teaspoon of the salt. Roast until almost cooked through, about 8 minutes. Remove from the oven and switch the oven to broil.

In a small bowl, combine the chili sauce and Sriracha. Brush the mixture over the fish and broil until the fish is cooked through, 1 to 2 minutes.

Heat a large nonstick wok or deep skillet over medium heat. Add the oil, garlic, and ginger and cook, stirring, until fragrant, about 30 seconds. Add the bok choy, mushrooms, and bell peppers. Increase the heat to medium-high, season with the remaining ½ teaspoon salt, and stir. Add 2 tablespoons water, cover, and cook until crisp-tender, 4 to 5 minutes.

To serve, divide the vegetables among 4 serving plates. Top with salmon and serve warm.

FOOD FACTS: EATING NATURE'S RAINBOW
Eating a variety of colorful vegetables gives your body a spectrum of nutrients. For example, the lycopene that gives red peppers their color can help improve your blood pressure, and the chlorophyll that makes bok choy green can help your liver and kidneys clean the body of toxins.

PER SERVING	1 piece salmon + ¾ cup vegetables
CALORIES	255
FAT	9 g
SATURATED FAT	1.5 g
CHOLESTEROL	60 mg
CARBOHYDRATE	17 g
FIBER	2.5 g
PROTEIN	26 g
SUGARS	11 g
SODIUM	627 mg

BAKED FISH and CHIPS   SERVES 4

Q GF

This all-time fish favorite gets a healthy makeover by skipping the deep-fryer (and the grease!). The mild white fish is breaded with panko and Parmesan for a crisp coating, and is finished off with a good squeeze of fresh lemon juice.

Olive oil spray (such as Bertolli) or a mister

CHIPS

4 medium russet or Yukon Gold potatoes (6 ounces each), cut into ¼-inch-thick slices

4 teaspoons olive oil

3 garlic cloves, crushed

1 teaspoon kosher salt

Freshly ground black pepper

1 tablespoon finely chopped fresh parsley

FISH

1 large egg

1 large egg white

1 tablespoon fresh lemon juice

⅛ teaspoon plus ½ teaspoon sweet paprika

⅛ teaspoon freshly ground black pepper

¾ cup panko bread crumbs*

1½ tablespoons freshly grated Parmesan cheese

1 tablespoon finely chopped fresh parsley

1 teaspoon grated lemon zest

4 (5-ounce) wild white fish fillets, such as Atlantic cod or haddock

¼ teaspoon kosher salt

4 lemon wedges, for serving

Read the label to be sure this product is gluten-free.

Adjust the oven racks in the center and bottom third and preheat the oven to 450°F. Line 2 large baking sheets with foil or parchment and spray the foil with oil.

For the chips: In a large bowl, toss the potatoes, oil, garlic, ½ teaspoon of the salt, and pepper. Arrange in a single layer on the prepared baking sheets. Bake until browned on the bottom, 12 to 14 minutes. Remove from the oven, flip the potatoes, and make room for the fish.

For the fish: In a medium bowl, whisk together the whole egg, egg white, lemon juice, ⅛ teaspoon of the paprika, and the pepper. In a shallow bowl, combine the panko, Parmesan, parsley, lemon zest, and remaining ½ teaspoon paprika.

Pat the fish dry and season with the salt. Dip the fish into the egg mixture and then into the panko. Place the fish on the baking sheets, nestled into the potatoes, and spray the tops with oil.

Bake until golden and the fish is cooked through, 10 minutes.

Sprinkle the potatoes with the remaining ½ teaspoon salt and the parsley. To serve, divide among 4 serving plates and serve with lemon wedges.

PER SERVING	1 piece fish + ¼ of the potatoes
CALORIES	368
FAT	7.5 g
SATURATED FAT	1.5 g
CHOLESTEROL	41 mg
CARBOHYDRATE	41 g
FIBER	3 g
PROTEIN	34 g
SUGARS	2 g
SODIUM	512 mg

VEGGIE-STUFFED FLOUNDER SHEET PAN DINNER SERVES 4

(Q) (GF)

Nothing is faster, healthier, and tastier than baked fish and veggies. Use prepared pesto to pull this dish together in just 20 minutes, and for easy cleanup, line the baking sheets with parchment or foil. The spiralized zucchini and squash are lovely in this dish, but if you want to add some color, you can incorporate some shredded or spiralized carrots into the veggie mix.

24 thin asparagus spears
(8 ounces), tough ends trimmed

Olive oil spray (such as Bertolli)
or a mister

Kosher salt and freshly ground
black pepper

4 (5½-ounce) flounder fillets

8 teaspoons basil pesto

3 ounces (about 1 cup) spiralized
zucchini

3 ounces (about 1 cup) spiralized
yellow squash

2 teaspoons seasoned panko
bread crumbs*

*Read the label to be sure this product is gluten-free.

Preheat the oven to 400°F.

Place 4 groups of 6 asparagus spears onto 2 large baking sheets. Spray with olive oil and season each group with ⅛ teaspoon salt and pepper to taste.

Season one side of each fish fillet with ⅛ teaspoon salt, then spread 1 teaspoon of pesto over each piece of fish. Place ½ cup spiralized vegetables in the center of each fillet, season with a pinch of salt and pepper, roll up, and place seam side down on top of the asparagus. Brush the tops of each rolled fish with 1 teaspoon pesto and sprinkle with the panko.

Bake in the center of the oven until the fish is cooked through, about 15 minutes. Switch the oven to broil. Move the pan to the second rack from the top and broil the fish until golden, about 3 minutes.

SKINNY SCOOP If you don't have a spiralizer, you can julienne the vegetables instead.

PER SERVING	1 stuffed fillet
CALORIES	213
FAT	7 g
SATURATED FAT	1.5 g
CHOLESTEROL	76 mg
CARBOHYDRATE	5 g
FIBER	2 g
PROTEIN	32 g
SUGARS	2 g
SODIUM	478 mg

ROASTED ASIAN STRIPED BASS   SERVES 4

Q GF DF

Soy, ginger, sesame, and lime—the flavors in this sauce will convert anyone in your house who isn't keen on fish. Another reason to reel in this recipe: It couldn't be any easier to make, as it uses ingredients you probably already have on hand. Start to finish, it takes about 15 minutes to throw together, so it's great for weeknights. I love the mild flavor of striped bass, but any flaky white fish will work.

2 tablespoons soy sauce*

1 tablespoon fresh lime juice

1 teaspoon honey

1 teaspoon toasted sesame oil

½ tablespoon chopped fresh ginger

1 teaspoon minced garlic

Cooking spray

4 (5-ounce) striped bass fillets

1 scallion, sliced, for garnish

*Read the label to be sure this product is gluten-free.

Preheat the oven to 450°F.

In a small bowl, combine the soy sauce, lime juice, honey, sesame oil, ginger, and garlic.

Coat a 9 x 13-inch baking dish with cooking spray. Arrange the fish in the dish and pour the sauce over each fillet.

Roast until the fish is cooked through and opaque in the center, 10 to 12 minutes, depending on the thickness. Serve the fish garnished with the scallions.

PER SERVING	1 fillet
CALORIES	161
FAT	4.5 g
SATURATED FAT	1 g
CHOLESTEROL	113 mg
CARBOHYDRATE	3 g
FIBER	0 g
PROTEIN	26 g
SUGARS	2 g
SODIUM	550 mg

FOOD FACTS: WHITE FISH
The American Heart Association recommends eating fish twice a week, and it's no wonder. Not only is fish a high-quality protein source, it's also low in saturated fat and is packed with an array of healthy vitamins and minerals. White fish, such as striped bass, is loaded with the B vitamins niacin (required to eliminate toxins from the body) and pyridoxine (needed for healthy skin).

PERFECT PAIRINGS This is great with brown rice and Pineapple Jicama Slaw (page 269).

BROILED WHOLE PORGIES SERVES 2

Q GF DF

Porgies are flaky and tender with a mild, delicate, clean flavor. While you can use any type of cooking method (grilling, frying, and so on), I find it easiest to broil them. Porgies benefit from marinating, if you have the extra time. If you can't find porgies where you live, you can use any small fresh whole fish, such as red snapper, branzino, sea bass, or even trout.

2 garlic cloves

1 tablespoon olive oil

Juice of ½ lime

2 sprigs of fresh thyme

½ teaspoon dried oregano

⅛ teaspoon ground cumin

1 teaspoon kosher salt

⅛ teaspoon freshly ground black pepper

2 whole porgies (about 1 pound each), gutted and cleaned

Olive oil spray (such as Bertolli) or a mister

½ cup reduced-sodium chicken broth*

1 tablespoon chopped fresh flat-leaf parsley

*Read the label to be sure this product is gluten-free.

Preheat the broiler to low. Adjust an oven rack in the top third of the oven and place a cast iron skillet on it to get hot.

In a small bowl, crush the garlic. Add the olive oil, lime juice, thyme leaves, oregano, cumin, salt, and pepper and stir to make a paste.

Pat the fish dry. Using a small sharp knife, make 3 cuts on both sides of each fish about 2 to 3 inches long. Using your hands, rub the spice paste over the entire fish, making sure to get it into the cuts. Carefully take the skillet out of the oven, spray it with a little oil, and place the fish into the skillet.

Broil until crisp, about 12 minutes per side.

Transfer the fish to a platter and place the skillet on the stove over medium-high heat. Add the broth and cook, stirring and scraping up any bits from the bottom of the pan, 3 to 4 minutes. Add the parsley and pour the pan drippings over the fish. Serve hot.

PERFECT PAIRINGS Serve this with a crisp green salad and fine dry white wine—chilled, of course.

PER SERVING	6 ounces fish
CALORIES	252
FAT	11.5 g
SATURATED FAT	2 g
CHOLESTEROL	89 mg
CARBOHYDRATE	2 g
FIBER	0.5 g
PROTEIN	33 g
SUGARS	0 g
SODIUM	776 mg

SLOW COOKER SHRIMP À LA CRIOLLA SERVES 6

SC GF DF

Yes, you can cook shrimp in the slow cooker! The key to avoiding *overcooking* the super seafood is to add them toward the end of cooking. This recipe—a simple stew of shrimp, tomatoes, peppers, garlic, and spices—was inspired by a meal I had at a restaurant on the beach in the Dominican Republic. The slow, low heat of the slow cooker is perfect for making the sauce. Then, at the end, I add the shrimp and olives, plus a little brine and fresh cilantro to brighten the dish.

STEW

4 medium plum tomatoes, chopped

1 large red bell pepper, chopped

1 (8-ounce) can tomato sauce

3 garlic cloves, crushed

¼ cup chopped fresh cilantro

½ teaspoon ground cumin

½ teaspoon kosher salt

2 bay leaves

SHRIMP

1½ pounds peeled and deveined jumbo shrimp

1 teaspoon olive oil

2 garlic cloves, crushed

½ teaspoon ground cumin

½ teaspoon kosher salt

⅛ teaspoon crushed red pepper flakes

¼ cup chopped green olives, plus 2 tablespoons brine

2 tablespoons chopped fresh cilantro, for garnish

For the stew: In a slow cooker, combine the tomatoes, bell pepper, tomato sauce, ½ cup water, the garlic, cilantro, cumin, salt, and bay leaves and stir. Cover and cook on low for 6 to 8 hours.

For the shrimp: In a medium bowl, combine the shrimp, olive oil, garlic, cumin, salt, and pepper flakes. Refrigerate until the stew has finished cooking.

When the stew is done, stir in the shrimp, olives, and brine. Cover and cook until the shrimp is opaque, 20 to 30 minutes on high. Discard the bay leaves. Serve immediately, garnished with the cilantro.

PERFECT PAIRINGS This is perfect served over rice with Baked Sweet Plantains with Cheese (page 259) on the side.

PER SERVING	1 cup
CALORIES	177
FAT	3.5 g
SATURATED FAT	0.5 g
CHOLESTEROL	136 mg
CARBOHYDRATE	13 g
FIBER	3 g
PROTEIN	22 g
SUGARS	7 g
SODIUM	716 mg

How to Reel in a Healthy Catch

With so many fish in the sea, which should you choose? Should you opt for wild or farmed? What about toxins? It's enough to make you seasick!

HERE ARE A FEW THINGS TO KEEP IN MIND:

- In general, wild fish—fish caught in the wild—are a better option than farmed fish, which are harvested in farms located either on land (in ponds, pools, or tanks) or in the ocean (in nets or mesh cages), because they're usually less contaminated and are better for the environment. Farmed salmon, for instance, can contain too many contaminants, pollute the environment, and squander resources.

- When it comes to varieties of fish or seafood that have been overfished (meaning, we're removing them from the ocean faster than they can reproduce), you're better off going with farmed versions. You may also want to consider buying other varieties of farmed fish that have been proven safe, including farmed mussels, oysters, and bay scallops.

- Enjoy variety. Experts recommend eating many different types of fish to reduce the impact of fishing or fish farming on the environment.

- Do your homework. Any reputable fishmonger at a fish market or fish counter should know about the sustainability and healthfulness of different types of fish and seafood, so don't be afraid to ask questions. Also, the Monterey Bay Aquarium Seafood Watch program (www.seafoodwatch.org) and the Environmental Defense Fund (www .seafood.edf.org) are invaluable resources for fish lovers. Finally, pay attention to advisories about the safety of local fish.

- Think small. Reduce the risk of toxic contaminants by eating fish that are "low on the food chain." This includes smaller fish, such as shrimp, sardines, and anchovies.

- Go fish! By choosing wild over farmed fish, you'll likely be getting a healthier catch, but the benefits of eating any fish, even farmed fish, far outweigh the health risks associated with forgoing fish.

SLOW COOKER POACHED SALMON WITH MEYER LEMON, CAPERS, AND PARSLEY SERVES 4

SC GF DF

My brother has a great recipe for salmon that's cooked in foil packets—my scribbled recipe card actually says "Ivan's Fish." Here, I've adapted it for the slow cooker. The low, slow heat of a slow cooker is actually perfect for shallow poaching. Rather than submerging the salmon in the poaching liquid, I rest it on a bed of Meyer lemons with parsley, shallots, and white wine so it cooks gently and absorbs all of the delicious flavors of the aromatics.

3 Meyer lemons

3 sprigs of fresh parsley

1 large shallot, thinly sliced

¼ cup dry white wine

1 pound skinless wild salmon fillets, 1 inch thick, cut into 4 pieces

¼ teaspoon kosher salt

Freshly ground black pepper

4 teaspoons capers, drained

Cut 2 pieces of parchment paper about 12 x 15 inches. Place them into the slow cooker lengthwise, one on top of the other, to create a sling that will make it easy to remove the salmon later.

Slice 2 of the lemons into ¼-inch-thick slices. Cut the remaining lemon into 4 wedges and set aside. Arrange the lemon slices in a single layer along the bottom of the slow cooker on top of the parchment. Top with the parsley sprigs and shallot slices. Pour in the wine and just enough water to get the level of the liquids even with the lemon, about ¼ cup.

Season the salmon with the salt and pepper to taste. Place the fish onto the lemon slices.

Cover and cook on low for 1 to 1½ hours, until the salmon is opaque throughout.

Using the parchment paper sling, transfer the salmon to a baking sheet. To serve, gently transfer a piece of salmon onto each of 4 plates, discarding the liquid, lemon, and herbs. Serve topped with the capers and with the reserved lemon wedges for squeezing.

SKINNY SCOOP Fish is best eaten when it is *really* fresh, so you should buy it from a fishmonger who knows his wares. If it arrived that morning, good—get it. If it's from yesterday, don't even bother. Another helpful hint is that if the fish smells "fishy," it's because it's old.

PER SERVING	1 piece
CALORIES	183
FAT	7.5 g
SATURATED FAT	1 g
CHOLESTEROL	62 mg
CARBOHYDRATE	3 g
FIBER	0.5 g
PROTEIN	23 g
SUGARS	1 g
SODIUM	207 mg

FAST

Q V GF Grilled Vegetable Caprese Salad **226**

Q V Grilled Cheese with Havarti, Brussels Sprouts, and Apple **229**

Q V Salad Pizza **230**

Q V Greek Panzanella Salad **233**

Q V GF Baked Pears with Greens, Blue Cheese, and Pecans **234**

Q V GF Baked Eggplant Parmesan Stacks **237**

Q V GF Easiest One-Pot Pasta and Broccoli **238**

Q V GF Coconut Veggie Curry **241**

Q V DF Dad's Peppers and Egg Sandwiches **242**

Q V Zucchini "Meatballs" **245**

SLOW

SC V GF Slow Cooker Loaded "Baked" Sweet Potatoes **246**

SC V GF FF Slow Cooker Chana Masala **248**

MEATLESS MAINS

GRILLED VEGETABLE CAPRESE SALAD

SERVES 2

Q V GF

Nothing screams summer like a caprese salad. It's traditionally made with fresh mozzarella, tomatoes, and basil, but here I went for a unique twist: I opted for lots of grilled vegetables instead of fresh tomatoes! The easiest way to grill vegetables outdoors is to use a grill tray, which prevents the veggies from falling through the grates. I prefer the ones that lie flat on the grill, as opposed to a grill basket.

½ pound asparagus (½ bunch), tough ends trimmed, cut into thirds

1 large zucchini (8 ounces), cut into ¼-inch-thick slices

1 large red bell pepper, cut into 2-inch pieces

½ teaspoon kosher salt

Freshly ground black pepper

2 tablespoons jarred pesto

Olive oil spray (such as Bertolli) or a mister

4 ounces fresh mini mozzarella balls (bocconcini), halved

2 tablespoons store-bought balsamic glaze (I love DeLallo)

12 small fresh basil leaves

In a large bowl, combine the asparagus, zucchini, and bell pepper and season with the salt and pepper. Add the pesto, toss well, and marinate for at least 15 minutes, or as long as overnight.

Preheat a grill to medium-high.

Working in batches, place the vegetables in a single layer on a large grill tray sprayed with oil and cook, turning constantly, until the edges of the vegetables are slightly charred, 6 to 8 minutes. Transfer to a plate and repeat with the remaining vegetables.

To serve, divide the vegetables between 2 plates. Add 2 ounces mozzarella to each dish and drizzle with the balsamic glaze. Top each with 6 fresh basil leaves.

SKINNY SCOOP You don't need a grill to make this dish. If you're cooking indoors, use a grill pan or roast the vegetables in the oven at 425°F for 7 to 8 minutes per side.

PER SERVING	1¾ cups
CALORIES	352
FAT	21 g
SATURATED FAT	9 g
CHOLESTEROL	47 mg
CARBOHYDRATE	25 g
FIBER	5.5 g
PROTEIN	19 g
SUGARS	19 g
SODIUM	786 mg

GRILLED CHEESE with HAVARTI, BRUSSELS SPROUTS, and APPLE

SERVES 2

Q V

I'm obsessed with this sandwich! Is there really anything better than a grilled cheese on those nights when you want comfort in a hurry? This sandwich will not disappoint. It's made with crisp, slightly charred Brussels sprouts and light Havarti, which melts beautifully compared with most low-fat cheese. Plus, because the cheese is light, I'm able to use *more* of it to create an extra-cheesy grilled cheese. The thin-sliced apples tucked in the center add the perfect shot of sweetness and tartness. Dig in!

1 teaspoon olive oil

1 tablespoon chopped shallot

2 cups (6 ounces) thinly shredded Brussels sprouts

¼ teaspoon salt

Freshly ground black pepper

Olive oil spray (such as Bertolli) or a mister

4 slices whole wheat Tuscan bread (1 ounce each)

4 ounces light Havarti cheese, shredded

2 Granny Smith apples, halved and cut into ⅛-inch-thick slices

Heat a medium skillet over medium heat. Add the oil and shallot and cook, stirring, until soft, about 1 minute. Add the Brussels sprouts, salt, and pepper to taste, and increase the heat to medium-high. Cook, stirring, until the sprouts are crisp and slightly browned on the edges, about 5 minutes. Remove the pan from the heat.

Heat a large nonstick skillet over medium-low heat. Spray one side of each slice of bread with olive oil and place 2 slices, oiled side down, into the skillet. Top each piece of bread with 1 ounce of the cheese. Divide the Brussels sprouts between the bread slices, then add a layer of apple slices and the remaining cheese. Top with the remaining bread, oiled side up, and cook until the bottom piece of bread is golden, 4 to 5 minutes. Using a spatula, carefully flip the sandwiches over. Cook until the second slices of bread are golden brown, 3 to 4 minutes. Serve immediately!

PERFECT PAIRINGS On soup and sandwich nights, pair this with a cup of Dad's Cauliflower Soup (page 40) or Cream of Zucchini Soup (page 43) for a satisfying, comforting meal.

PER SERVING	1 sandwich
CALORIES	449
FAT	13.5 g
SATURATED FAT	7 g
CHOLESTEROL	30 mg
CARBOHYDRATE	63 g
FIBER	10.5 g
PROTEIN	25 g
SUGARS	23 g
SODIUM	822 mg

MEATLESS MAINS

SALAD PIZZA SERVES 4

Q V

New York is known for great pizza. But believe it or not, one of my favorite slices from my local pizzeria isn't topped with extra cheese or pepperoni, but with *salad*. It's light and healthy and tastes so good. I've created a version that's pretty close to the original, only as smaller individual pies. I especially love the balsamic glaze that gets brushed onto the crust—it adds sweetness and flavor to every bite—and the crumbled Gorgonzola cheese is a must. This is also great grilled outdoors in the summer.

Olive oil spray (such as Bertolli) or a mister

12 ounces whole wheat pizza dough, at room temperature

All-purpose flour, for dusting

¼ cup coarsely chopped red onion

2 vine tomatoes, cut into 1-inch pieces

1 tablespoon olive oil

1½ tablespoons white balsamic vinegar

½ teaspoon kosher salt

Freshly ground black pepper

6 cups mixed baby greens

4 teaspoons store-bought balsamic glaze (I love DeLallo)

2 ounces Gorgonzola cheese, crumbled

Preheat the oven to 450°F. Spray 2 baking sheets with olive oil.

Cut the pizza dough into 4 pieces that are 3 ounces each. Sprinkle a work surface with a little flour and, using a rolling pin or your hands, stretch each piece of dough into a rectangle about 4½ x 9½ inches. Place them on the prepared baking sheets. Using a fork, poke a few holes in the center of the dough to prevent bubbles.

Bake until the crusts are golden, 8 to 12 minutes.

Meanwhile, in a large bowl, combine the onion, tomatoes, olive oil, vinegar, salt, and pepper to taste. Add the greens and toss well.

Remove the crusts from the oven and let cool for 5 minutes. Brush each crust with 1 teaspoon of the balsamic glaze. Divide the salad among the crusts (about 1 heaping cup each) and top each with ½ ounce of the Gorgonzola.

TIME-SAVING TIP Making your own pizza dough is pretty simple, but if you want to keep the prep and cook times under 30 minutes, buy dough from the supermarket or ask your local pizzeria, as many sell their dough.

PER SERVING	1 pizza
CALORIES	**335**
FAT	**12.5 g**
SATURATED FAT	**4 g**
CHOLESTEROL	**15 mg**
CARBOHYDRATE	**47 g**
FIBER	**4.5 g**
PROTEIN	**14 g**
SUGARS	**11 g**
SODIUM	**798 mg**

GREEK PANZANELLA SALAD

SERVES 4

I'm in love with Greek preoiled flatbreads used for gyros—they're so moist and heavenly. In fact, they inspired this Greek version of a panzanella salad. Rather than using lettuce, I opt for a big bowl of chopped cucumbers, tomatoes, bell peppers, and Kalamata olives. Using high-quality ingredients is key to making this taste exceptional. I use a superb cold-pressed extra-virgin olive oil, and rather than buying precrumbled feta, which is usually dry and chalky, I buy a block and crumble it myself. One bite and (yum!) you'll see that it's totally worth the extra effort.

2 (7-inch) pre-oiled gyro breads, such as Kontos (naan would also work)

Olive oil spray (such as Bertolli) or a mister

2 English cucumbers (11 ounces each), peeled and chopped

1 green bell pepper, chopped

1½ cups halved grape tomatoes

15 pitted Kalamata olives, quartered

¼ cup sliced red onion

5 teaspoons extra-virgin olive oil

Juice of ½ lemon

1 tablespoon red wine vinegar

2 teaspoons finely chopped fresh oregano

½ teaspoon kosher salt

Freshly ground black pepper

3 ounces feta cheese, crumbled

Preheat a grill to medium (or preheat a grill pan over medium heat). Lightly spritz the bread on both sides with oil and grill for about 1 minute per side. Transfer to a cutting board and cut into 1-inch pieces.

In a large bowl, combine the cucumbers, bell pepper, tomatoes, olives, and red onion. Add the olive oil, lemon juice, vinegar, oregano, salt, and pepper to taste and toss well. Add the feta and bread and toss. Divide among 4 bowls, and serve.

PER SERVING	2 cups salad + ½ gyro bread
CALORIES	321
FAT	18 g
SATURATED FAT	5 g
CHOLESTEROL	19 mg
CARBOHYDRATE	33 g
FIBER	5 g
PROTEIN	9 g
SUGARS	7 g
SODIUM	1,065 mg

BAKED PEARS with GREENS, BLUE CHEESE, and PECANS SERVES 4

Q **V** **GF**

Pears baked with a drizzle of honey and a sprinkle of cinnamon are an easy and flavorful dessert. But turning them into a savory dish by putting them over a bed of greens and adding a simple vinaigrette, crumbled blue cheese, and pecans is *outstanding*. Both savory and sweet, it's definitely a dish that will impress. It's great served warm or chilled.

Olive oil spray (such as Bertolli) or a mister

2 large ripe pears, such as Royal Riviera or Anjou

Kosher salt and freshly ground black pepper

1½ tablespoons olive oil

2 teaspoons Dijon mustard

1½ tablespoons white balsamic vinegar

1 teaspoon honey

5 cups baby watercress or arugula

2 ounces blue cheese or Gorgonzola, crumbled

½ cup pecan halves, toasted (see Skinny Scoop)

Preheat the oven to 350°F. Spray a baking sheet with oil.

Halve the pears lengthwise (I cut a sliver off the bottom end so they sit upright) and, using a measuring spoon or melon baller, scoop out the core. Season with a pinch of salt and pepper and place cut side down on the prepared baking sheet. Bake until soft, about 30 minutes. Let cool for 10 minutes.

Meanwhile, in a small bowl, whisk together the oil, mustard, vinegar, honey, ¼ teaspoon salt, and pepper to taste.

To serve, divide the watercress among 4 plates. Top each with a pear half (cut side up), ½ ounce blue cheese, 2 tablespoons pecans, and 1 tablespoon vinaigrette.

SKINNY SCOOP To toast the pecans, place them in a small skillet over medium heat, stirring occasionally, until fragrant, 3 to 5 minutes.

PER SERVING	1 salad
CALORIES	266
FAT	18.5 g
SATURATED FAT	4 g
CHOLESTEROL	11 mg
CARBOHYDRATE	22 g
FIBER	5 g
PROTEIN	6 g
SUGARS	14 g
SODIUM	367 mg

BAKED EGGPLANT PARMESAN STACKS   SERVES 4

Q V GF

This dish is lighter and easier to make than traditional eggplant Parmesan, which is usually breaded and fried before going into the oven. I skipped the breading and layered each stack with a blend of part-skim ricotta, mozzarella, and Pecorino Romano, as well as spinach and tomato sauce. It bakes quickly, just until everything is hot and melted. Simple, delicious, and a wonderful meatless main dish.

Olive oil spray (such as Bertolli) or a mister

2 large eggplants (about 3 pounds total)

½ teaspoon kosher salt

Freshly ground black pepper

1 cup part-skim ricotta cheese

¾ cup shredded part-skim mozzarella cheese*

½ cup freshly grated Pecorino Romano cheese

3 tablespoons finely chopped fresh basil

1½ cups marinara sauce, homemade (see page 52) or store-bought

32 baby spinach leaves

Read the label to be sure this product is gluten-free.

Preheat the oven to 450°F. Lightly spray 2 nonstick baking sheets with oil.

Trim the ends off the eggplant and slice each crosswise into twelve ½-inch-thick rounds to get 24 rounds total. Arrange the eggplant on the prepared baking sheets. Lightly spritz both sides with olive oil and season both sides with the salt and pepper to taste.

Bake until golden brown on both sides, 8 to 9 minutes per side. Transfer all but the 8 largest slices of eggplant to a plate.

Meanwhile, in a medium bowl, combine the ricotta, mozzarella, Romano, and basil.

Make stacks by ladling 1 tablespoon marinara sauce onto each of the 8 eggplant slices on the baking sheet. Top with 1 tablespoon of the cheese mixture and 2 spinach leaves. Repeat to make a second layer and finish each stack with one of the reserved eggplant slices. Top each with 1 tablespoon tomato sauce and the remaining cheese mixture.

Bake until the cheese is melted and the stacks are heated throughout, 8 to 10 minutes. Serve hot.

FOOD FACTS: EGGPLANT
This purple vegetable is full of beneficial nutrients. The fiber, potassium, vitamin C, vitamin B$_6$, and phytonutrients in eggplants all support heart health. And thanks to nasunin, a potent antioxidant abundant in their skin, this veggie may help fight aging and cancer when consumed.

PER SERVING	2 stacks
CALORIES	340
FAT	13.5 g
SATURATED FAT	8 g
CHOLESTEROL	42 mg
CARBOHYDRATE	33 g
FIBER	15 g
PROTEIN	24 g
SUGARS	10 g
SODIUM	832 mg

EASIEST ONE-POT PASTA AND BROCCOLI SERVES 6

(Q) (V) (GF)

With just five ingredients (not counting salt and pepper) and one pot, you'll have an easy dinner on the table in just about 15 minutes. Madison won't eat cooked broccoli on its own, but she *loves* this dish. (Let's just say that it's not by accident that it gets all mashed up.) Because the broccoli is used to create a pesto-like sauce, it sticks to the pasta and the kids can't pick it out. I made this dish weekly for Madison when she got her first set of teeth, using ditalini pasta, a small size that is easy for toddlers to eat. Nowadays, I use shells because they hold more of the yummy sauce, but any pasta shape works fine. Leftovers are great reheated the next day.

Kosher salt

12 ounces medium pasta shells*

6½ cups broccoli florets

2 tablespoons olive oil

5 garlic cloves, roughly chopped

¼ cup freshly grated Pecorino Romano cheese, plus more for serving (optional)

Freshly ground black pepper

Read the label to be sure this product is gluten-free.

Bring a large pot of salted water to a boil. Add the pasta and broccoli at the same time and cook until the pasta is al dente according to package directions. Reserving about 1 cup of the water, drain the pasta and broccoli.

Return the pot to the stove and set over high heat. Add 1 tablespoon of the olive oil and the garlic. Cook, stirring, until golden brown, about 1 minute. Reduce the heat to low and add the pasta and broccoli. Add the remaining 1 tablespoon olive oil, the Romano, ½ teaspoon salt, and pepper to taste. Stir well, smashing any large pieces of broccoli into smaller pieces. Add ½ cup of the reserved pasta water and stir, adding more as needed to loosen the sauce.

Divide among 6 pasta bowls and serve with additional grated cheese on the side, if desired.

SKINNY SCOOP Since this recipe relies on just a few ingredients, it's important to use good-quality grated cheese such as Pecorino Romano or Parmesan. If you like a little spice, add some crushed red pepper flakes.

PER SERVING	1½ cups
CALORIES	277
FAT	7.5 g
SATURATED FAT	1.5 g
CHOLESTEROL	4 mg
CARBOHYDRATE	47 g
FIBER	8.5 g
PROTEIN	13 g
SUGARS	4 g
SODIUM	190 mg

COCONUT VEGGIE CURRY SERVES 4

Q V GF

Coconut and basil are two of Tommy's favorite ingredients, so I can never go wrong making this curry in my house. Super simple and veggie-packed, this recipe is light on the spices, but warm and comforting. The beauty of this dish is that you can use any combination of vegetables you like. I like to keep it colorful and eat the rainbow, but feel free to use any combination you like, including sugar snap peas, spinach, broccoli, zucchini, or eggplant.

1 teaspoon coconut or grapeseed oil

½ cup chopped onions

¼ teaspoon kosher salt

1 tablespoon grated fresh ginger

2 garlic cloves, crushed

2 tablespoons Thai red curry paste

1 (14-ounce) can light coconut milk

2 teaspoons reduced-sodium soy sauce*

1 cup carrot slices (¼ inch thick)

1 teaspoon raw sugar

1 medium red bell pepper, cut into ¼-inch-wide strips

1 medium yellow squash, cut into ¼-inch-thick half-moons

1 cup cauliflower florets

1½ cups bok choy slices (1 inch wide; about 1 medium)

1 teaspoon fresh lime juice

Chopped fresh basil

3 cups cooked jasmine rice

Chili garlic sauce, for serving (optional)

*Read the label to be sure this product is gluten-free.

Heat a large, deep nonstick skillet or wok over medium heat. Add the oil, onions, and salt and cook, stirring, until soft, about 3 minutes. Add the ginger, garlic, and curry paste and cook, stirring, until fragrant, about 30 seconds. Add the coconut milk, ¼ cup water, the soy sauce, carrots, and sugar and bring to a boil. Reduce the heat to medium-low, cover, and cook until the carrots are almost tender, 5 minutes.

Add the bell pepper, squash, cauliflower, and bok choy and cook until crisp-tender, 8 to 10 minutes. Remove the pan from the heat and stir in the lime juice and basil.

To serve, divide the rice among 4 plates (¾ cup each) and top with 1 cup of the curry. Serve with chili garlic sauce for a spicy kick, if desired.

PER SERVING	1 cup curry + ¾ cup rice
CALORIES	278
FAT	6.5 g
SATURATED FAT	5 g
CHOLESTEROL	0 mg
CARBOHYDRATE	48 g
FIBER	4 g
PROTEIN	6 g
SUGARS	7 g
SODIUM	409 mg

DAD'S PEPPERS AND EGG SANDWICHES   SERVES 4

(Q) (V) (DF)

I always look forward to eating this dish when I visit Tommy's parents, since my father-in-law, a Brooklyn Italian, often makes it for us. It's mostly peppers and onions, with just two eggs—that's not a mistake! Dad says the secret to his peppers is adding a splash of vinegar at the end. Cubanelles are Italian sweet frying peppers, and they really are a must for this dish. Tommy likes his with some grated Pecorino Romano on top, but Dad says if you top it with a slice of Swiss, it's out of this world. Personally, I love it as is, or with a dash of hot sauce.

1 tablespoon plus 1 teaspoon extra-virgin olive oil

1 medium onion, cut into ¼-inch-thick slices

1 teaspoon kosher salt

Freshly ground black pepper

1 medium red bell pepper, cut into ¼-inch-wide slices

4 medium green cubanelle peppers, cut into ¼-inch-wide slices

1 teaspoon distilled white vinegar

2 large eggs

8 ounces whole wheat baguette, cut into 4 pieces

In a large skillet, heat 1 tablespoon of the olive oil over medium heat. Add the onion, ¼ teaspoon of the salt, and pepper to taste and cook, stirring, until soft but not browned, 6 to 7 minutes. Add the bell and cubanelle peppers, the remaining 1 teaspoon olive oil, ½ teaspoon of the salt, and pepper to taste. Cover, reduce the heat to medium-low, and cook, stirring every 5 minutes, until the peppers are soft, about 20 minutes. Stir in the vinegar.

In a small bowl, beat the eggs with the remaining ¼ teaspoon salt. Pour the eggs over the peppers and cook, stirring, until set, 2 to 3 minutes.

To serve, slice open the bread pieces. Put ½ cup peppers and eggs on the bottom pieces and top with the tops.

PER SERVING	1 sandwich
CALORIES	263
FAT	9 g
SATURATED FAT	2 g
CHOLESTEROL	93 mg
CARBOHYDRATE	37 g
FIBER	5.5 g
PROTEIN	10 g
SUGARS	5 g
SODIUM	602 mg

ZUCCHINI "MEATBALLS" SERVES 4

Q V

The first time I tried eggplant meatballs at a neighborhood restaurant, I fell in love. I quickly figured out how to re-create them myself, and when I shared them on my blog and with friends and neighbors, everyone asked the same question: Can you make them with zucchini? So, I went back into my kitchen to experiment, and boy, am I glad I did. These zucchini meatballs are a *huge* hit, even with my husband, who usually prefers his meatballs made with beef.

Cooking spray

1¼ pounds zucchini, unpeeled

1 teaspoon olive oil

2 garlic cloves, crushed

¼ teaspoon kosher salt

⅛ teaspoon freshly ground black pepper

1 cup Italian seasoned bread crumbs

1 large egg, beaten

1 ounce Parmesan cheese, grated (¼ cup)

3 tablespoons chopped fresh basil, plus leaves for garnish

2 cups marinara sauce, homemade (see page 52) or store-bought

Preheat the oven to 375°F. Coat a large rimmed baking sheet with cooking spray.

Grate the zucchini using the large holes of a box grater into a kitchen cloth or paper towels. Squeeze very tightly to remove as much liquid as possible from the zucchini.

Heat a large nonstick skillet over medium heat. Add the oil and garlic and cook, stirring, until golden, about 30 seconds. Add the zucchini, salt, and pepper. Increase the heat to high and cook, stirring, until the water evaporates from the skillet, 4 to 5 minutes. Transfer to a colander to drain any excess water (zucchini has a ton of water in it), then transfer to a large bowl and let cool.

Add the bread crumbs, egg, Parmesan, and basil; mix well. Using wet hands, form the zucchini mixture into 16 balls, each about 1 ounce, rolling tightly. Arrange on the prepared baking sheet. Coat the tops with cooking spray. Bake until firm and browned, 20 to 25 minutes.

Meanwhile, in a large deep skillet, warm the marinara sauce over low heat, covered, for about 3 minutes.

When the meatballs are done, add to the sauce and simmer, covered, for 5 minutes. Serve garnished with fresh basil leaves.

SKINNY SCOOP Many cheeses contain animal rennet, an ingredient used to make milk coagulate. To make this recipe vegetarian, look for Parmesan cheese made with vegetable rennet, such as Organic Valley Parmesan Cheese.

PER SERVING	4 meatballs + ½ cup sauce
CALORIES	245
FAT	7 g
SATURATED FAT	2 g
CHOLESTEROL	52 mg
CARBOHYDRATE	34 g
FIBER	5 g
PROTEIN	12 g
SUGARS	7 g
SODIUM	1,136 mg

MEATLESS MAINS

SLOW COOKER LOADED "BAKED" SWEET POTATOES

SERVES 4

SC   V   GF

I'm going to let you in on a little secret: The best way to make baked sweet potatoes is in the slow cooker, not in the oven! They come out moist and delicious every time. And the best part is that there's no prep aside from washing the potatoes—no need to poke them or wrap them in foil. I like my sweet potatoes on the savory side, so these loaded ones are my go-to meatless meal when I need something that requires very little work. The spicy filling is a great complement to the sweetness of the potatoes, and the melted cheese and avocados are the icing on the cake.

4 medium sweet potatoes (about 7 ounces each)

½ cup canned black beans,* rinsed and drained

½ cup corn kernels, fresh or frozen

⅓ cup canned tomato sauce

2 tablespoons chopped scallions

½ teaspoon ground cumin

¼ teaspoon cayenne pepper

½ teaspoon kosher salt

½ cup shredded pepper Jack cheese*

1 small Hass avocado (4 ounces), chopped

2 tablespoons chopped fresh cilantro

4 tablespoons 0% Greek yogurt (optional)

*Read the labels to be sure these products are gluten-free.

Wash and dry the sweet potatoes. Place them in a slow cooker, cover, and cook on high for 4 hours or on low for 8 hours.

In a medium bowl, combine the black beans, corn, tomato sauce, scallions, cumin, cayenne, and salt.

Remove the potatoes from the slow cooker and cut each potato lengthwise three-fourths of the way through. Pull apart to create an opening and gently mash the flesh with a fork. Divide the bean filling among the potatoes and gently mix it into the potato flesh. Top each with 2 tablespoons pepper Jack, return to the slow cooker, cover, and cook on high until the filling is hot and the cheese melts, about 15 minutes.

Transfer the potatoes to 4 serving plates. Top with the avocado, cilantro, and yogurt (if using) and eat right away.

PER SERVING	1 sweet potato
CALORIES	379
FAT	14.5 g
SATURATED FAT	4.5 g
CHOLESTEROL	13 mg
CARBOHYDRATE	54 g
FIBER	11.5 g
PROTEIN	11 g
SUGARS	15 g
SODIUM	491 mg

SLOW COOKER CHANA MASALA

SERVES 8

SC V GF FF

Prior to making Skinnytaste a full-time career, I worked in Manhattan as a digital retoucher, and one of my coworkers, Sebastian, who was from India, often brought this dish to office potlucks. He served it over basmati rice, and I just loved it. Of course, I had to have the recipe! It turns out he used a box of premixed spices from a local Indian market. Luckily, he brought me a box with all the ingredients listed, and I kept it so I could re-create the dish myself. I've made some tweaks by using spices that are readily available, and I toned it down a bit more for my taste buds. If you prefer to spice things up, simply add more chile peppers!

½ tablespoon vegetable oil

1 medium onion, finely chopped

3 garlic cloves, minced

2 teaspoons grated fresh ginger

2 hot green chile peppers, minced

1 tablespoon ground coriander

1 tablespoon ground cumin

1½ teaspoons ground turmeric

1 teaspoon garam masala*

½ teaspoon ground cardamom

3 (15.5-ounce) cans chickpeas,* rinsed and drained

1 (15-ounce) can petite diced tomatoes

1 tablespoon tomato paste

1¼ teaspoons kosher salt

Juice of ½ lemon

⅓ cup chopped fresh cilantro

Read the labels to be sure these products are gluten-free.

In a medium nonstick skillet, heat the oil over medium heat. Add the onion, garlic, ginger, and chile peppers and cook, stirring, until golden, about 5 minutes. Reduce the heat to medium-low and add the coriander, cumin, turmeric, garam masala, and cardamom. Cook, stirring, for about 2 minutes. Transfer to a slow cooker. Add 2 cups water, the chickpeas, tomatoes, and tomato paste, and stir.

Cover and cook on high for 2 to 3 hours or on low for 4 to 6 hours. When done, add the salt, lemon juice, and cilantro.

PERFECT PAIRINGS Serve with garlic naan or steamed basmati rice.

PER SERVING	generous ¾ cup
CALORIES	193
FAT	3.5 g
SATURATED FAT	0 g
CHOLESTEROL	0 mg
CARBOHYDRATE	32 g
FIBER	9 g
PROTEIN	10 g
SUGARS	3 g
SODIUM	543 mg

Make It a Meatless Monday

ONE DAY A WEEK, CUT OUT THE MEAT

Meatless Monday is an international campaign that encourages people to skip eating meat on Mondays to increase the amount of plant-based foods you eat, thereby improving your health and the health of the planet. If you replaced just one meat-based meal a week with a meat-free alternative, you could:

BOOST YOUR HEALTH. Plant-based protein is loaded with good-for-you-nutrients, like folate, zinc, fiber, and magnesium. People who follow a diet that's rich in fruits, vegetables, and other plant-based foods have a lower risk for cancer, whereas people who eat a lot of red or processed meat are at a greater risk for cardiovascular disease, certain cancers, and diabetes. Indeed, one study in the *JAMA Archives of Internal Medicine* found that people who had fish, poultry, nuts, legumes, low-fat dairy or whole grains in place of one red meat serving per day decreased their risk of death by up to 19 percent.

SAVE CASH. A plant-based diet is often less pricey than one rich in animal foods.

CUT CALORIES. People who eat little to no meat weigh less than frequent meat eaters.

PROTECT YOUR PUMPER. Vegetarians have a significantly lower risk for heart disease than meat eaters, according to research.

HELP MOTHER EARTH. The meat industry is tough on our planet. Consider these facts: It takes way more water to raise animals than it does to grow grains or vegetables. Also, the meat industry creates more greenhouse gas emissions than the transportation industry, and it uses up way more fossil fuel than plant-based proteins.

FAST

Q V GF Italian House Salad with Dijon Vinaigrette **252**

Q V GF DF Burnt Broccoli **255**

Q V GF DF Zucchini Wedges with Lemon and Fresh Oregano **256**

Q V GF Baked Sweet Plantains with Cheese **259**

Q V GF Cauliflower "Fried Rice" **260**

Q V GF Roasted Acorn Squash with Parmesan **263**

Q V GF Whipped Parmesan Cauliflower Puree **264**

Q V GF DF Braised Red Cabbage with Vinegar **265**

Q V GF Spaghetti Squash with Garlic and Oil **266**

Q V GF DF Pineapple Jicama Slaw **269**

Q V GF DF Sesame Roasted Cabbage Steaks **270**

SLOW

SC V GF Creamy Slow Cooker Buttermilk Mashed Potatoes **273**

SC Slow Cooker Sausage-Herb Stuffing **274**

ON THE
SIDE

ITALIAN HOUSE SALAD WITH DIJON VINAIGRETTE

SERVES 4

Q V GF

There's a chain of Italian restaurants that serves this awesome dish as their house salad. I love the combination of chickpeas, Kalamata olives, mozzarella, and red onion tossed with crisp romaine lettuce. It's a big and pretty substantial bowl—you could easily turn it into a main dish by increasing the eggs and chickpeas. Dig in!

VINAIGRETTE

1½ tablespoons extra-virgin olive oil

1½ tablespoons red wine vinegar

2 teaspoons Dijon mustard

¼ teaspoon kosher salt

Freshly ground black pepper

SALAD

5 cups chopped romaine lettuce

½ cup canned chickpeas,* rinsed and drained

¼ small red onion, sliced

¼ cup pitted Kalamata olives, quartered

1 hard-boiled egg, quartered

1 medium vine tomato, quartered

¼ cup shredded part-skim mozzarella cheese*

Read the labels to be sure these products are gluten-free.

For the vinaigrette: In a small bowl, whisk together the oil, vinegar, mustard, salt, and pepper to taste.

For the salad: Arrange the lettuce in a large bowl. Top with the chickpeas, red onion, and olives. Arrange the egg, tomato, and mozzarella on top. When ready to serve, toss with the vinaigrette.

PER SERVING	1¾ cups
CALORIES	148
FAT	9.5 g
SATURATED FAT	2 g
CHOLESTEROL	50 mg
CARBOHYDRATE	9 g
FIBER	3.5 g
PROTEIN	6 g
SUGARS	2 g
SODIUM	316 mg

BURNT BROCCOLI SERVES 4

(Q) (V) (GF) (DF)

This may be the one time you can burn a dish and actually get away with it! That's because the charred, crisp edges of the broccoli are what makes this side such a hit. We love it alongside everything from grilled fish to steaks, chops, and chicken. Some of my favorite neighborhood Italian restaurants have this on their menu, and I laugh because a few of them charge extra for it.

1 bunch broccoli spears (about 14 ounces)

6 garlic cloves, peeled

3 tablespoons extra-virgin olive oil

½ teaspoon kosher salt

Pinch of crushed red pepper flakes (optional)

Adjust the oven racks in the bottom and upper third and preheat the oven to 450°F.

Trim about 1 inch off the ends of the broccoli spears and discard. Slice each broccoli spear lengthwise into 8 pieces total. If your spears are thick, you may need to quarter each spear into 4 pieces.

Place the broccoli, cut side up, and the garlic cloves on a large rimmed baking sheet and drizzle broccoli with the olive oil. Season both sides with the salt and pepper flakes (if using).

Roast on the bottom rack until the broccoli is browned on the bottom, about 10 minutes. Flip the broccoli and garlic and roast until tender and browned, 10 more minutes.

Turn on the broiler. Put the pan on the higher rack and broil until the broccoli just begins to char and crisp, about 2 minutes. Keep a close eye to make sure you don't overburn it! Serve immediately.

PER SERVING	2 pieces
CALORIES	130
FAT	10.5 g
SATURATED FAT	1.5 g
CHOLESTEROL	0 mg
CARBOHYDRATE	8 g
FIBER	2.5 g
PROTEIN	3 g
SUGARS	2 g
SODIUM	69 mg

ON THE SIDE

ZUCCHINI WEDGES WITH LEMON AND FRESH OREGANO

SERVES 4

(Q) (V) (GF) (DF)

Sprinkling fresh oregano and lemon zest over these sautéed zucchini wedges is a great way to enjoy the summer's bounty. Cooking the zucchini in a hot skillet gets the edges browned and slightly charred—a recipe for deliciousness! Just be careful not to overcook, or they'll get too soft.

2 medium zucchini (about 7 ounces each)

2 teaspoons olive oil

¾ teaspoon kosher salt

Freshly ground black pepper

2 small garlic cloves, crushed

1½ teaspoons fresh oregano leaves

Zest of 1 small lemon

1 teaspoon fresh lemon juice

Trim the ends off the zucchini, halve it lengthwise, and then quarter the halves lengthwise to give you 16 wedges total.

In a large nonstick skillet, heat the oil over medium-high heat. Add the zucchini wedges, ½ teaspoon of the salt, and pepper to taste. Cook, turning occasionally, until the wedges begin to brown, about 5 minutes. Add the garlic and oregano and cook, stirring, for 1 minute. Remove the pan from the heat. Sprinkle with the remaining ¼ teaspoon salt, pepper to taste, the lemon zest, and lemon juice and serve.

PERFECT PAIRING You can serve these wedges with just about anything. Try them with my Asiago-Crusted Chicken Breasts (page 148).

PER SERVING	4 wedges
CALORIES	41
FAT	2.5 g
SATURATED FAT	0.5 g
CHOLESTEROL	0 mg
CARBOHYDRATE	4 g
FIBER	1.5 g
PROTEIN	1 g
SUGARS	3 g
SODIUM	218 mg

BAKED SWEET PLANTAINS WITH CHEESE   SERVES 4

Q V GF

When I was a kid, on the nights Mom made Colombian meat dishes like Colombian shredded beef (see Slow Cooker Carne Desmechada, page 195) or rice and beans, she always served sweet plantains on the side. Different from green plantains, which are underripe and more savory when cooked, sweet plantains are overripe and are especially delicious when baked and topped with cheese, as in this recipe, for a savory-sweet combo.

Olive oil spray (such as Bertolli) or a mister

1 medium overripe plantain, peeled

⅛ teaspoon kosher salt

½ cup shredded part-skim mozzarella cheese*

Chopped fresh cilantro, for garnish

*Read the label to be sure this product is gluten-free.

Preheat the oven to 425°F. Line a baking sheet with foil and lightly spray with oil.

Slice the plantain on an angle into 16 pieces that are about ¼ inch thick. Place the plantain slices on the prepared baking sheet and lightly spray with oil. Sprinkle with the salt.

Bake until golden on the bottom, about 12 minutes. Flip the plantains and bake for 5 more minutes. Top the plantains with the mozzarella and bake until the cheese is melted, 3 more minutes. Serve immediately, garnished with cilantro.

SKINNY SCOOP You'll want to purchase yellow plantains and let them sit until the skin turns almost entirely black. They should also feel soft and give in a little without being mushy.

PER SERVING	4 slices
CALORIES	97
FAT	3 g
SATURATED FAT	2 g
CHOLESTEROL	8 mg
CARBOHYDRATE	15 g
FIBER	1 g
PROTEIN	4 g
SUGARS	7 g
SODIUM	111 mg

FOOD FACTS: PLANTAINS Plantains are lesser-known members of the banana family. A staple in African and Caribbean countries, they're not only exotic and tasty, but are also extremely nutritious. Fiber-rich plantains are starchier and lower in sugar than bananas, and they're an excellent source of potassium and vitamins A, C, and B$_6$.

CAULIFLOWER "FRIED RICE"   SERVES 4

Q V GF

I *love* fried rice—I can eat a great big bowl and call it a meal. I often whip it up using leftover brown rice; but on days when I want to cut carbs or balance out a more decadent dish, I replace the rice with cauliflower "rice." I shared this quick and light recipe on my blog and everyone went nuts . . . in a good way. They raved about how their cauliflower-hating husbands and kids gobbled it up! You can easily turn this into a main dish by adding any protein—chicken, shrimp, you name it.

1 medium head cauliflower, or 24 ounces cauliflower florets

Cooking spray

2 large eggs

Pinch of kosher salt

1 tablespoon toasted sesame oil

½ small onion, finely chopped

5 scallions, chopped, whites and greens kept separate

½ cup frozen peas and carrots

2 garlic cloves, minced

¼ cup reduced-sodium soy sauce,* or more to taste

*Read the label to be sure this product is gluten-free.

Remove and discard the core of the cauliflower. Coarsely chop it into florets, then place half of the cauliflower into a food processor. Pulse until the cauliflower resembles grains of rice (don't overprocess or it will get mushy). Set aside and repeat with the remaining cauliflower.

Heat a large nonstick pan or wok over medium heat and spray it with oil. In a small bowl, beat the eggs with the salt. Pour the eggs into the pan and cook, turning a few times, until set, 1 to 2 minutes. Transfer to a plate.

To the pan, add the sesame oil, onion, scallion whites, peas and carrots, and garlic. Cook, stirring, until soft, 3 to 4 minutes. Increase the heat to medium-high. Add the cauliflower "rice" and soy sauce. Stir, cover, and cook, stirring frequently, until the cauliflower is slightly crispy on the outside but tender on the inside, 5 to 6 minutes. Add the egg, remove the pan from the heat, and stir in the scallion greens. Divide among 4 bowls and serve hot.

PER SERVING	1¼ cups
CALORIES	138
FAT	6 g
SATURATED FAT	1.5 g
CHOLESTEROL	93 mg
CARBOHYDRATE	15 g
FIBER	5.5 g
PROTEIN	8 g
SUGARS	6 g
SODIUM	653 mg

ROASTED ACORN SQUASH WITH PARMESAN   SERVES 4

Q V GF

When I want my family to eat their veggies, I pull out my secret weapon: roasting! Cooking vegetables in the oven until they're crisp and browned on the edges is usually a sure way to win everyone over. But when I *really* want to pull out all the stops, I bust out the Parmesan . . . and no one can resist! This squash recipe has the perfect balance of savory and sweet.

Cooking spray

2 acorn squash (about 16 ounces each)

1½ tablespoons olive oil

Leaves from 3 sprigs of fresh thyme

¾ teaspoon kosher salt

½ teaspoon garlic powder

Freshly ground black pepper

2 tablespoons freshly grated Parmesan cheese

Preheat the oven to 425°F. Lightly coat 2 large nonstick baking sheets with cooking spray.

Halve the squash lengthwise and scoop out the seeds with a spoon. Slice each half crosswise into ¼-inch-thick half-moons and place them in a large bowl. Add the olive oil, thyme, salt, garlic powder, and pepper to taste and toss to coat. Arrange the squash on the prepared baking sheets.

Bake until golden brown, 20 to 24 minutes, flipping them halfway through. Remove the pan from the oven, top with the Parmesan, and serve hot.

FOOD FACTS: ACORN SQUASH

Like all winter squash, acorn squash is a great source of beta-carotene, an important nutrient for your eyes and skin, and for a healthy immune system.

PER SERVING	½ squash
CALORIES	134
FAT	6 g
SATURATED FAT	1 g
CHOLESTEROL	2 mg
CARBOHYDRATE	20 g
FIBER	3.5 g
PROTEIN	3 g
SUGARS	5 g
SODIUM	258 mg

WHIPPED PARMESAN CAULIFLOWER PUREE SERVES 4

Q V GF

I love creamy polenta and wanted to create a vegetable puree with the same buttery texture, but without all the calories and carbs. That's how this dish was born. Cauliflower is such a versatile vegetable when it comes to low-carb swaps. It's the secret ingredient in my Cauliflower "Fried Rice" (page 260) and faux mashed potatoes, so why not polenta? This dish is wonderful served with braised meats that have gravies or sauce, such as pictured with my Slow Cooker Osso Buco (page 199).

1 medium head cauliflower (about 1½ pounds), cut into florets

3 garlic cloves, peeled

¼ cup 2% milk

⅓ cup freshly grated Parmesan cheese

1 tablespoon whipped butter

½ teaspoon kosher salt

Freshly ground black pepper

¼ cup grated light Havarti cheese

Bring a large pot of water to a boil. Add the cauliflower and garlic and boil until the cauliflower is soft, 15 to 20 minutes. Drain, and return the vegetables to the pot.

Add the milk, Parmesan, butter, salt, and pepper to taste. Puree the mixture right in the pot with an immersion blender until smooth (or in a regular blender in batches). Stir in the Havarti until it has melted, and serve hot.

PER SERVING	¾ cup
CALORIES	123
FAT	6 g
SATURATED FAT	3.5 g
CHOLESTEROL	17 mg
CARBOHYDRATE	11 g
FIBER	4.5 g
PROTEIN	9 g
SUGARS	5 g
SODIUM	391 mg

BRAISED RED CABBAGE WITH VINEGAR SERVES 6

Q V GF DF

My father is from the Czech Republic, so I grew up eating many traditional Czech, German, and Austrian dishes, most of which involved some form of cooked cabbage. This is an easy side dish that we often enjoyed with Pork Tenderloin with Potatoes and Caraway Seeds (page 191). When the cabbage is well seasoned and simmered until tender, it ends up being a totally scrumptious side!

1 teaspoon olive oil

½ medium onion, chopped

½ head red cabbage (14 ounces), cut into ¼-inch-wide shreds

¼ teaspoon caraway seeds

½ teaspoon sugar

¼ teaspoon kosher salt

Freshly ground black pepper

¾ cup reduced-sodium chicken broth*

2 tablespoons red wine vinegar

Read the label to be sure this product is gluten-free.

In a medium pot, heat the oil over medium-high heat. Add the onion and cook, stirring, until golden, 3 to 5 minutes. Add the cabbage, caraway seeds, sugar, salt, and pepper to taste. Cook, tossing occasionally, until the cabbage is wilted, about 5 minutes. Add the broth and vinegar, cover, and reduce the heat to medium-low. Simmer until the cabbage is tender, 15 to 20 minutes.

PERFECT PAIRINGS This is a great side for Pork Tenderloin with Potatoes and Caraway Seeds (page 191), and I also love it with roasted chicken or pork chops.

PER SERVING	½ cup
CALORIES	35
FAT	1 g
SATURATED FAT	0 g
CHOLESTEROL	0 mg
CARBOHYDRATE	6 g
FIBER	1.5 g
PROTEIN	1 g
SUGARS	3 g
SODIUM	137 mg

SPAGHETTI SQUASH WITH GARLIC AND OIL   SERVES 4

(Q) (V) (GF)

This recipe was inspired by my favorite pasta dish: spaghetti with garlic and oil. By swapping the spaghetti squash for pasta, I was able to cut calories and carbs. This has become one of my favorite ways to eat this kind of squash, and it's such an easy side to whip up. You can make it a main dish by adding some sautéed chicken or shrimp. Dinner is served!

2 tablespoons extra-virgin olive oil

4 garlic cloves, thinly sliced

¼ teaspoon crushed red pepper flakes

4 cups cooked spaghetti squash (see below)

1 teaspoon kosher salt

1 tablespoon chopped fresh flat-leaf parsley

¼ cup freshly grated Parmigiano-Reggiano cheese

Heat a large skillet over medium heat. Add the olive oil and garlic and cook, stirring, until the garlic softens and turns golden, about 2 minutes. Add the pepper flakes and cook 30 more seconds. Add the cooked spaghetti squash, season with the salt, and toss well.

Transfer the squash to a large serving dish, add the parsley and Parmigiano, and serve.

HOW TO COOK SPAGHETTI SQUASH

Shredded spaghetti squash is delicious on its own, and it's an awesome low-calorie and nutrient-packed pasta swap, because the strands look just like, well, spaghetti! Start by poking holes all over a 2¼-pound squash. Here's the fast or slow way to make it:

MICROWAVE. Microwave it on high for 6 minutes. Turn the squash and microwave until the shell is tender, 6 to 8 minutes. Let cool for 8 to 10 minutes.

SLOW COOKER. Cook on high for 4 to 5 hours or on low for 6 to 7, until very soft and flimsy.

Halve the squash lengthwise. Remove the seeds and use a fork to scrape out the spaghetti-like strands of squash. Season with 1 teaspoon salt and pepper to taste.

PER SERVING	1 cup
CALORIES	134
FAT	9 g
SATURATED FAT	2 g
CHOLESTEROL	6 mg
CARBOHYDRATE	11 g
FIBER	2.5 g
PROTEIN	4 g
SUGARS	4 g
SODIUM	695 mg

FOOD FACTS: JICAMA
Also known as the Mexican water chestnut, this bulbous root vegetable is an excellent source of fiber and vitamin C.

PINEAPPLE JICAMA SLAW SERVES 6

Q V GF DF

So light and refreshing, this recipe is a fantastic summertime side and pairs perfectly with fish tacos or grilled chicken. It holds up well at a potluck, too, since it doesn't have mayonnaise in the dressing. Try serving it alongside my Ahi Tuna Poke Jicama Tacos (page 132).

1 tablespoon unseasoned rice vinegar

2 tablespoons pineapple juice

Pinch of kosher salt

Freshly ground black pepper

2 cups shredded cabbage

1 cup julienned jicama (from 1 small)

1 cup finely chopped fresh pineapple

¼ cup sliced scallions

3 tablespoons chopped fresh cilantro

In a medium bowl, whisk together the rice vinegar, pineapple juice, salt, and pepper to taste. Add the cabbage, jicama, pineapple, scallions, and cilantro. Toss well and serve.

SKINNY SCOOP The easiest way to julienne jicama is to peel it, then cut it using a mandoline fitted with a julienne blade. If you don't have a mandoline, use a very sharp knife to cut the jicama into ⅛-inch-thick slices, then cut the slices into thin strips. It can also be spiralized, if you have a spiralizer.

PER SERVING	¾ cup
CALORIES	32
FAT	0 g
SATURATED FAT	0 g
CHOLESTEROL	0 mg
CARBOHYDRATE	8 g
FIBER	2 g
PROTEIN	0.5 g
SUGARS	4 g
SODIUM	18 mg

ON THE SIDE

SESAME ROASTED CABBAGE STEAKS SERVES 4

Q V GF DF

Can you guess the one vegetable that you'll always find in my fridge? Cabbage! We eat lots of it, and in many different preparations. My family loves it raw, shredded, and tossed with olive oil and vinegar. We also whip up quick slaws for topping tacos. And, of course, Braised Red Cabbage with Vinegar (page 265) is always a winner. In this recipe, I've cut the cruciferous veggie into large slabs and roasted it. The slightly charred edges and sesame flavor are wonderful. But don't take my word for it—try it yourself!

Cooking spray

4 slices (1 inch thick) green cabbage, cut from the center (10 ounces each)

4 teaspoons toasted sesame oil

1/2 teaspoon kosher salt

1/2 teaspoon black and white sesame seeds

Adjust an oven rack in the bottom third and preheat the oven to 400°F. Lightly coat a large rimmed baking sheet with cooking spray.

Place the cabbage on the prepared baking sheet and drizzle it with the sesame oil. Season with 1/4 teaspoon of the salt.

Roast on the bottom rack until the bottoms are slightly charred, about 20 minutes. Carefully flip the cabbage, season with the remaining 1/4 teaspoon salt, and roast until tender and browned on the bottom, 10 more minutes. Sprinkle with the sesame seeds and serve hot.

PER SERVING	1 "steak"
CALORIES	113
FAT	5 g
SATURATED FAT	1 g
CHOLESTEROL	4 mg
CARBOHYDRATE	17 g
FIBER	7 g
PROTEIN	4 g
SUGARS	9 g
SODIUM	191 mg

FOOD FACTS: CABBAGE
While the humble cabbage certainly isn't the most glamorous vegetable at the farmers' market, it is chock-full of good-for-you vitamins and minerals including calcium, iron, magnesium, phosphorus, potassium, vitamin C, vitamin K, folate, and fiber (just to name a few).

CREAMY SLOW COOKER BUTTERMILK MASHED POTATOES SERVES 6

SC V GF

Yukon Gold potatoes are buttery in color and texture, which makes them perfect for whipping into mashed potatoes. This recipe is a perfect match for a slow cooker, because the cooking is completely hands-off and then the potatoes stay in the cooker to keep warm until (and during) serving. Here, I've given my basic recipe, but you can swap low-fat milk for the buttermilk, if you wish, or try other variations. For instance, sometimes I add roasted garlic at the end, or swap thyme or sage for the chives.

2 pounds Yukon Gold potatoes (about 8 medium), peeled and cut into 1-inch pieces

3 cups reduced-sodium chicken broth*

1/3 cup low-fat buttermilk

1/4 cup light sour cream (I like Breakstone's)

2 tablespoons whipped butter (I like Land O'Lakes)

3/4 teaspoon kosher salt

Freshly ground black pepper

1 tablespoon chopped fresh chives

*Read the label to be sure this product is gluten-free.

Put the potatoes into a slow cooker and pour the broth over the top. Cover and cook on high for 4 hours or on low for 8 hours, until the potatoes are cooked and soft.

Drain the potatoes, reserving some of the broth, and return them to the slow cooker. Add the buttermilk, sour cream, butter, salt, and pepper to taste and mash with a potato masher. Stir in the chives and keep warm until ready to serve. It's best to eat right away, but if you're eating them later and the potatoes get dry, add some of the reserved broth to soften them.

PER SERVING	3/4 cup
CALORIES	148
FAT	4 g
SATURATED FAT	2.5 g
CHOLESTEROL	11 mg
CARBOHYDRATE	25 g
FIBER	3.5 g
PROTEIN	4 g
SUGARS	2 g
SODIUM	274 mg

ON THE SIDE

SLOW COOKER SAUSAGE-HERB STUFFING SERVES 12

SC

Hands down, my favorite part of Thanksgiving dinner is the stuffing. I like to make it in the slow cooker because it comes out extra moist with crisp edges. Prep perk: This comes in handy when you run out of oven space for large family gatherings. Because the lid of the slow cooker traps a lot of condensation, I place a kitchen towel under the cover, which catches the steam, so the stuffing doesn't get mushy.

14 ounces whole wheat French bread or baguette, cut into ½-inch cubes

1½ tablespoons unsalted butter

1¾ cups chopped celery (about 4 medium stalks)

1½ cups chopped yellow onion

¼ cup chopped fresh sage

¼ cup chopped fresh parsley

1 tablespoon chopped fresh thyme

14 ounces sweet Italian chicken sausage, casings removed

1¾ cups reduced-sodium chicken broth*

1 large egg, beaten

½ teaspoon kosher salt

Freshly ground black pepper

Cooking spray

Read the label to be sure this product is gluten-free.

Spread the bread out onto a rimmed baking sheet and let it dry overnight. If you want to speed up the process, bake it in a 350°F oven for about 20 minutes, until the bread is dried out.

In a large nonstick skillet, melt the butter over medium heat. Add the celery, onion, sage, parsley, and thyme and cook, stirring occasionally, until soft, 5 to 8 minutes. Transfer to a large bowl.

In the same skillet, cook the sausage over medium heat, using a wooden spoon to break the meat into small pieces as it browns, about 10 minutes. Transfer the sausage to the bowl with the onion mixture. Add the bread and stir well. Add the broth, egg, salt, and pepper to taste and stir well.

Coat the inside of a slow cooker with cooking spray. Transfer the stuffing to the slow cooker, place a kitchen towel over the top, and cover. Cover and cook on low for 4 to 5 hours, until browned at the edges.

SKINNY SCOOP Slow cookers are not all created equal. Some brands run hotter than others, so get to know your slow cooker and adjust the cook times as needed.

PER SERVING	⅔ cup
CALORIES	170
FAT	5.5 g
SATURATED FAT	2 g
CHOLESTEROL	45 mg
CARBOHYDRATE	20 g
FIBER	2.5 g
PROTEIN	10 g
SUGARS	2 g
SODIUM	483 mg

THE SWEETER SIDE

FAST

Q V Banana Pudding Cups **279**

Q V GF Macerated Berries with Whipped Cream **280**

Q V GF Easy No-Cook Mango Fool **283**

Q V GF DF Grilled Piña Colada Delight **284**

Q V GF Vanilla Bean Cheesecake Shooters **287**

SLOW

SC V GF Slow Cooker Peach-Strawberry Crumble **288**

SC V GF DF Slow Cooker Vanilla Bean Pear Butter **291**

SC V GF Crustless Slow Cooker Apple Pie à la Mode **292**

SC V Slow Cooker Blueberry Slump **295**

SC V GF Slow Cooker Triple-Almond Flourless Brownies **296**

SC V GF Slow Cooker Pumpkin Flan **298**

BANANA PUDDING CUPS   SERVES 6

(Q) (V)

Banana pudding is one of my favorite desserts, so while testing this recipe for my cookbook, I may have eaten more than I should have (oops!). Although it's tempting to buy instant pudding, trust me when I say that vanilla pudding made from scratch is on a totally different taste level. It's silky and light, and the flavor is so wonderful, you, too, may be tempted to eat more than just one (hey, I'm not judging!).

¼ cup cold heavy whipping cream

¼ cup 0% Greek yogurt

2 tablespoons cornstarch

5 tablespoons sugar

1 cup fat-free milk

1 large egg yolk, beaten

1 teaspoon vanilla extract

2 medium firm bananas, sliced

6 vanilla wafer cookies

Place a medium metal bowl and the metal whisk attachments of a hand mixer into the freezer for 10 to 15 minutes.

Remove the bowl and attachments from the freezer. Put the cream in the bowl. Using the hand mixer, beat at medium speed until the cream holds stiff peaks, 2 to 3 minutes. Gently whisk in the yogurt until incorporated, about 15 seconds.

In a medium saucepan, combine the cornstarch and sugar. Whisk in the milk until smooth. Set the pan over medium-high heat and cook, whisking, until thickened and bubbling, about 2 minutes. Reduce the heat to low and cook until thick, 2 to 3 more minutes. Remove the pan from the heat.

Stir ¼ cup of the hot milk mixture into the egg yolk and quickly stir to combine. Pour the mixture back into the pan. While whisking constantly, bring the mixture to a gentle boil over medium heat. Cook, whisking constantly, for 2 more minutes. Remove the pan from the heat and stir in the vanilla. Transfer to a medium bowl, cover with plastic wrap, and let cool to room temperature, 8 to 10 minutes. Once cool, fold into the whipped cream mixture.

In the bottom of clear glass cups, make a layer of banana slices. Top with 2 tablespoons pudding. Repeat the layers. Top with vanilla wafers. Cover and refrigerate for at least 1 hour before serving.

PER SERVING	1 cup
CALORIES	178
FAT	5.5 g
SATURATED FAT	3 g
CHOLESTEROL	46 mg
CARBOHYDRATE	29 g
FIBER	1 g
PROTEIN	4 g
SUGARS	18 g
SODIUM	45 mg

THE SWEETER SIDE

MACERATED BERRIES
WITH WHIPPED CREAM SERVES 6

(Q) (V) (GF)

I love bringing a big bowl of these juicy berries to a backyard gathering, especially in the summer when berries are at their peak. This easy dessert doesn't require any cooking, and is always a crowd-pleaser. You can use any combination of berries, but my favorites are blackberries, raspberries, and strawberries. My trick to making homemade whipped cream with less fat is folding in some Greek yogurt, which also adds a slight tang that's quite delicious with the berries.

BERRIES

2½ cups (6 ounces) raspberries

2½ cups (6 ounces) blackberries

2½ cups (10 ounces) strawberries, hulled and halved

¼ cup sugar

WHIPPED CREAM

2 tablespoons sugar

⅓ cup cold heavy whipping cream

½ teaspoon vanilla extract

⅓ cup 0% Greek yogurt

For the berries: In a large bowl, combine ½ cup each of the raspberries, blackberries, and strawberries. Add the sugar and mash with a potato masher until the sugar dissolves. Gently stir in the remaining whole berries. Let sit at room temperature, tossing occasionally, until the berries are juicy, at least 30 minutes or up to 2 hours.

For the whipped cream: Place a medium metal bowl and the metal whisk attachments of a hand mixer into the freezer for 10 to 15 minutes.

Remove the bowl and attachments from the freezer. Put the sugar, cream, and vanilla in the bowl. Using the hand mixer, beat at medium speed until the cream holds stiff peaks, 2 to 3 minutes. Gently whisk in the yogurt until incorporated, about 15 seconds.

To serve, divide the berries among 6 serving bowls. Divide the whipped cream over the berries.

SKINNY SCOOP The berries and the cream can be made a few hours ahead and kept covered, separately, in the refrigerator.

PER SERVING	1 cup berries + 2½ table-spoons cream
CALORIES	141
FAT	5.5 g
SATURATED FAT	3 g
CHOLESTEROL	18 mg
CARBOHYDRATE	23 g
FIBER	4 g
PROTEIN	2 g
SUGARS	18 g
SODIUM	9 mg

EASY NO-COOK MANGO FOOL   SERVES 4

Q V GF

Summers in New York are hot and humid, so when I need an easy dessert that won't heat up my kitchen, looks gorgeous, and tastes amazing, nothing beats a fruit fool. This no-cook version utilizes sweet, delicious mangoes that you simply puree in the blender. To lighten up the cream, I fold in Greek yogurt, which also adds a wonderful tartness to the dessert. I like to serve it in small glass cups or jars so you can see the layers—beautiful and delish. With only five ingredients, you'd be, well, foolish not to make this!

2½ cups chopped mango (from about 3)

2 tablespoons sugar

⅓ cup cold heavy whipping cream

½ teaspoon vanilla extract

⅓ cup 0% Greek yogurt

Reserve ½ cup of the mango and pulse the remaining 2 cups in a blender until slightly pureed.

Place a small metal bowl and the whisk attachments of an electric hand mixer in the freezer for 10 to 15 minutes.

Remove the bowl and whisk from the freezer, and place the sugar, cream, and vanilla into the bowl. Using the hand mixer, beat at medium speed until the mixture holds stiff peaks, 2 to 3 minutes. Beat in the yogurt until incorporated, about 15 seconds.

Divide half of the mango puree among 4 small glass jars or cups. Divide the whipped cream among them and top with the remaining mango puree. Garnish with the reserved chopped mango. Chill in the refrigerator and serve.

SKINNY SCOOP While any variety of mango will work in this recipe, Kent or Keitt mangoes are best since they have virtually no fibers. If you're having friends over for dinner, you can make these a few hours ahead and refrigerate until you're ready to serve.

PER SERVING	1 jar
CALORIES	155
FAT	7.5 g
SATURATED FAT	4.5 g
CHOLESTEROL	28 mg
CARBOHYDRATE	22 g
FIBER	2 g
PROTEIN	2 g
SUGARS	19 g
SODIUM	14 mg

THE SWEETER SIDE

GRILLED PIÑA COLADA
DELIGHT SERVES 4

Q V GF DF

Fresh pineapple is pretty perfect on its own, but grilling it intensifies the flavors and caramelizes the sugars—you just have to try it. Here, I put a tropical spin on it to create a simple, delicious dessert.

1 (13.6-ounce) can unsweetened coconut milk	Cooking spray	¼ teaspoon ground cinnamon
¼ cup sweetened coconut flakes*	4 slices (½-inch-thick) fresh pineapple	3 tablespoons confectioners' sugar

*Read the label to be sure this product is gluten-free.

Put the can of coconut milk in the refrigerator—without shaking or moving it—and chill overnight (24 hours is best).

In a small skillet, toast the coconut flakes over medium heat until slightly browned, 3 to 4 minutes.

Preheat a grill to medium (or preheat a grill pan over medium heat). Oil the grates or spray the grill pan with cooking spray. Sprinkle the pineapple with the cinnamon and grill the pineapple until grill marks appear, 3 minutes per side.

Open the can without shaking it and spoon out the thick cream that rose to the top of the can. Put the cream into a medium bowl (discard the liquid). Add the sugar and, using a hand mixer, beat on high until creamy and thick, about 1 minute. Refrigerate, covered, until ready to use. The whipped coconut cream is best if used within 2 hours. If it stays longer and hardens, simply whip it again.

Put one pineapple slice on each of 4 plates; top with 1 tablespoon toasted coconut and 2 tablespoons whipped coconut cream.

SKINNY SCOOP You can sweeten the coconut cream with granulated sugar, stevia, or even honey. It's also yummy with a little vanilla extract. Only full-fat coconut milk will work here, so don't bother with the light stuff.

PER SERVING	1 pineapple slice + 2 tablespoons coconut cream
CALORIES	129
FAT	7 g
SATURATED FAT	6 g
CHOLESTEROL	0 mg
CARBOHYDRATE	17 g
FIBER	2 g
PROTEIN	1 g
SUGARS	13 g
SODIUM	24 mg

VANILLA BEAN CHEESECAKE SHOOTERS SERVES 8

Q V GF

I love dessert shooters of all kinds. These miniature works of art are the perfect size to satisfy your sweet tooth without tempting you to undo your diet. Cheesecake shooters are one of my favorites (who's with me here?). And because there's no baking, they are super easy to make. Get ready to indulge!

4 graham cracker squares (not the full rectangles)*

¼ cup cold heavy whipping cream

⅓ cup 0% Greek yogurt

1 (8-ounce) package ⅓-less-fat cream cheese, at room temperature

⅓ cup sugar

1 teaspoon fresh lemon juice

1 vanilla bean, split lengthwise

8 raspberries

*Read the label to be sure this product is gluten-free.

Turn the graham crackers into crumbs by putting them in a zip-top plastic bag and crushing them with a rolling pin, or process in a food processor. Place ½ tablespoon of the crumbs in the bottom of each of 8 shot glasses.

Place a medium metal bowl and the metal whisk attachments of a hand mixer into the freezer for 10 to 15 minutes. Remove the bowl and attachments from the freezer. Put the cream in the bowl. Using the hand mixer, beat at medium speed until the cream holds stiff peaks, 2 to 3 minutes. Gently whisk in the yogurt until incorporated, about 15 seconds.

In a separate bowl, combine the cream cheese, sugar, and lemon juice. Scrape the vanilla seeds into the bowl. Using the hand mixer, beat until smooth. Gently stir in the whipped cream until combined. Put the mixture into a pastry bag fitted with a large plain tip and pipe the mixture into the shot glasses. Top each with a raspberry. Refrigerate until ready to eat.

PER SERVING	1 shooter
CALORIES	149
FAT	9 g
SATURATED FAT	6 g
CHOLESTEROL	18 mg
CARBOHYDRATE	12 g
FIBER	0 g
PROTEIN	3 g
SUGARS	11 g
SODIUM	148 mg

SLOW COOKER PEACH-STRAWBERRY CRUMBLE

SERVES 8

SC · V · GF

Fruit desserts such as crumbles, cobblers, and pies are my absolute favorite. There's something irresistible about warm fruit topped with a sweet-crisp topping (especially when it's finished off with a scoop of frozen yogurt or whipped cream . . . double yum!). This is best to make in the summer when strawberries and peaches are in season and at their sweetest. And, because this is made in a slow cooker, it doesn't heat up your kitchen!

FILLING

Cooking spray

6 yellow peaches (1½ pounds total), pitted, peeled, and cut into ½-inch-thick slices

1 cup (5 ounces) hulled and quartered strawberries

¼ cup raw honey, preferably local

1 tablespoon fresh orange juice

2 teaspoons cornstarch

TOPPING

¾ cup quick-cooking oats* (I like Bob's Red Mill Quick Gluten Free Oats)

½ cup chopped roasted almonds

¼ cup packed light brown sugar

1 tablespoon flour*

¼ teaspoon kosher salt

3 tablespoons unsalted butter

Frozen yogurt or whipped cream, for serving (optional)

Read the labels to be sure these products are gluten-free.

Lightly coat the inside of a slow cooker with cooking spray.

For the filling: In a large bowl, combine the peaches, strawberries, honey, and orange juice. Sprinkle with the cornstarch and toss until coated. Transfer to the slow cooker.

For the topping: In a medium bowl, using a fork, combine the oats, almonds, brown sugar, flour, salt, and butter. Sprinkle over the fruit.

Cover and cook on low until the fruit is tender, about 3 hours.

To serve, scoop the cobbler out into 8 bowls and top with frozen yogurt or whipped cream, if desired.

PER SERVING	generous ½ cup
CALORIES	230
FAT	10.5 g
SATURATED FAT	3 g
CHOLESTEROL	11 mg
CARBOHYDRATE	33 g
FIBER	3.5 g
PROTEIN	4 g
SUGARS	24 g
SODIUM	72 mg

SKINNY SCOOP To easily peel the peaches, bring a large pot of water to a boil. Score an X on the bottom of each peach and blanch them in the boiling water for 1 minute, making sure they are submerged. Remove with a slotted spoon, let cool, and the skin will come off easily.

SLOW COOKER VANILLA BEAN PEAR BUTTER

MAKES 2 CUPS · SERVES 32

SC V GF DF

Bypass regular butter and whip up this sweet spread instead. This thick fruit butter is great stirred into oatmeal, Greek yogurt, or cottage cheese. It's also wonderful spread over pancakes or waffles for breakfast, or dolloped onto frozen yogurt for dessert. Or you can try my favorite combination: with almond butter on a piece of whole-grain toast. Wonderful any time of day.

3½ pounds large ripe pears (about 6), such as Bartlett or Royal Riviera, peeled, cored, and finely chopped

½ cup packed light brown sugar

3 tablespoons raw sugar

1 vanilla bean, halved lengthwise

Place the pears in a slow cooker and sprinkle the sugars over them. Scrape the vanilla seeds into the slow cooker. Stir well and add the vanilla bean halves.

Cover and cook on high for 4 hours, stirring once halfway, until the pears are tender and dark brown.

Uncover, remove the vanilla bean halves, and puree with an immersion blender. Cook on high, uncovered, for 3 hours, stirring occasionally, until thickened. Serve warm or cold. The pear butter will keep in an airtight container in the refrigerator for up to 1 week.

PER SERVING	1 tablespoon
CALORIES	42
FAT	0 g
SATURATED FAT	0 g
CHOLESTEROL	0 mg
CARBOHYDRATE	11 g
FIBER	1.5 g
PROTEIN	0 g
SUGARS	8 g
SODIUM	1 mg

CRUSTLESS SLOW COOKER APPLE PIE À LA MODE   SERVES 8

SC V GF

Nothing says fall like the scent of apples and cinnamon filling up your home. These slow-cooked apples have all the delicious flavor of apple pie without the crust—or the extra calories. They're delicious warm right out of the slow cooker with a scoop of vanilla frozen yogurt—simply divine! But there are so many other ways to enjoy these apples, too: Try them over waffles, oatmeal, or pancakes for breakfast.

2¼ pounds (about 6) apples (I like Honeycrisp), peeled, cored, and cut into ¼-inch-thick slices

⅓ cup packed light brown sugar

1 tablespoon cornstarch

1 teaspoon ground cinnamon

¼ teaspoon ground nutmeg

4 cups nonfat frozen vanilla yogurt, for serving (I like Stonyfield)

Place the apples, brown sugar, cornstarch, cinnamon, and nutmeg in a slow cooker. Stir to combine.

Cover and cook on high for 2 hours or on low for 4 hours, until the apples are bubbling and tender.

To serve, put ½ cup of the apples in each of 8 small bowls. Top each with ½ cup frozen yogurt.

PER SERVING	½ cup apples + ½ cup frozen yogurt
CALORIES	194
FAT	0 g
SATURATED FAT	0 g
CHOLESTEROL	5 mg
CARBOHYDRATE	45 g
FIBER	3 g
PROTEIN	4 g
SUGARS	38 g
SODIUM	68 mg

SLOW COOKER BLUEBERRY SLUMP

SERVES 8

SC **V**

Cobblers, crisps, buckles, and slumps are all similar—they're warm desserts with fruit on the bottom and some sort of sweet topping. Ask me which is my favorite and I honestly couldn't tell you; I love them all. A slump is like a cobbler, only instead of being baked in the oven, it's made on the stovetop. I played around with it to make it in the slow cooker. It has a cake-like topping over the warm gooey berries, and it slumps onto your plate when you serve it. Simple and unfussy, it's a true comfort food.

FRUIT

Cooking spray

5 cups (26 ounces) blueberries

1/3 cup raw sugar

1 tablespoon cornstarch

1 teaspoon grated lemon zest

TOPPING

3/4 cup all-purpose flour (I like King Arthur)

1/3 cup raw sugar

1 1/2 teaspoons baking powder

1/2 teaspoon grated lemon zest

Pinch of kosher salt

2 tablespoons cold whipped butter

1/2 cup 2% milk

1 teaspoon vanilla extract

For the fruit: Coat a 5- or 6-quart slow cooker with cooking spray. Combine the blueberries, sugar, cornstarch, and lemon zest in the slow cooker.

For the topping: In a medium bowl, whisk together the flour, sugar, baking powder, lemon zest, and salt. Using a fork or a pastry blender, cut in the butter until it resembles coarse crumbs.

In a small bowl, combine the milk and vanilla. Add it to the flour mixture and stir with a spatula until combined. Spoon the topping over the blueberries and spread it out evenly.

Cover and cook on low for 4 hours, until the blueberries are bubbling and the topping is set. Let stand for 20 minutes before serving.

FOOD FACTS: BLUEBERRIES
Packed with compounds and nutrients that can help protect your heart, brain, eyes, and more, the blueberry is a small but mighty superfood. Not only does eating blueberries ward off diseases like diabetes, cancer, and heart disease, it also provides anti-inflammatory benefits.

PER SERVING	1/2 cup
CALORIES	**185**
FAT	**2.5 g**
SATURATED FAT	**1.5 g**
CHOLESTEROL	**7 mg**
CARBOHYDRATE	**40 g**
FIBER	**2.5 g**
PROTEIN	**3 g**
SUGARS	**26 g**
SODIUM	**131 mg**

SLOW COOKER TRIPLE-ALMOND FLOURLESS BROWNIES SERVES 6

SC V GF

Moist and chocolaty, these brownies are surprisingly free of oil, butter, and flour! I use almond meal instead of flour, along with some almond extract to bump up the flavor, and slivered almonds for crunch. It may never have occurred to you that you can bake in your slow cooker, but yes, you can—as long as your slow cooker is large enough to hold an 8½ x 4½-inch loaf pan. And since this recipe makes a small batch, it's the perfect way to satisfy your sweet tooth without the temptation to overindulge.

Cooking spray

1 large egg white, beaten

½ cup finely ground almond meal (I like Bob's Red Mill)

¼ cup unsweetened cocoa powder

½ teaspoon baking soda

⅛ teaspoon kosher salt

3 tablespoons agave syrup

½ teaspoon vanilla extract

½ teaspoon almond extract

2½ ounces semisweet chocolate chips*

3 tablespoons (1 ounce) slivered almonds

*Read the label to be sure this product is gluten-free.

Pour about 2 cups water into a slow cooker and place a foil "rack" (see Skinny Scoop) in the bottom. Cut a piece of parchment 8½ x 12 inches and place it into an 8½ x 4½-inch nonstick loaf pan. Coat with cooking spray.

In a small bowl, whisk the egg white until foamy.

In a medium bowl, whisk together the almond meal, cocoa powder, baking soda, and salt. Gently fold in the egg white using a spatula. Add ¼ cup water, the agave, vanilla extract, and almond extract and stir until combined.

In a small microwave-safe bowl, melt the chocolate in the microwave in 30-second increments, stirring after each, until the chocolate is melted and soft. Fold the chocolate and half of the almonds into the batter. Pour the batter into the prepared pan, top with the remaining almonds, and set the pan on the foil "rack" in the slow cooker.

Bake on high for 3 to 4 hours, until a toothpick inserted in the center comes out clean. Remove the pan from the slow cooker and let cool at least 1 hour. Using the parchment paper, lift the brownies out of the pan and transfer to a cutting board. Cut the brownies into 6 squares and serve.

SKINNY SCOOP To make a rack out of foil, loosely roll a 24 x 12-inch piece of foil into a 1-inch cylinder. Bend the cylinder into an oval-shaped rack.

PER SERVING	1 brownie
CALORIES	179
FAT	11 g
SATURATED FAT	3 g
CHOLESTEROL	0 mg
CARBOHYDRATE	21 g
FIBER	3.5 g
PROTEIN	5 g
SUGARS	15 g
SODIUM	141 mg

SLOW COOKER PUMPKIN FLAN SERVES 6

(SC) (V) (GF)

Confession: I've eaten *a lot* of flan in my day. My mom makes it every year for the holidays, both to eat and to give away as gifts, and my mother-in-law is probably her most grateful recipient. Made with canned pumpkin and a few minor swaps, this lighter version is creamy, is rich in flavor, and has a nice spice that's so great during the holidays.

½ cup sugar

½ teaspoon fresh lemon juice

5 tablespoons fat-free sweetened condensed milk

½ cup 2% milk

½ cup canned unsweetened pumpkin puree

3 large eggs

1 teaspoon vanilla extract

¼ teaspoon grated lemon zest

½ teaspoon pumpkin pie spice

Pinch of kosher salt

In a small, heavy nonstick saucepan, combine the sugar, lemon juice, and 2 tablespoons water. Set over medium-high heat and set a timer for 7 minutes. Cook, whisking constantly to dissolve the sugar as it comes to a boil, about 1 minute (of the 7 minutes). Stop whisking and continue cooking, undisturbed, until the timer goes off. Immediately remove the pan from the heat and swirl the caramel in the pan for 1 minute, until it turns amber in color, being careful not to burn it, as the heat from the pan will continue cooking the caramel.

Dividing evenly, carefully pour a scant tablespoon of the caramel into each of six 4-ounce ramekins. Working quickly, tilt each ramekin to coat the sides of the cup. If the caramel hardens too quickly, you can reheat the ramekin in the microwave for about 5 seconds to loosen. Set aside to cool.

In a blender, combine the condensed milk, 2% milk, pumpkin puree, eggs, vanilla, lemon zest, pumpkin pie spice, and salt. Blend well. Pour a scant ⅓ cup into each ramekin.

Pour 3 cups hot water into the bottom of a slow cooker and place the ramekins inside. Cover and cook on low for 3 hours. Remove the ramekins from the slow cooker right away and let cool for 10 minutes. Cover with plastic wrap and refrigerate overnight.

To serve, run a very thin knife or metal spatula all around the edges of the ramekins to loosen. Invert a ramekin onto each of 6 small plates, and tap and shake lightly until the flan comes out. If any caramel remains in the ramekin, you can microwave a few seconds to loosen, then pour over each flan.

SKINNY SCOOP You'll need 6 mini (4-ounce) ramekins and a 6-quart oval slow cooker for this recipe. Note that the caramel will be very hot, so be careful not to get it on your skin.

PER SERVING	1 flan
CALORIES	166
FAT	3 g
SATURATED FAT	1 g
CHOLESTEROL	95 mg
CARBOHYDRATE	30 g
FIBER	0.5 g
PROTEIN	6 g
SUGARS	29 g
SODIUM	80 mg

ACKNOWLEDGMENTS

It takes an entire team to create a cookbook, and I owe many thanks to the people who helped make this book happen. First and foremost, to Skinnytaste fans, without you the blog, the book—none of this—would be possible. Thank you for allowing me to do what I love every single day.

To my parents, who taught me how to cook at a very young age and instilled in me a love of food and cooking. To my husband, my biggest supporter and toughest taste-tester, thanks for all your patience while I worked long hours and for trying all my recipe creations (the good and the bad!). And to my children, who are always open to trying new foods and who made sacrifices for Mommy's busy schedule.

A huge thank-you to Heather K. Jones, R.D., for working with me once again on the book; I can't imagine doing it without you! You add so much value to this book and your positive attitude is always contagious. To my aunt Ligia, my devoted recipe tester, thank you for all the hours you invested with me, I couldn't have done this without you. Rene, Nina, and Camila, for offering to be my taste-testers. And, of course, to my agent, Janis Donnaud, thank you for your guidance. I am always grateful to have you in my corner.

A tremendous thank-you to my dream team at Clarkson Potter: Ashley Phillips Meyer, Carly Gorga, and Erica Gelbard, I won the lottery when I got assigned to work with the three of you. And to all the folks at Potter who were involved with this book: Rica Allannic, Doris Cooper, Ian Dingman, Stephanie Huntwork, Marysarah Quinn, Patricia Shaw, Kim Tyner, and Aaron Wehner.

To my amazing photography team, thank you for making my food look beautiful; photographer Helene Dujardin, food stylist Tami Hardeman, assistant food stylist Abby Gaskins, and prop stylist Kim Phillips. It was a pleasure getting to spend so much time with you all in amazing Charleston, South Carolina. To Angela Hall Designs for letting me wear your gorgeous jewelry, Bunny Hall for letting me use your fabulous kitchen, Mark and Jen Hatala for letting us shoot in your lovely home on Kiawah Island, and Ruth McSweeney (aka Mama Ruth) for your southern hospitality.

To the vendors who loaned their beautiful props: CBFB Tablescapes, Henry Street Studio, Marite Acosta, and Claykat Ceramics. And a big thanks to Harry & David, for providing such beautiful pears.

To Danielle Hazard, your nutrition and culinary background (and love of food!) really made you a unique and awesome part of the book team, and to Donna Fennessy, editor and writer extraordinaire!

And last but not least, to my girlfriends who make me laugh after a long day and help keep me sane: Nalini, Joanne, Denise H, Katia, Raquel, Doreen, Denise P, Gabbie, Roseanne, Nicole, and Julia. I am forever grateful for our friendships.

INDEX

Note: Page references in *italics* indicate recipe photographs.

Apple:
Brussels Sprouts, and Havarti, Grilled Cheese with, *228*, *229*
-Butternut Soup, Slow Cooker, with Crispy Leeks, *56*, *57*
Pie à la Mode, Crustless Slow Cooker, *292*, *293*
Artichoke and Shrimp Quinoa Bowls, *88*, 89
Arugula:
Baked Pears with Greens, Blue Cheese, and Pecans, *234*, *235*
Salad, Grilled Veal Chop Milanese with, *186*, *187*
Asparagus:
Grilled Vegetable Caprese Salad, 226, *227*
Veggie-Stuffed Flounder Sheet Pan Dinner, *214*, *215*
Avocado(s):
Ahi Tuna Poke Jicama Tacos, 132, *133*
Ranch Sauce, 154, *155*
Rice and Sunny-Side-Up Egg Bowls, *90*, *91*
and Shrimp Salad, Zesty Lime, *208*, *209*
Slow Cooker Loaded "Baked" Sweet Potatoes, *246*, *247*
Spicy Lump Crab and Charred Corn Flaco "Tacos," *150*, *151*
Toast, Five Ways, 22, *23–25*

Banana(s):
-Almond Smoothie Bowl, *30*, *31*
Breakfast Banana Split, *34*, 34
Chocolate Swirl Bread, Slow Cooker, *36*, *37*
Coconut, and Blueberries, Slow Cooker "Baked" Oatmeal with, 35
Pudding Cups, *278*, *279*
Split, Breakfast, *34*, 34
Bean(s):
Black, Brazilian, with Collard Greens, 185
Black, Tacos, Slow Cooker Vegetarian, *144*, 145
Italian House Salad with Dijon Vinaigrette, *252*, *253*
Pasta e Fagioli, *46*, *47*
Slow Cooker Chana Masala, 248
Slow Cooker Chicken Burrito Bowls, *92*, 93
Slow Cooker Chicken Taco Chili, *62*, 63
Slow Cooker Loaded "Baked" Sweet Potatoes, *246*, *247*

Spiralized Lemon-Basil Zucchini Mason Jar Salads, *98*, *99*
Two-, and Beef Chili, Slow Cooker, *66*, 67
White, and Italian Sausage Soup, Slow Cooker, with Escarole, 51
White, Turkey, and Pumpkin Chili, Slow Cooker, *64*, 65
Beef. *See also* Veal:
Fork-and-Knife Cheeseburgers, *180*, 181
Grilled Cumin-Rubbed Skirt Steak Tacos with Pickled Red Onions, *128*, 129
Ragu, Slow Cooker, with Pappardelle, *122*, 123
Roast, Perfect Medium-Rare, in the Slow Cooker, *196*, *197*
Slow Cooker Bolognese Sauce, 120, *121*
Slow Cooker Brisket with Onions, *192*, 193
Slow Cooker Carne Desmechada, *194*, 195
Slow Cooker Hamburger Stroganoff, *118*, *119*
Slow Cooker Stuffed Cabbage Rolls, 200, *201*
Slow Cooker Stuffed Pepper Soup, 50
Steak and Onions, *182*, *183*
Stew, Slow Cooker, with Sweet Potatoes, 69
Stock in the Slow Cooker, 73
Tacos, Madison's Favorite, *138*, 139
Tacos, Slow Cooker Korean-Style, 140, *141*
and Two-Bean Chili, Slow Cooker, *66*, 67
Beet, Spiralized, Salad with Seared Scallops and Orange, 110
Blueberry(ies):
Banana-Almond Smoothie Bowl, *30*, *31*
Coconut, and Bananas, Slow Cooker "Baked" Oatmeal with, 35
Slump, Slow Cooker, *294*, *295*
Bok choy:
Egg Roll Bowls, *84*, *85*
Sweet 'n' Spicy Salmon with Stir-Fried Veggies, *210*, 211
Breads:
Avocado Toast Five Ways, 22, *23–25*
Chocolate Swirl Banana, Slow Cooker, *36*, *37*
Greek Panzanella Salad, *232*, 233
Slow Cooker Sausage-Herb Stuffing, *274*, 275
Broccoli:
Burnt, *254*, 255
and Melted Mozzarella, Chicken Scaloppine with, *152–53*, 153
and Pasta, Easiest One-Pot, 238, *239*

Brownies, Slow Cooker Triple-Almond Flourless, *296*, 297
Brussels Sprout(s):
Hash with Bacon and Eggs, 26, *27*
Havarti, and Apple, Grilled Cheese with, *228*, *229*
Roasted, with Spicy Sausage, 82

Cabbage:
Egg Roll Bowls, *84*, *85*
Red, Braised, with Vinegar, 265
Rolls, Stuffed, Slow Cooker, 200, *201*
Slow Cooker Hawaiian Pork Tacos with Charred Pineapple Salsa, *4*, 142–43
Steaks, Sesame Roasted, 270, *271*
Carrots:
Greek Chicken Sheet Pan Dinner, 158, *159*
and Radishes, Pickled, *94*, 95
Cauliflower:
"Fried Rice," 260, *261*
-Potato Tacos with Lime-Cilantro Chutney, *134*, 135
Puree, Whipped Parmesan, *193*, 264
Soup, Dad's, 40, *41*
Teriyaki Chicken Bowls, *80*, 81
Cheese:
Asiago-Crusted Chicken Breasts, 148, *149*
Baked Eggplant Parmesan Stacks, 236, 237
Baked Sweet Plantains with, *258*, 259
Blue, Dressing, 172
Blue, Greens, and Pecans, Baked Pears with, *234*, *235*
Chicken Scaloppine with Broccoli and Melted Mozzarella, *152–53*, 153
Fork-and-Knife Cheeseburgers, *180*, 181
Grilled, with Havarti, Brussels Sprouts, and Apple, *228*, *229*
Grilled Vegetable Caprese Salad, 226, *227*
Pizza-Stuffed Chicken Roll-Ups, 156, *157*
Roasted Acorn Squash with Parmesan, 262, *263*
Salad Pizza, 230, *231*
Slow Cooker Lasagna Soup, *52*, 53
Vanilla Bean Cheesecake Shooters, *286*, 287
Whipped Parmesan Cauliflower Puree, *193*, 264
Zoodles with Shrimp and Feta, *104*, 105
Chicken. *See also* Sausage(s):
Bowls, Teriyaki, *80*, 81
Breasts, Asiago-Crusted, 148, *149*
Buffalo, Lettuce Wraps, Slow Cooker, *172*, *173*

Chicken (continued):
  Burrito Bowls, Slow Cooker, 92, 93
  Cacciatore, Slow Cooker, 112, 113
  Cold Peanut-Sesame, and Spiralized
    Cucumber Noodle Salad, 100, 101
  and Couscous Bowls with Piri Piri, 78–79,
    79
  Drumsticks, Slow Cooker Maple-Dijon,
    166, 167
  and Dumpling Soup, Slow Cooker, 54, 55
  Grilled Greek, Tostadas, 126, 127
  Lettuce Wraps, Korean-Inspired, 150, 151
  Paprikash, Slow Cooker Czech, 170, 171
  and Peas, Slow Cooker Indian, 164, 165
  Pressure Cooker Three-Cup, 160
  Roasted, Stock in the Slow Cooker, 72
  Roll-Ups, Pizza-Stuffed, 156, 157
  Salsa Verde Taquitos, Slow Cooker, 136,
    137
  Scaloppine with Broccoli and Melted
    Mozzarella, 152–53, 153
  Sheet Pan Dinner, Greek, 158, 159
  Slow Cooker Adobo, with Sriracha,
    Ginger, and Scallions, 162, 163
  Slow Cooker BBQ Pulled, 168
  Slow Cooker Pollo in Potacchio, 114, 115
  Soup, Pressure Cooker, for My Soul, 44
  Taco Chili, Slow Cooker, 62, 63
  Tikka Masala, Slow Cooker, 161
  and Zucchini Noodles with Black Bean
    Sauce, 102, 103
Chili:
  Beef and Two-Bean, Slow Cooker, 66,
    67
  Chicken Taco, Slow Cooker, 62, 63
  Turkey, White Bean, and Pumpkin, Slow
    Cooker, 64, 65
Chocolate:
  Slow Cooker Triple-Almond Flourless
    Brownies, 296, 297
  Swirl Banana Bread, Slow Cooker, 36, 37
Chutney, Lime-Cilantro, 134, 135
Cilantro:
  -Lime Chutney, 134, 135
  Sofrito, 184
Coconut:
  Grilled Piña Colada Delight, 284, 285
  Veggie Curry, 240, 241
Corn:
  Charred, and Spicy Lump Crab Flaco
    "Tacos," 130, 131
  Pressure Cooker Chicken Soup for My
    Soul, 44
  Slow Cooker Chicken Burrito Bowls,
    92, 93
  Slow Cooker Chicken Taco Chili, 62, 63
  Slow Cooker Loaded "Baked" Sweet
    Potatoes, 246, 247
Couscous and Chicken Bowls with Piri
    Piri, 78–79, 79
Crab, Spicy Lump, and Charred Corn
    Flaco "Tacos," 130, 131

Crêpes, Whole Wheat, with Strawberry
    Sauce, 20–21
Cucumber(s):
  Chicken and Couscous Bowls with Piri
    Piri, 78–79, 79
  Greek Panzanella Salad, 232, 233
  Noodle, Spiralized, and Cold Peanut-
    Sesame Chicken Salad, 100, 101
  Tomato, and Lox Toast, 22, 25

Eggplant Parmesan Stacks, Baked, 236,
    237
Egg Roll Bowls, 84, 85
Egg Rolls, Santa Fe Turkey, with Avocado
    Ranch Sauce, 154–55, 155
Egg(s):
  and Bacon, Brussels Sprout Hash with,
    26, 27
  Cauliflower "Fried Rice," 260, 261
  Kale Caesar and Grilled Chicken Bowls,
    76, 77
  Karina's Special, 22, 24
  Mexican Huevos Shakshukos, 28, 29
  and Peppers Sandwiches, Dad's, 243
  Poached, and Pancetta, Butternut
    Squash Noodles with, 108, 109
  Put an Egg on It!, 22, 23
  Savory Quinoa Breakfast Bowls, 32, 33
  South of the Border Huevos Revueltos,
    22, 25
  Sunny-Side-Up, and Avocado Rice
    Bowls, 90, 91

Fennel and Shallots, Braised, Skillet Pork
    Chops with, 188, 189
Fish:
  Ahi Tuna Poke Jicama Tacos, 132, 133
  Broiled Whole Porgies, 218, 219
  and Chips, Baked, 212, 213
  Cucumber, Tomato, and Lox Toast, 22, 25
  Drunken Seafood Stew, 48, 49
  Roasted Asian Striped Bass, 216, 217
  Slow Cooker Poached Salmon with
    Meyer Lemon, Capers, and Parsley,
    222, 223
  Spicy Seared Tuna Sushi Bowls, 86, 87
  sustainable or wild, buying, 221
  Sweet 'n' Spicy Salmon with Stir-Fried
    Veggies, 210, 211
  Veggie-Stuffed Flounder Sheet Pan
    Dinner, 214, 215
Flan, Slow Cooker Pumpkin, 298, 299
Flounder, Veggie-Stuffed, Sheet Pan
    Dinner, 214, 215
Fridge and freezer essentials, 11
Fruits. See also specific fruits:
  seasonal, buying, 10

Garlic:
  and Oil, Spaghetti Squash with, 266, 267
  Sofrito, 184
Grains. See Oatmeal; Quinoa; Rice

Greens. See also Arugula; Lettuce:
  Collard, Brazilian Black Beans with, 185
  Kale Caesar and Grilled Chicken Bowls,
    76, 77
  Salad Pizza, 230, 231
  Slow Cooker Italian Sausage and White
    Bean Soup with Escarole, 51

Jicama:
  Pineapple Slaw, 268, 269
  Tacos, Ahi Tuna Poke, 132, 133

Kale Caesar and Grilled Chicken Bowls,
    76, 77

Lamb Ragu with Penne, Slow Cooker
    Spicy Harissa, 111
Lettuce:
  Italian House Salad with Dijon
    Vinaigrette, 252, 253
  Spicy Lump Crab and Charred Corn
    Flaco "Tacos," 130, 131
  Wraps, Buffalo Chicken, Slow Cooker,
    172, 173
  Wraps, Chicken, Korean-Inspired, 150, 151

Mango Fool, Easy No-Cook, 282, 283
Meal planning, 10
Meatballs, Slow Cooker Italian Turkey-
    Zucchini, 116, 117
"Meatballs," Zucchini, 244, 245
Meatless Monday campaign, 249
Meatloaf, Turkey, Slow Cooker, 176, 177
Menus, for four weeks, 14–17
Mushrooms:
  Fork-and-Knife Cheeseburgers, 180, 181
  Pizza-Stuffed Chicken Roll-Ups, 156, 157
  Roasted Brussels Bowls with Spicy
    Sausage, 82
  Slow Cooker Asian Pork with, 205
  Slow Cooker Chicken Cacciatore, 112,
    113
  Slow Cooker Hamburger Stroganoff,
    118, 119

Oatmeal, Slow Cooker "Baked," with
    Coconut, Blueberries, and Bananas,
    35
Onions:
  Red, Pickled, 128, 129
  Slow Cooker Brisket with, 192, 193
  Steak and, 182, 183

Pantry staples, 11
Pasta:
  and Broccoli, Easiest One-Pot, 238, 239
  Chicken and Couscous Bowls with Piri
    Piri, 78–79, 79
  e Fagioli, 46, 47
  Roasted Pepper and Orzo Soup, 45
  Slow Cooker Beef Ragu with
    Pappardelle, 122, 123

Slow Cooker Lasagna Soup, 52, 53
Slow Cooker Spicy Harissa Lamb Ragu with Penne, 111
Peach-Strawberry Crumble, Slow Cooker, 288, 289
Peanut Butter:
Banana-Almond Smoothie Bowl, 30, 31
Cold Peanut-Sesame Chicken and Spiralized Cucumber Noodle Salad, 100, 101
Pear(s):
Baked, with Greens, Blue Cheese, and Pecans, 234, 235
Butter, Vanilla Bean, Slow Cooker, 290, 291
Slow Cooker Stuffed Turkey Tenderloins with Gravy, 174-75, 175
Pepper(s):
Chicken and Couscous Bowls with Piri Piri, 78-79, 79
and Egg Sandwiches, Dad's, 243
Greek Panzanella Salad, 232, 233
Grilled Vegetable Caprese Salad, 226, 227
Roasted, and Orzo Soup, 45
Slow Cooker Chicken Cacciatore, 112, 113
Slow Cooker Shrimp à la Criolla, 220
Slow Cooker Spicy Harissa Lamb Ragu with Penne, 111
Sofrito, 184
Spicy Lump Crab and Charred Corn Flaco "Tacos," 130, 131
Stuffed, Soup, Slow Cooker, 50
Sweet 'n' Spicy Salmon with Stir-Fried Veggies, 210, 211
Pineapple:
Breakfast Banana Split, 34, 34
Charred, Salsa, 4, 142-43
Grilled Piña Colada Delight, 284, 285
Jicama Slaw, 268, 269
Pizza, Salad, 230, 231
Plantains, Baked Sweet, with Cheese, 258, 259
Porgies, Broiled Whole, 218, 219
Pork:
Asian, with Mushrooms, Slow Cooker, 205
Brazilian Black Beans with Collard Greens, 185
Chops, Skillet, with Braised Fennel and Shallots, 188, 189
Egg Roll Bowls, 84, 85
Slow Cooker Banh Mi Rice Bowls, 94, 95
Slow Cooker Goulash with Sauerkraut, 202
Slow Cooker Pernil, 203
Tacos, Slow Cooker Hawaiian, with Charred Pineapple Salsa, 4, 142-43
Tenderloin with Potatoes and Caraway Seeds, 190, 191

Potato(es). See also Sweet Potatoes:
Baked Fish and Chips, 212, 213
Buttermilk Mashed, Creamy Slow Cooker, 272, 273
and Caraway Seeds, Pork Tenderloin with, 190, 191
-Cauliflower Tacos with Lime-Cilantro Chutney, 134, 135
Greek Chicken Sheet Pan Dinner, 158, 159
Pudding Cups, Banana, 278, 279
Pumpkin:
Flan, Slow Cooker, 298, 299
Turkey, and White Bean Chili, Slow Cooker, 64, 65

Quinoa:
Bowls, Shrimp and Artichoke, 88, 89
Breakfast Bowls, Savory, 32, 33

Radishes and Carrots, Pickled, 94, 95
Raspberries:
Macerated Berries with Whipped Cream, 280, 281
Vanilla Bean Cheesecake Shooters, 286, 287
Rice:
Bowls, Slow Cooker Banh Mi, 94, 95
Bowls, Sunny-Side-Up Egg and Avocado, 90, 91
Brazilian Black Beans with Collard Greens, 185
Brown, Perfect, in the Slow Cooker, 50
Coconut Veggie Curry, 240, 241
Korean-Inspired Chicken Lettuce Wraps, 150, 151
Slow Cooker Chicken Burrito Bowls, 92, 93
Slow Cooker Stuffed Cabbage Rolls, 200, 201
Slow Cooker Stuffed Pepper Soup, 50
Spicy Seared Tuna Sushi Bowls, 86, 87

Salad Pizza, 230, 231
Salads:
Baked Pears with Greens, Blue Cheese, and Pecans, 234, 235
Greek Panzanella, 232, 233
Grilled Vegetable Caprese, 226, 227
Italian House, with Dijon Vinaigrette, 252, 253
Kale Caesar and Grilled Chicken Bowls, 76, 77
Lime Shrimp and Avocado, Zesty, 208, 209
Peanut-Sesame Chicken and Spiralized Cucumber Noodle, Cold, 100, 101
Spiralized Beet, with Seared Scallops and Orange, 110
Spiralized Lemon-Basil Zucchini Mason Jar, 98, 99
Salmon:
Cucumber, Tomato, and Lox Toast, 22, 25

Slow Cooker Poached, with Meyer Lemon, Capers, and Parsley, 222, 223
Sweet 'n' Spicy, with Stir-Fried Veggies, 210, 211
Salsa:
Charred Pineapple, 4, 142-43
Pico de Gallo, 92, 93
Salt, note about, 11
Sandwiches:
Grilled Cheese with Havarti, Brussels Sprouts, and Apple, 228, 229
Peppers and Egg, Dad's, 243
Sauces:
Avocado Ranch, 154, 155
BBQ, Homemade, 169
Bolognese, Slow Cooker, 120, 121
Quick Marinara, 52
Slow Cooker Beef Ragu with Pappardelle, 122, 123
Slow Cooker Chicken Cacciatore, 112, 113
Slow Cooker Spicy Harissa Lamb Ragu with Penne, 111
Sauerkraut, Slow Cooker Goulash with, 202
Sausage(s):
-Herb Stuffing, Slow Cooker, 274, 275
Italian, and White Bean Soup, Slow Cooker, with Escarole, 51
Slow Cooker Lasagna Soup, 52, 53
Spicy, Roasted Brussels Bowls with, 82
Scallops, Seared, and Orange, Spiralized Beet Salad with, 110
Shellfish. See also Shrimp:
Drunken Seafood Stew, 48, 49
Spicy Lump Crab and Charred Corn Flaco "Tacos," 130, 131
Spiralized Beet Salad with Seared Scallops and Orange, 110
Shrimp:
and Artichoke Quinoa Bowls, 88, 89
and Avocado Salad, Zesty Lime, 208, 209
Drunken Seafood Stew, 48, 49
and Feta, Zoodles with, 104, 105
à la Criolla, Slow Cooker, 220
and Summer Squash Noodles Baked in Foil, 106, 107
Slaw, Pineapple Jicama, 268, 269
Sofrito, 184
Soups. See also Stews:
Butternut-Apple, Slow Cooker, with Crispy Leeks, 56, 57
Cauliflower, Dad's, 40, 41
Chicken, Pressure Cooker, for My Soul, 44
Chicken and Dumpling, Slow Cooker, 54, 55
Italian Sausage and White Bean, Slow Cooker, with Escarole, 51
Lasagna, Slow Cooker, 52, 53
Pasta e Fagioli, 46, 47

Soups (continued):
Roasted Pepper and Orzo, 45
Stuffed Pepper, Slow Cooker, 50
Tomato, Slow Cooker Creamy, 58, 59
Vegetable Yellow Split Pea, Slow
Cooker, 60, 61
Zucchini, Cream of, 42, 43
Squash. See also Zucchini:
Acorn, Roasted, with Parmesan, 262, 263
Butternut, Noodles with Pancetta and
Poached Egg, 108, 109
Shrimp and Summer Squash Noodles
Baked in Foil, 106, 107
Slow Cooker Butternut-Apple Soup
with Crispy Leeks, 56, 57
Slow Cooker Pumpkin Flan, 298, 299
Slow Cooker Stuffed Turkey Tenderloins
with Gravy, 174–75, 175
Slow Cooker Turkey, White Bean, and
Pumpkin Chili, 64, 65
spaghetti, how to cook, 266
Spaghetti, with Garlic and Oil, 266, 267
Veggie-Stuffed Flounder Sheet Pan
Dinner, 214, 215
Stews:
Beef, Slow Cooker, with Sweet Potatoes,
69
Drunken Seafood, 48, 49
Slow Cooker Carne Desmechada, 194,
195
Slow Cooker Shrimp à la Criolla, 220
Venison, Slow Cooker, 70, 71
Stocks:
Beef, in the Slow Cooker, 73
Roasted Chicken, in the Slow Cooker, 72
Strawberry(ies):
Banana-Almond Smoothie Bowl, 30, 31
Breakfast Banana Split, 34, 34
Macerated Berries with Whipped
Cream, 280, 281
-Peach Crumble, Slow Cooker, 288, 289
Sauce, Whole Wheat Crêpes with, 20–21
Striped Bass, Roasted Asian, 216, 217
Stuffing, Slow Cooker Sausage-Herb, 274,
275

Sweet Potatoes:
Slow Cooker Beef Stew with, 69
Slow Cooker Loaded "Baked," 246, 247

Tacos:
Beef, Madison's Favorite, 138, 139
Beef, Slow Cooker Korean-Style, 140,
141
Black Bean, Slow Cooker Vegetarian,
144, 145
Cauliflower-Potato, with Lime-Cilantro
Chutney, 134, 135
Grilled Cumin-Rubbed Skirt Steak, with
Pickled Red Onions, 128, 129
Jicama, Ahi Tuna Poke, 132, 133
Pork, Slow Cooker Hawaiian, with
Charred Pineapple Salsa, 4, 142–43
"Tacos," Flaco, Spicy Lump Crab and
Charred Corn, 130, 131
Taquitos, Slow Cooker Salsa Verde
Chicken, 136, 137
Tomato(es):
Greek Panzanella Salad, 232, 233
Mexican Huevos Shakshukos, 28, 29
Pico de Gallo, 92, 93
Quick Marinara, 52
Slow Cooker Beef Ragu with
Pappardelle, 122, 123
Slow Cooker Bolognese Sauce, 120, 121
Slow Cooker Italian Turkey-Zucchini
Meatballs, 116, 117
Slow Cooker Pollo in Potacchio, 114, 115
Slow Cooker Shrimp à la Criolla, 220
Slow Cooker Stuffed Pepper Soup, 50
Soup, Slow Cooker Creamy, 58, 59
Tostadas, Grilled Greek Chicken, 126, 127
Tuna:
Ahi, Poke Jicama Tacos, 132, 133
Spicy Seared, Sushi Bowls, 86, 87
Turkey:
Egg Rolls, Santa Fe, with Avocado
Ranch Sauce, 154–55, 155
Meatloaf, Slow Cooker, 176, 177
Slow Cooker Stuffed Cabbage Rolls,
200, 201

Tenderloins, Slow Cooker Stuffed, with
Gravy, 174–75, 175
White Bean, and Pumpkin Chili, Slow
Cooker, 64, 65
-Zucchini Meatballs, Slow Cooker
Italian, 116, 117

Veal:
Chop, Grilled, Milanese with Arugula
Salad, 186, 187
Slow Cooker Osso Buco, 198, 199
Vegetable(s). See also specific
vegetables:
Coconut Veggie Curry, 240, 241
seasonal, buying, 10
Yellow Split Pea Soup, Slow Cooker,
60, 61
Venison Stew, Slow Cooker, 70, 71

Yellow Split Pea Vegetable Soup, Slow
Cooker, 60, 61
Yogurt:
Breakfast Banana Split, 34, 34
Crustless Slow Cooker Apple Pie à la
Mode, 292, 293

Zucchini:
Grilled Vegetable Caprese Salad, 226,
227
"Meatballs," 244, 245
Noodles and Chicken with Black Bean
Sauce, 102, 103
Shrimp and Summer Squash Noodles
Baked in Foil, 106, 107
Soup, Cream of, 42, 43
Spiralized Lemon-Basil, Mason Jar
Salads, 98, 99
-Turkey Meatballs, Slow Cooker Italian,
116, 117
Veggie-Stuffed Flounder Sheet Pan
Dinner, 214, 215
Wedges with Lemon and Fresh
Oregano, 256, 257
zoodles, how to make, 120
Zoodles with Shrimp and Feta, 104, 105

Copyright © 2016 by
Gina Homolka
Photographs copyright
© 2016 by Helene Dujardin

All rights reserved.
Published in the United States by
Clarkson Potter/Publishers, an imprint of
the Crown Publishing Group, a division of
Penguin Random House LLC, New York.
crownpublishing.com
clarksonpotter.com

CLARKSON POTTER is a trademark
and POTTER with colophon is a
registered trademark of
Penguin Random House LLC.

Skinnytaste™ is a trademark of
Skinnytaste, Inc.

Library of Congress
Cataloging-in-Publication Data
is available upon request.

ISBN 978-0-553-45960-9
eBook ISBN 978-0-553-45961-6

Printed in China

Book and jacket design by
Ian Dingman

10 9 8 7 6 5 4 3 2 1

First Edition